Canadian Industrial Policy in Action

This is Volume 4 in the series of studies commissioned as part of the research program of the Royal Commission on the Economic Union and Development Prospects for Canada.

The studies contained in this volume reflect the views of their authors and do not imply endorsement by the Chairman or Commissioners.

Canadian Industrial Policy in Action

D.G. McFetridge
Research Coordinator

Published by the University of Toronto Press in cooperation with the Royal Commission on the Economic Union and Development Prospects for Canada and the Canadian Government Publishing Centre, Supply and Services Canada

University of Toronto Press
Toronto   Buffalo   London

Grateful acknowledgment is made to the following for permission to reprint previously published and unpublished material: Butterworth & Co. (Canada) Ltd.; Economic Council of Canada; Electrical and Electronic Manufacturers Association of Canada; Harvard University Graduate School of Business Administration; Minister of Supply and Services Canada; Pergamon Press Inc.; Praeger Publishers; Bruce Scott, Esq.; Professor R. Nelson, Institute for Social and Policy Studies, Yale University.

Printed in Canada
ISBN 0-8020-7244-5
ISSN 0829-2396
Cat. No. Z1-1983/1-41-4E

CANADIAN CATALOGUING IN PUBLICATION DATA

Main entry under title:
Canadian industrial policy in action

(*The Collected research studies / Royal Commission on the Economic Union and Development Prospects for Canada,*
ISSN 0829-2396 ; 4)
Includes bibliographical references.
ISBN 0-8020-7244-5

1. Industry and state — Canada — Addresses, essays, lectures. 2. Government business enterprises — Canada — Addresses, essays, lectures. 3. Canada — Economic policy — Addresses, essays, lectures. I. McFetridge, D.G., 1945– II. Royal Commission on the Economic Union and Development Prospects for Canada. III. Series: The Collected research studies (Royal Commission on the Economic Union and Development Prospects for Canada) ; 4.

HD3616.C33C36 1985   338.971   C85-099243-5

PUBLISHING COORDINATION: Ampersand Communications Services Inc.
COVER DESIGN: Will Rueter
INTERIOR DESIGN: Brant Cowie/Artplus Limited

CONTENTS

When the members of the Rowell-Sirois Commission began their collective task in 1937, very little was known about the evolution of the Canadian economy. What was known, moreover, had not been extensively analyzed by the slender cadre of social scientists of the day.

When we set out upon our task nearly 50 years later, we enjoyed a substantial advantage over our predecessors; we had a wealth of information. We inherited the work of scholars at universities across Canada and we had the benefit of the work of experts from private research institutes and publicly sponsored organizations such as the Ontario Economic Council and the Economic Council of Canada. Although there were still important gaps, our problem was not a shortage of information; it was to interrelate and integrate — to synthesize — the results of much of the information we already had.

The mandate of this Commission is unusually broad. It encompasses many of the fundamental policy issues expected to confront the people of Canada and their governments for the next several decades. The nature of the mandate also identified, in advance, the subject matter for much of the research and suggested the scope of enquiry and the need for vigorous efforts to interrelate and integrate the research disciplines. The resulting research program, therefore, is particularly noteworthy in three respects: along with original research studies, it includes survey papers which synthesize work already done in specialized fields; it avoids duplication of work which, in the judgment of the Canadian research community, has already been well done; and, considered as a whole, it is the most thorough examination of the Canadian economic, political and legal systems ever undertaken by an independent agency.

The Commission's research program was carried out under the joint direction of three prominent and highly respected Canadian scholars: Dr. Ivan Bernier (*Law and Constitutional Issues*), Dr. Alan Cairns (*Politics and Institutions of Government*) and Dr. David C. Smith (*Economics*).

Dr. Ivan Bernier is Dean of the Faculty of Law at Laval University. Dr. Alan Cairns is former Head of the Department of Political Science at the University of British Columbia and, prior to joining the Commission, was William Lyon Mackenzie King Visiting Professor of Canadian Studies at Harvard University. Dr. David C. Smith, former Head of the Department of Economics at Queen's University in Kingston, is now Principal of that University. When Dr. Smith assumed his new responsibilities at Queen's in September 1984, he was succeeded by Dr. Kenneth Norrie of the University of Alberta and John Sargent of the federal Department of Finance, who together acted as Co-directors of Research for the concluding phase of the Economics research program.

I am confident that the efforts of the Research Directors, research coordinators and authors whose work appears in this and other volumes, have provided the community of Canadian scholars and policy makers with a series of publications that will continue to be of value for many years to come. And I hope that the value of the research program to Canadian scholarship will be enhanced by the fact that Commission research is being made available to interested readers in both English and French.

I extend my personal thanks, and that of my fellow Commissioners, to the Research Directors and those immediately associated with them in the Commission's research program. I also want to thank the members of the many research advisory groups whose counsel contributed so substantially to this undertaking.

DONALD S. MACDONALD

At its most general level, the Royal Commission's research program has examined how the Canadian political economy can better adapt to change. As a basis of enquiry, this question reflects our belief that the future will always take us partly by surprise. Our political, legal and economic institutions should therefore be flexible enough to accommodate surprises and yet solid enough to ensure that they help us meet our future goals. This theme of an adaptive political economy led us to explore the interdependencies between political, legal and economic systems and drew our research efforts in an interdisciplinary direction.

The sheer magnitude of the research output (more than 280 separate studies in 72 volumes) as well as its disciplinary and ideological diversity have, however, made complete integration impossible and, we have concluded, undesirable. The research output as a whole brings varying perspectives and methodologies to the study of common problems and we therefore urge readers to look beyond their particular field of interest and to explore topics across disciplines.

The three research areas — *Law and Constitutional Issues*, under Ivan Bernier; *Politics and Institutions of Government*, under Alan Cairns; and *Economics*, under David C. Smith (co-directed with Kenneth Norrie and John Sargent for the concluding phase of the research program) — were further divided into 19 sections headed by research coordinators.

The area *Law and Constitutional Issues* has been organized into five major sections headed by the research coordinators identified below.

- Law, Society and the Economy — *Ivan Bernier and Andrée Lajoie*
- The International Legal Environment — *John J. Quinn*
- The Canadian Economic Union — *Mark Krasnick*

- Harmonization of Laws in Canada — *Ronald C.C. Cuming*
- Institutional and Constitutional Arrangements — *Clare F. Beckton and A. Wayne MacKay*

Since law in its numerous manifestations is the most fundamental means of implementing state policy, it was necessary to investigate how and when law could be mobilized most effectively to address the problems raised by the Commission's mandate. Adopting a broad perspective, researchers examined Canada's legal system from the standpoint of how law evolves as a result of social, economic and political changes and how, in turn, law brings about changes in our social, economic and political conduct.

Within *Politics and Institutions of Government*, research has been organized into seven major sections.

- Canada and the International Political Economy — *Denis Stairs and Gilbert Winham*
- State and Society in the Modern Era — *Keith Banting*
- Constitutionalism, Citizenship and Society — *Alan Cairns and Cynthia Williams*
- The Politics of Canadian Federalism — *Richard Simeon*
- Representative Institutions — *Peter Aucoin*
- The Politics of Economic Policy — *G. Bruce Doern*
- Industrial Policy — *André Blais*

This area examines a number of developments which have led Canadians to question their ability to govern themselves wisely and effectively. Many of these developments are not unique to Canada and a number of comparative studies canvass and assess how others have coped with similar problems. Within the context of the Canadian heritage of parliamentary government, federalism, a mixed economy, and a bilingual and multicultural society, the research also explores ways of rearranging the relationships of power and influence among institutions to restore and enhance the fundamental democratic principles of representativeness, responsiveness and accountability.

Economics research was organized into seven major sections.

- Macroeconomics — *John Sargent*
- Federalism and the Economic Union — *Kenneth Norrie*
- Industrial Structure — *Donald G. McFetridge*
- International Trade — *John Whalley*
- Income Distribution and Economic Security — *François Vaillancourt*
- Labour Markets and Labour Relations — *Craig Riddell*
- Economic Ideas and Social Issues — *David Laidler*

Economics research examines the allocation of Canada's human and other resources, the ways in which institutions and policies affect this allocation, and the distribution of the gains from their use. It also considers the nature of economic development, the forces that shape our regional and industrial structure, and our economic interdependence with other countries. The thrust of the research in economics is to increase our comprehension of what determines our economic potential and how instruments of economic policy may move us closer to our future goals.

One section from each of the three research areas — The Canadian Economic Union, The Politics of Canadian Federalism, and Federalism and the Economic Union — have been blended into one unified research effort. Consequently, the volumes on Federalism and the Economic Union as well as the volume on The North are the results of an interdisciplinary research effort.

We owe a special debt to the research coordinators. Not only did they organize, assemble and analyze the many research studies and combine their major findings in overviews, but they also made substantial contributions to the Final Report. We wish to thank them for their performance, often under heavy pressure.

Unfortunately, space does not permit us to thank all members of the Commission staff individually. However, we are particularly grateful to the Chairman, The Hon. Donald S. Macdonald; the Commission's Executive Director, J. Gerald Godsoe; and the Director of Policy, Alan Nymark, all of whom were closely involved with the Research Program and played key roles in the contribution of Research to the Final Report. We wish to express our appreciation to the Commission's Administrative Advisor, Harry Stewart, for his guidance and advice, and to the Director of Publishing, Ed Matheson, who managed the research publication process. A special thanks to Jamie Benidickson, Policy Coordinator and Special Assistant to the Chairman, who played a valuable liaison role between Research and the Chairman and Commissioners. We are also grateful to our office administrator, Donna Stebbing, and to our secretarial staff, Monique Carpentier, Barbara Cowtan, Tina DeLuca, Françoise Guilbault and Marilyn Sheldon.

Finally, a well-deserved thank you to our closest assistants: Jacques J.M. Shore, *Law and Constitutional Issues*; Cynthia Williams and her successor Karen Jackson, *Politics and Institutions of Government*; and I. Lilla Connidis, *Economics*. We appreciate not only their individual contribution to each research area, but also their cooperative contribution to the research program and the Commission.

IVAN BERNIER
ALAN CAIRNS
DAVID C. SMITH

The papers in this volume of the Commission's research series discuss the Canadian experience with two types of industrial policy instruments — economic regulation and government enterprise. A description of Canadian industrial adjustment policies and an assessment of their efficacy can be found in the study by Marcia Chandler and Michael Trebilcock in volume 5. André Blais also describes recent Canadian industrial policies and evaluates them in a political context in his study in volume 45.

Three papers in this volume deal with the past effects and future prospects of various types of economic regulation. Harold Crookell assesses the effects of restrictions on foreign ownership and regional development policies on the rationalization of production in the large electrical appliance industry. He finds that restrictions on foreign acquisitions and on plant closures in particular regions not only were ultimately futile but also slowed the rationalization process and weakened the industry's ability to compete internationally.

John Chant surveys the problems associated with the regulation of financial intermediaries and of financial markets in general. These problems are illustrative of those faced by regulators or would-be regulators in general. Changes in technology are making the enforcement of regulations increasingly costly and necessitating a virtually continuous process of revision. Disputes continue to arise as to which jurisdiction should make and enforce various regulations. These issues are also addressed in the Commission monograph by Richard Schultz and Alan Alexandroff (volume 42).

Chant's study also provides insight into a number of industrial policy issues. As noted in both the Chandler-Trebilcock study and Donald Lecraw's study in volume 5, a number of critiques of the industrial policies of various countries focus on their respective financial systems. Economies in which financial intermediaries have large and sometimes controlling interests in industrial companies are said by some to have better adaptive properties than economies such as Canada's, in which intermediaries are largely confined to a lending role. Other critiques focus on entry restrictions and the lack of competition among intermediaries. The implication of Chant's analysis is that giving financial intermediaries a more conspicuous role in economic development — either by reducing restrictions on the financial and real assets they can hold or by easing entry into intermediation — entails a potentially costly incentive (conflict of interest) problem in the financial system itself. This problem is often ignored in the industrial policy literature.

Keith Acheson surveys the recent literature on non-financial economic regulation in Canada. He discusses a number of studies of the costs of regulation and concludes that they should be interpreted with caution. He notes that these studies often compute regulatory costs as if the alternative were no government intervention and as if many of the price and quantity restrictions observed in a regulatory context would not be observed in an unregulated, competitive market. Acheson argues that the alternative to regulation is often some other form of intervention such as taxation and subsidization, and that the relevant question is whether the political system is predisposed to adopt an inappropriate — that is, wasteful — form of intervention. He also argues that the incidence of regulatory costs and benefits is often unclear even after detailed study and that the price, quantity and quality restrictions observed in regulated markets could be motivated as much by a desire to minimize the cost of transacting as by monopolistic intent. The implication is that it may be more difficult than is commonly supposed to make the case that regulation is for redistributive purposes and that, if that is the purpose, regulation is an inferior means of achieving it.

Taken together, the papers of Chant and Acheson provide little to support arguments for wholesale deregulation. The existence of much of Canada's regulatory apparatus may be explained, in their view, in terms other than rent seeking. It is interesting to ponder whether these authors might also find efficiency defences for the regulation of foreign ownership.

Two papers in this volume deal with government enterprise. Sandford Borins and Barry Boothman focus on the economic efficiency of commercial Crown corporations. They argue that government enterprises need not, in theory, be less efficient than widely held private corporations. Their evaluation of the empirical evidence is that government enterprises — two of the most prominent being Air Canada and Canadian National — are at least as efficient as their private sector counterparts. They conclude, more generally, that it is the structure of the market, including the regulatory environment, rather than ownership which is the principal determinant of corporate efficiency.

Donald McFetridge concentrates on the efficiency of Crown corporations and so-called mixed enterprise in which government has only a partial ownership interest as public policy instruments. His paper also summarizes and comments on the discussion which took place at a seminar on government enterprise organized by the Royal Commission. McFetridge argues that the identity and distribution of corporate ownership is more important than Borins and Boothman — and indeed most of the literature — suggest. He concludes that the fixed ownership structure of government enterprise may reduce its adaptive properties and make it unsuited for rapidly evolving industries. He finds that government enterprise has some important advantages over regulation as a public policy instrument but that this advantage is not shared by mixed enterprise. Indeed, the latter may combine the worst rather than the best features of government and private enterprise.

The overview paper focusses on some of the broader issues of industrial strategy. The overview addresses the problems posed by interprovincial industrial policy rivalry, the pros and cons of targetted industrial assistance, and the role of industrial policy in facilitating economic adjustment. In their briefest form, the conclusions are that interprovincial industrial policy rivalry has not been a serious problem, that targetting has little to recommend it, and that adjustment assistance should be oriented primarily to individuals rather than firms or industries.

Readers interested in industrial strategy might also find interesting the Commission papers by Donald Lecraw, Reuven Brenner and Léon Courville, Marcia Chandler and Michael Trebilcock in volume 5 and the monograph by Richard Harris (volume 13).

D.G. McFetridge

ACKNOWLEDGMENTS

The Research Advisory Group on the Economics of Industrial Structure played an important role in the development of the material presented in this volume. Their contributions are gratefully acknowledged. Members of the Group were John R. Baldwin, Léon Courville, Donald J. Daly, Dennis P. De Melto, Steven Globerman, Paul Gorecki, Christopher Green, Richard G. Harris, Donald Lecraw, George Lermer, Frank Mathewson, and Michael Trebilcock.

D.G.M.

The Economics of Industrial Policy
An Overview

D.G. MCFETRIDGE

Introduction

Thousands of pages have been written on industrial policy during the last few years.[1] The topic is a controversial one. Opinion is essentially divided between those who see industrial policy as at least potentially wealth-increasing and those who see it as a form of redistribution which is collectively wealth-reducing.

The first group is concerned about the unwillingness of governments to formulate and adhere to the appropriate industrial strategy. The second group questions both the existence of a wealth-increasing industrial strategy and the ability of democratic governments, especially in federal systems, to implement one.

This paper discusses the three central issues in the industrial policy debate as it relates to Canada. These are: (a) the problems posed by federal-provincial and interprovincial industrial policy rivalry; (b) the pros and cons of targetting or picking winners; and (c) the role of proactive industrial and other policies in a positive adjustment program.

Defining Industrial Policy

In this paper, industrial policies are defined as those government policies which are intended to have a direct effect on a particular industry or firm. Davenport et al. (1983, p.1) describe industrial policy as " any government program that directly affects the economic activity of an industry, company or plant. Industrial policies are designed to change economic structures, behavior and/or performance."

Industrial policies are the embodiment of efforts by the state to encourage particular types of industrial activity. They may involve encouraging the use of particular inputs such as scientists or engineers, the production of certain goods or services such as shoes or ships or software, or the adoption of certain organizational forms such as a small business or a Canadian-owned business.

Industrial policies should be distinguished from regional development policies. In principle, industrial policies are concerned with certain types of industrial activity regardless of where they are located, while regional development policies are concerned with the interregional distribution of economic activity regardless of industrial composition. In practice, this distinction is difficult to make. Many industries receive assistance not because of what they produce or how they produce it but because of *where* they produce it. The support of coalmining in Cape Breton or textile and clothing production in Quebec reflects a concern with sustaining economic activity in those regions rather than simply with sustaining those particular types of industrial activity. When analyzing industrial policies it is important to keep in mind that most will have a geographic dimension and that this will affect the standards by which they are to be judged.

This paper does not distinguish between industrial policy and industrial strategy. The usual distinction is that a strategy is a set of policies which are mutually consistent ex post. Most observers argue that Canada does not have now and has never had an industrial strategy — with the possible exception of the C.D. Howe years.

Bliss (1982) states that even the National Policy of the nineteenth century cannot be regarded as an industrial strategy:

> One of the most common views of nineteenth century industrial policies is that the major policies . . . the tariff, transcontinental railway, homestead and immigration policies . . . coalesced or cohered into or were planned as part of one grand national development strategy, usually called the National Policy. . . .
>
> In fact . . . the term "National Policy" was used by the politicians who invented it to refer to the policy of tariff protection. . . . Throughout the nineteenth century the term did not refer to the other national development policies. Nor, at the time of its implementation or for many years afterwards was the tariff policy conceived or defended as furthering the creation of a transcontinental economy. (pp. 16–17)

Insofar as the present day is concerned, the unanimous conclusion is that Canada (and the United States) have no industrial strategy. The conclusion reached by Maule (1984, pp. 22–23) is typical — "If one could start from scratch, no sane individual would or could construct the barrage of industrial policies that presently exist in Canada, with their duplication, overlap, unknown interaction and unmeasured effect."

The problem with this sort of evaluation is that it is not enough to say ex post that a set of policies does not merge into a coherent whole. It is also necessary to look at the constraints that existed ex ante. It is not particularly productive to worry about whether or not the set of policies now in place can be regarded as a strategy, if we do not know what objectives or constraints existed when they were put in place.

Industrial Policy in Perspective

Industrial policies must be distinguished from general factor or product market policies which also affect the nature and amount of industrial activity. While these general policies may have the effect of encouraging the expansion of some industries and the contraction of others, they are not put in place explicitly to do so.

These general or framework policies operate on what Bruce Scott (1984) calls the "generic incentives" in an economy. Some examples include:

- labour market policies — such as unemployment insurance, other income support schemes, and minimum wage rates — which can change incentives and hence decisions about work, leisure and migration;
- tax policies, which can affect choices between consumption and investment and the pattern of investment;
- tariff policies, which can affect prices and production costs directly in all traded goods industries and indirectly in other industries; and
- monetary or, more generally, macroeconomic management policies, which can affect investment decisions in all industries.

It is at least arguable that generic incentives and the stability of the macroeconomic environment are more important, in terms of their effects on industrial and economic activity in general, than the sum of all industrial policies could ever be.

For example, Robin Boadway and Steven Clarke, in their study in volume 21 of the Commission's research series, cite evidence to the effect that the replacement of taxes on capital income by a tax on consumption expenditures would ultimately result in a 17 percent increase in annual per capita consumption.[2] Similarly, Harris and Cox (1983, p. 146) estimate that multilateral free trade would have the effect of increasing Canadian GNP by between 8 and 10 percent and Canadian real wages by between 20 and 25 percent. Even unilateral free trade would increase Canadian GNP by between 2 and 5 percent.

The effects of unemployment insurance and regional differences in UI benefits on the incidence of layoffs, time spent on job search, and decisions to migrate are examined by Jean-Michel Cousineau (1985) and

John Vanderkamp (1985), in volumes 1 and 64 respectively of the Commission series. These authors suggest reforms which would have significant output-increasing effects.

There is a general consensus, even among advocates of interventionist industrial policies, that the first priority is to have the appropriate general incentives to work, to save, and to direct investment toward its most productive ends. For example, Scott (1984) argues:

> The debate on U.S. industrial policy is clouded by the fact that those, such as Magaziner and Reich, who took a lead in pointing out our less than competitive policies, have built their notion of industrial policy on the premise that existing policies can be made more competitive by making them more rational and more coherent without a fundamental re-ordering of priorities and particularly without the need for sacrifice in consumer subsidies and entitlements. . . . There is little evidence that industrial policy has bloomed successfully in the climate of any welfare state. There is a good deal of evidence to the contrary. Over time it becomes another welfare program to help the disadvantaged who, in this case, rather than being supported in their existing activities should be encouraged to move to others. At the extreme, targeting becomes a panacea, no more deserving of serious attention than the Laffer curve of Reaganomics. (pp. 53–54)

In his Royal Commission study in volume 3, Edwin Mansfield concludes that:

> It seems more likely that a nation's policies concerning economic growth and investment, competition and protection, taxes and entrepreneurship have much more effect on its rate of innovation than its policies concerning research and development. Thus, if one wants to stimulate innovation, the former areas may be more important than R&D.

In sum, industrial policy is no substitute for establishing and maintaining the appropriate generic incentives. There is agreement on this. There is less agreement however as to whether, given the appropriate framework incentives, additional benefits can be derived from the encouragement of certain firms or industries.

Goals of Industrial Policy

The essential feature of industrial policies is that they alter market outcomes by changing either the pattern of production (resource reallocation) or the distribution of wealth (income redistribution) or both. The most common justification for industrial policy is that it can improve on market outcomes in the sense of making some individuals better off while leaving none worse off. That is, if markets do not direct resources to their highest valued uses, industrial policy could be invoked to correct this market failure.

Markets fail when, for some reason, exchanges which would be beneficial to the parties involved cannot be consummated. This failure of mutually beneficial exchange to occur is what is defined in economics as an externality. The first instinct of an economist seeking to rationalize the existence of an industrial policy is to look for the externality it is intended to eliminate (internalize).

Examples of externalities include, first, the public goods externality. Providers of new information, technology or on-the-job training are not able to obtain appropriate compensation from the beneficiaries of these services and, as a consequence, less of these services is provided than would be the case if compensation could be arranged. It is often argued that the solution to this problem lies in the support of innovation or training or of industries which provide general training to workers (infant-industry argument) by government.

Second, individuals may not be able to hold a sufficiently wide variety of financial assets to exploit fully the available opportunities for risk reduction through portfolio diversification. It is often argued that government can diversify more fully and/or at lower cost than can individuals and that it should therefore undertake the risk-bearing function.

Third, due perhaps to minimum wage rates or the existence of national union wage scales, job-seekers in some regions may be unable to offer their services at wage rates which are attractive to potential employers. The difference between the wage a potential employer is required to pay and a worker's alternative earnings (his opportunity cost) is sometimes called the labour externality. The labour externality is often adduced as a rationale for subsidizing industrial development projects.

While markets undeniably do fail relative to some ideal, it is the view of some economists, including myself, that the market failure justification for industrial policy and government intervention in general has been used to excess — that is, applied to situations in which it is simply not valid. This has occurred for several reasons.

First, market failure has often been adduced in support of intervention without serious study of the market in question. In many cases, externalities which for theoretical reasons are thought to exist, are in fact being internalized by market participants. A generation of economists used the example of apiaries and apple orchards to illustrate the case of a positive externality requiring government subsidization. Later investigation by Cheung (1973) revealed the existence of a well-developed set of contractual relationships between the owners of apiaries and orchards which effectively internalized this externality without government intervention. Less whimsically, investigation of a wide variety of situations in which externalities could exist — from technology transfer to urban land use — reveals that there are market arrangements to cope with them. These arrangements may be inferior to the government alternative but this should not be presumed.[3]

This raises the second issue, which is that in many cases it is not a question of market failure but of a more generalized institutional failure. Market arrangements may not be particularly satisfactory, but the effectiveness of government may be impaired for the same reasons.

Thus, it is not particularly productive to adopt what Demsetz has termed the "Nirvana approach" of comparing a stylized perfect government with an imperfect market or vice versa. There is a continuum of incentive systems each involving a different degree of government participation and different advantages and disadvantages. The problem is not so much one of market failure as of finding the form of state participation which is most productive in each situation.

Finally, many discussions of market failure have nothing to do with the failure of market mechanisms per se. Often the source of a perceived failure lies in restrictions placed on the market by governments. A good example would be the "gaps" in the residential mortgage and business term-lending markets that led to the creation of the Canada Mortgage and Housing Corporation and the Industrial Development Bank (later the Federal Business Development Bank), respectively. Had the chartered banks been allowed to take real property as security (as they now can), it is unlikely that these government lenders would have been necessary. It may be that existing restrictions on the development of markets cannot be removed, but it should nevertheless be recognized that their removal is an alternative to further intervention and that the perceived failure does not lie in the market mechanism itself.

The types of market failure that have been discussed so far are general in the sense that they apply to market activity in any country. Another line of argument is that while markets in some industrial countries may function efficiently, Canadian markets do not. An example is the Science Council's view that Canadian firms are truncated or underdeveloped and are thus incapable of perceiving and acting in their long-term self-interest. For this reason, Canadian firms are thought to need guidance and assistance which would not be required by firms in other countries. Taken to the extreme, the argument suggests that government must be the source of entrepreneurship, acting not only to guide business firms but to start them as well.

Another common rationale for industrial policy is that it serves to redistribute income in society. The underlying view here is that while market processes may be efficient, they may lead to a distribution of wealth which the community finds inequitable. Government intervention is deemed necessary to offset these inequities. Watson (1983) labels this a "market mega-failure" rationale for government intervention. Some of this intervention takes the form of industrial policies. Various forms of assistance to declining industries, whether in the form of tariff or quota protection or modernization subsidies, can be viewed as an income transfer to victims of technological change or changes in the extent of international competition.

Michael Trebilcock, in his Commission monograph (volume 8), considers the ethical arguments for wealth redistributing industrial policies. He finds "that large unanticipated private losses (principally those incurred by labour), probably whatever the source, should be subject to a compensation principle . . . directed specifically at the least-advantaged victims of change."

Trebilcock contends that ethical arguments lead to a compensation of labour rather than capital, which implies that industrial policies designed to support firms or entire industries in the name of compensating the victims of changing economic conditions are not based on strong philosophical ground. He concedes, however, that whether the compensation takes the appropriate forms and is correctly targetted depends on the cost of doing so. Sometimes industry-wide measures (such as import quotas) which impede change as well as compensating the victims of it may be the best that can be done.

Wealth-transferring industrial policies may also be instituted not because of an ethical commitment to compensate losers, but as the price demanded by them for allowing change to occur. Indeed, much of what we call industrial policy may reflect the success of various groups in using the power of the state to extort wealth from the rest of society. In this view, industrial policy has little to do with improving on market outcomes or achieving a "fairer" distribution of income. It is simply the sum of current and past rent-seeking activities. Its increasing prominence could be a reflection of the increasing prevalence and power of interest or lobby groups, which Olson (1982) argues will characterize the aging of democratic regimes.

Many of the critics of North American and European industrial policies decry the incoherence of these policies and argue for an industrial strategy or overall plan as a remedy. If industrial policy is in large measure merely the manifestation of rent seeking, it will indeed seem incoherent when viewed through an allocative efficiency lens. It will seem a good deal more coherent when viewed through an interest group or political power lens. The mere existence of an overarching industrial strategy will not change this situation. The problem lies not in the absence of a strategy but in the power of various lobbies to extract concessions. The solution lies not in the promulgation of a strategy but in measures which would render the political process less vulnerable to capture.

Trebilcock's Commission study in volume 12 makes a number of useful suggestions in this regard. His suggestions, which are considered in greater detail in subsequent sections, are of two varieties. The first relates to the policy process. He suggests that the process of setting tariffs or quotas be made more formal and open so that the contending interests may be seen and explicitly and publicly weighed. His second suggestion relates to the form of support which is provided. The support should not contribute to the creation of a new interest group. Assistance to the victims of economic change should be made contingent on evidence that recipients have taken measures to adjust to their new circumstances. Contingent adjustment assistance, also known as a policy of "positive adjustment," is based on the notion that if recipients of adjustment assistance turn to different economic activities, perhaps in different geographic areas, they will not form a continuing lobby for assistance. Applying the same logic, Trebilcock argues that a policy of targetting "winners" and favouring them with assistance will also have the effect of creating a lobby from which it will be impossible to withdraw assistance.

While the capture theory yields useful insights, there is more to most industrial policies than a simple transfer to a well-defined interest group. Restrictions on import competition and on entry of new domestic competitors are often used in combination to create pools of monopoly profit which are then transferred to a variety of groups. These may include some classes of consumers, the employees or owners of specialized resources used by protected firms, or the owners of the firms themselves. The monograph by Richard Schultz and Alan Alexandroff (volume 42 of the Commission research series) labels this process "planning regulation." Keith Acheson's study in this volume notes that the incidence of the benefits of the complex series of transfers effected by planning regulation is often difficult to discern. It is thus difficult to determine who has done the capturing and, for that matter, where redistribution backed by broad political consensus ends and capture begins.

The National Oil Policy provides one example. Some analysts argue that this policy was the result of capture of the federal government by the multinational oil companies. Others maintain that it was promulgated by the western-dominated government of the time in order to increase exports of relatively costly western Canadian crude to the United States. As Baldwin (1982) points out, the multinational oil companies benefitted from the NOP in their capacity as owners of crude oil but lost in their capacity as refiners. On balance, the multinationals as a group gained very little. Ontario and western consumers lost, but there was a mechanism to minimize consumer losses in Ontario and western provincial governments gained petroleum revenues both on foreign and domestic sales. Who gained and who lost? Who captured whom?

If the net redistribution of income resulting from industrial policy is obscure, it may occasionally also be unintentional. Industrial policy may reflect neither a desire to improve upon the market nor a desire to redistribute income. It may be a form of collective consumption.

Bliss (1982, p. 11) states that from the earliest days of the Dominion, most industrial policy has been motivated by a desire to build the kind of industrial structure it was thought a "mature" or "developed" nation should have. Then as now, being a "developed" nation was associated with having a large secondary manufacturing sector, having an industrial R&D capability, and exporting manufactured goods.

Industrial policies may well reflect a political consensus in favour of the collective purchase of an industrial structure that properly functioning markets would not generate. Bliss argues that this type of "nation-building" consensus existed in Canada between 1945 and 1957 under the leadership of C.D. Howe.

Arguments for support of self-serving interest groups can, of course, be cloaked in "nation-building" terms. Daly and Globerman (1976) find, for example, that Canadian science policy has been oriented more toward providing employment opportunities for scientists than to improving the technological capacities of Canadian industry.

Goals Versus Instruments

The purpose, then, of industrial policy is to change the composition of industrial activity for the purpose of either increasing or redistributing national income. The means by which this can be accomplished are almost limitless. Industrial policy instruments have the common feature of favouring certain firms or industries at the expense of others, either by protecting them from competition or by subsidizing their operation.

Protective measures may be directed against some or all imports from other countries (or provinces), against the entry of new domestic rivals or the expansion of existing ones. Protection can be provided by means of tariffs, quotas and procurement policy administered directly by the government. It can be provided by restrictions on output, imports or on interprovincial trade, administered by marketing boards or other regulatory bodies. It can be and often is combined with restrictions on the entry of new competitors, administered by various regulatory bodies and by investment screening agencies.

Subsidies may be provided directly in the form of payments to firms engaged in particular activities (e.g., R&D, capital investment) or indirectly through the tax system in the form of earlier or larger deductions, tax credits or lower tax rates. Subsidies may also be implicit, taking the form of financing or other services provided at below market prices. Prominent in this regard are loans, loan guarantees and equity provided at below market rates of return.

This list of possible industrial policy instruments and combinations thereof could be extended indefinitely. Classification difficulties will also arise with a number of policies which are both means and ends, instruments and goals. The control of foreign ownership may, for example, be an end in itself, Canadian ownership perhaps being desirable for its own sake. It may also be a means in that domestic ownership may be thought to lead to better economic performance. At another level there remains the question of how domestic ownership is to be encouraged and foreign ownership discouraged. Similarly, competition policy also has both means and ends components.

Instrument classification can occur at a number of levels. At the most general level, a distinction may be made between protecting and subsidizing instruments. At a second and more operational level, subsidies can be classified in terms of the activity (investment, employment, production, R&D, and so on) to which the subsidy is tied. A third classification might involve the framework within which support or protection is administered (government department, enterprise, regulatory tribunal, marketing board, and so on). A similar (two level) mode of classification is used by André Blais in his research monograph for the Royal Commission (volume 45):

> A more promising avenue would be to consider the destination and the type of government assistance. The simplest and most fundamental distinction would appear to be the one between domestic assistance, which is specifically targetted to domestic production, and "exterior" aid to the protection, exercised at the borders . . . which strikes imports and stimulates national production through higher prices charged for these imports because of the restrictions on their quantity.
>
> Domestic assistance and protection are themselves made up of specific instruments particular to each type of assistance. Domestic assistance can be either financial or technical. Financial assistance can be direct (grants, loans, loan guarantees) or indirect, either through tax measures or government procurement policies. As for protection, the principle could have been the one that distinguishes between policies affecting the price of imports and policies that determine their quantity.

Blais defines protection more narrowly than I have, but the basic issues concerning choice of instrument remain — whether to protect or subsidize and how to protect or subsidize.

Blais argues further that the apparent increase in industrial policy intervention in recent years is more a substitution of support for protection, especially tariff protection. The net result, in his view, has been a liberalization of international trade. That is, while various forms of industrial policy support have been put in place by governments as a replacement for declining tariffs, the degree of intervention, measured in terms of net protection or support supplied, has declined.

In this connection, Blais' work raises two important points. The first is that the degree of industrial policy intervention is properly measured only if all instruments are taken into account. Blais is probably correct in his contention that the increase in support conveyed by subsidies and government enterprise and the like does not compensate for the decline in support conveyed via the tariff mechanism.

Second, the possibility of replacing some of the protection formerly provided by the tariff, at least temporarily, with other forms of support may be a precondition for trade liberalization. Thus, as Trebilcock also suggests, industrial policy can be viewed as compensation to groups adversely affected either by exogenous change or by policy-induced change such as tariff reduction.

As Reuven Brenner and Léon Courville observe in their Commission study in volume 5, many industrial policies may seem inefficient relative to the ideal but are not necessarily worse than the alternative of no change at all.

While comparatively little attention has been paid to it, the manner in which decisions are made to support a particular activity, firm or industry may be as important as the means by which this support is conveyed. Many argue that the categorization of decision making as involving either the government or the market is too simplistic. McMillan (1984) and Ouchi (1984), among others, describe the process by which government and business collaborate to form and administer industrial policy in Japan. There is not the same adversarial relationship as is said to exist in North America and western parts of Europe.

Many argue that there is nothing special about the industrial policy instruments applied in Japan. They are the familiar procurement policies, below-market and/or forgivable loans, subsidies, and tax credits used in other countries. What many feel is special is the extent to which these instruments have been administered in pursuit of efficiency rather than redistributive goals. The Japanese industrial policy apparatus seems somehow less vulnerable to rent seeking than is the case in North America and much of Europe.

A number of suggestions have been made as to how various societies — the Japanese in particular — are able to constrain rent seeking. Olson (1982) suggests that peak or all-encompassing interest groups (such as employers' associations) neutralize their component special interests and present the government with an agenda which better reflects the common good. Marcia Chandler and Michael Trebilcock, in their study in volume 5 of the Commission series, discuss this idea and find it wanting in many respects.

Ouchi (1984) also sees the solution to the problem in terms of broader interest groups, a closer integration between these interest groups and the government, and more effective interaction among the interest groups themselves:

> The nation will be able to resolve its differences and move ahead only if the interest groups confront one another directly and frequently and settle their disputes. . . . It must be the task of government that we create and maintain a dialogue among interest groups within the policy so that hundreds and thousands of lesser but still important disputes can be settled among those who will gain or lose by the settlement. (pp. 210–11)

For McMillan, the success of Japanese industrial policy can be explained in terms of willingness to plan industrial structure with the overriding goal of achieving global competitiveness and a planning process which is characterized by:

- thorough discussions and information exchange between industry and government; and
- coordination of the instruments of government policy toward the agreed upon ends.

Again the role of industry associations, peak association (the Keidanren) and advisory councils and the salutary effect of the dialogue occurring within them is emphasized as having contributed to the success of industrial policy in Japan.

Provincial Industrial Policies

In a federal state, industrial policies can be administered by different levels of government. This raises problems concerning not only choice of instrument but also level of jurisdiction.

Decentralizing administration of industrial policy may be beneficial in that industrial policy objectives may be simpler and clearer and performance evaluation may be easier at the provincial level of government. On the other hand, it may be difficult to coordinate the policies of individual provinces, and to prevent the policies of one province from imposing costs on others.

The essential issue in the discussion of provincial industrial policies is the nature, extent and potential cost of industrial policy rivalry among provinces and, of course, between federal and provincial levels. This issue is addressed by Jenkin (1983) and Tupper (1985), among others.

The emergence of provincial industrial policies in Ontario and Quebec after 1960 is described by Faucher et al. (1983) and Davenport et al. (1983). Both provinces experienced significant growth in their transfers to business for industrial development purposes during the 1967–75 period and apparently relatively little growth thereafter (Faucher et al., 1983, p. 70).

These provinces differ with respect to the types of transfers made, with Quebec tending to rely relatively more on subsidies and loan guarantees and Ontario more on loans. Quebec's intervention has been greater than Ontario's in the sense that transfers to business relative to total business investment are larger (Faucher et al., 1983, p. 68; Davenport et al., 1983, pp. 12–20).

Cash transfers represent a relatively small portion of the assistance granted by these provinces to business. They are also small relative to provincial GDP and to federal transfers made for the same purpose. Indeed, Jenkin (1983, pp.152–53) finds that federal transfers to business for economic development are approximately three times as large as those of all ten provinces.

Provincial support is also conveyed through the subsidization of business services such as electricity and waste disposal and through procurement and regulatory arrangements which protect local business from competition from abroad or from other provinces. Government and mixed enterprises are increasingly used as a means of subsidizing local production. In this case, the subsidy takes the form of the acceptance by a provincial government of a lower-than-normal return on its equity in firms which engage in certain activities within the province.

Some provinces have begun to articulate industrial strategies. The province of Ontario details its efforts and plans for the encouragement of technological innovation in a paper published by the Ministry of Treasury and Economics (Grossman, 1984). It emphasizes education and training, innovation and technology centres, and the supply of capital to innovative firms. The most prominent provincial initiatives in this regard have been establishment of the IDEA Corporation, a provincial Crown corporation which finances technological innovation; the Small Business Development Corporation's program which offers tax credits for equity investment in small business; and six provincial technology centres which assist local businesses in adopting new technologies.

The province of Alberta details its proposed industrial strategy in a white paper (Alberta, 1984). The essence of the proposed Alberta strategy is:

- cooperation with the private sector in undertaking large-scale projects such as oil sands, and heavy oil plants and transportation facilities utilizing assistance measures, which would include royalty deferrals, loans, loan guarantees, and direct equity involvement;
- selection of specific sectors for special support, with support being directed to sectors that offer security and expansion of primary and secondary jobs (high technology and resource processing fields "should be prime candidates for support"; tax incentives should be the primary means of support with subsidies to be used where tax incentives would be inadequate);
- government initiation of export consortia, provided prospects for foreign sales are improved as a consequence; and
- development of a procurement policy to give advantage to Alberta-based suppliers and contractors.

Support for export-oriented high-technology activity would also be provided by new government-supported institutions, including an export corporation, an international business institute, and an innovation centre.

Alberta's proposed industrial strategy is analyzed in detail by a number of industrial policy authorities (see Walker, 1984). Comment on some of its fundamental assumptions, specifically regarding the gains from picking high-tech winners, also appears below in the section on targetting. For the present, however, it is enough to illustrate the extent and nature of provincial industrial policy activism. The recent activities of Saskatchewan (in resource and high technology fields) and Quebec (in virtually all fields) provide additional illustrations.

The extent and nature of provincial barriers to the free movements of goods, people and capital are discussed by Jenkin (1983, pp. 89–94) and exhaustively catalogued by Trebilcock et al. (1983, pp. 243–351). Whalley (1983, pp. 161–200) measures the welfare cost of these barriers. Jenkin cites the three major barriers — procurement policy, control over capital flows, and control over resource extraction.

Quebec, Newfoundland, Nova Scotia, British Columbia and Alberta maintain preferences of 10 to 15 percent for local suppliers. Many provinces require that a portion of private pension fund and insurance company assets be invested within the province. Provinces have occasionally intervened to block the sale of locally prominent corporations to "outside" interests (Credit Foncier, MacMillan Bloedel). More recently, some provinces have used provincial holding companies and pension fund money to acquire control of companies regarded as crucial to provincial development. The most important example is the 30 and 12 percent interests in Domtar held by the Caisse de dépot et placement du Québec and the Société Général du Financement, respectively. Finally, provinces have sometimes used their jurisdiction over resource extraction to control the amounts of some resources (crude oil, potash) available either elsewhere in Canada or abroad.

While these and other restrictions have received considerable attention, the general consensus is that they are not important. Jenkin (1983) notes:

> The barrier issue seems of limited important. And the degree to which it has attracted the attention of policy makers is probably the result of the few isolated and spectacular cases which have arisen. Barriers are still the exception rather than the rule. . . . (p. 94)

Whalley provides estimates of the welfare losses resulting from provincial barriers to the movement of goods, labour and capital. He concludes that with respect to goods flows, "A working hypothesis . . . is that the potential welfare costs involved in the distortions of interprovincial goods trade in Canada are quite small, perhaps in the region of one-half of one percent of GNP" (1983, p. 191).

With respect to barriers to labour flows, Whalley concludes that the welfare cost is insignificant, perhaps 0.04 percent of GNP. Barriers to the flow of capital are also deemed to be inconsequential: "Save for energy policies, interprovincial capital market distortions are small and some supposed distortions are not distortions at all. On this basis an educated guess could be that the annual welfare costs are unlikely to exceed those for labour distortions" (1983, p. 193). Thus, measures to protect provincial industry are generally regarded as having no significant efficiency consequences.

Provincial industrial development subsidies and subsidy programs are detailed by Trebilcock et al. (1983). Jenkin notes an emerging tendency for provinces to offer corporate tax incentives in the area of small business (in Ontario and Quebec), R&D (in Quebec), and equity investment (in Quebec).

Jenkin also notes that provincial industrial subsidies can result in the fragmentation of an industry, leading to smaller scales of operation and higher costs. This problem is not confined to provincial subsidies. Federal subsidies to new entrants in a number of industries have led to the bankruptcy of existing producers in some cases and excess capacity in others.[4]

It is generally agreed that this problem has not been severe, because provincial subsidies to industry have been relatively small and because the provinces do not often compete for the same type of industrial activity. This may change as more provinces attempt to attract "high-tech" industries.

For Allan Tupper, in his study in volume 44 of the Commission series, provincial industrial policy rivalry is cause for concern:

> Interprovincial rivalries and conflicts of interest add to the incoherence of Canadian industrial policy. As the provincial economic role has expanded, fairly frequent and intense international competition for industry has emerged. Provincial governments are now concerned with offering concessions to industry that are comparable with their neighbours. And in the modern era at least three governments seek to nurture provincial petrochemical industries while another six harbour ambitions in steel. In its most extreme form, interprovincial competition for industry has degenerated into spectacular instances of "bidding wars" for new industry. A revealing example of this seemingly irrational activity occurred in 1978, when Ontario, Quebec and several American states openly bid for new automobile plants. Perhaps more shocking is the admission by several provincial governments that they seek to influence firms to relocate in Canada . . . corporations tend to be the major beneficiaries of interprovincial rivalries.

Tupper appears to be inferring the existence of widespread and economically significant interprovincial industrial policy rivalry from a few events. Apart from this, however, there is the question of whether a provincial bidding rivalry for new industry would necessarily be a bad thing, if it did exist.

As suggested earlier, when labour is immobile and institutional restrictions keep wage rates from adjusting to clear the labour market, what has come to be called a labour externality may exist. Specifically, an employer may be willing to pay a wage which is better than a worker's best alternative but less than the institutionally determined minimum, and so there is no offer of employment.

In this case, a third-best alternative may be to subsidize potential employers in the amount of the difference between what they must pay a worker and what the worker's output is worth to them. This type of subsidy is, in effect, "buying jobs." There will then be a "market for jobs" in which governments are the buyers and footloose firms — those not tied to some particular production location — are the sellers. The governments involved will bid up to the amount of the labour externality involved to attract these firms. The winning bidder will be the jurisdiction with the greatest externality. In the simple case described here, that would be the jurisdiction in which the alternatives for labour and other resources are the least favourable.

The possibility that this type of bidding for jobs could occur on an international scale is discussed by Conklin (1984). It could also occur on a national scale. In either case, the process is efficient in the restricted sense that the jurisdiction with the greatest "need" — that is, the greatest excess of the wage rate over opportunity cost — gets the firm. Bidding for industry is thus a substitute for wage flexibility and/or labour mobility.

While bidding for industry is potentially beneficial in that industry locates where the need is greatest, the bidding process may also have distributive consequences. Specifically, a firm — Bell Helicopter, for example — may be in a position to demand subsidies equal to the entire benefit derived by the jurisdiction in which it locates in return for locating there. All the surplus resulting from the transaction goes to the (possibly foreign-owned) firm and none to the jurisdiction in which it ultimately locates. Hence, while the "market for industrial location" leads to efficient locational decisions, the winning jurisdiction is not better off for having attracted the new industry. In this sense, Tupper's fears are not groundless and there would be gains to provinces and nations from coordinating their bidding activity to achieve the same locational outcome but at a lower price.

At the risk of complicating what the reader may already consider an excessively abstract analysis, I must add that the conclusion reached above assumes that Bell Helicopter is somehow unique as a provider of jobs. This is generally not the case. Many firms are in a position to provide the high-skill or technology-intensive or meaningful jobs that most jurisdictions are seeking to attract. The market for industrial location may be competitive on both sides, and if Bell Helicopter wants too much, then perhaps 3M will locate a plant in the same jurisdiction for less. In this case, the winning jurisdiction need not be left without surplus and is the better off for having attracted the new industry. There may still be gains from international coordination of bidding for industry of the type which exists in the European Economic Community (see Conklin, 1984, pp.11–13) or from interprovincial coordination, but these gains will be smaller than when the suppliers of jobs are unique.

It should be reemphasized that "bidding for jobs" makes some sense only if the resources involved are assumed to be immobile and their prices inflexible. It is not necessarily preferable to policies, such as those advocated by Trebilcock (1985b), which encourage relocation of workers to areas in which their employment need not be subsidized. Indeed, it is possible that the emergence of jurisdictional bidding for new industry has reduced labour mobility and wage flexibility and that, as a consequence, there will be even more of it in the future.

Targetting

The Theory of Targetting

Industrial policy, as we have defined it, always involves encouraging certain industrial activities at the expense of others. In this sense, all industrial policy involves targetting — choosing those firms or industries that will receive support in the form of subsidization and/or protection and those that will not.

What targetting has come to mean in recent years, however, is that industrial policy can be used to improve on market outcomes — that is, to increase rather than simply redistribute national income.

The impetus for targetting has come from observation of the apparent success Japan has had as a consequence of orienting its industrial production toward goods and services characterized by high technological content, high value-added and a quickly expanding world market.

Targetting is also known as "engineering a comparative advantage." The essence of this notion is that the pattern of a nation's trade can be determined by forces other than its factor endowment (natural resources, labour and capital). While it is true that, given a sufficient expenditure, Canada can export bananas, this is not what the proponents of targetting are arguing. They are arguing that, given the appropriate strategy, Canada is as able to export technology-intensive goods profitably as any other industry country.

The proponents of targetting are making two arguments which require detailed consideration. First, there are gains to be realized by any industrialized or newly industrialized country from timely specialization in goods and services characterized by rapidly growing world demand and relatively high technological intensity and rate of technological progress.[5] Second, left to themselves, business firms will not find it in their interest to specialize in this fashion, so they must be encouraged to do so by public policy.

Analysis begins with the properties of high-growth, technology-intensive goods and services that make their production so attractive. The reason these goods promise long-term supranormal profits is that their production is thought to be characterized by a learning or experience curve, or by what some analysts have called dynamic cost advantages. An experience curve is simply a relationship between the cost of production and accumulated production volume. The greater the accumulated volume, the lower the per unit costs. A firm which is the first to enter a market and which builds up sufficient production volume (experience) can confront potential rivals with a production cost advantage that will deter them from entering. This is called pre-emption of the market. Successful pre-emption implies a monopoly, perhaps a worldwide monopoly, of the market in question.

Notice that it is the technological progress or learning curve aspect which is important. The learning which has served to lower unit costs is, in the parlance of contemporary industrial organization, a sunk or market-specific asset. It is this "sunkness" which serves as the barrier to the entry of new competition as the market develops.

Successful pre-emption may, but need not necessarily, result in excess profits. The market may fail to develop. Rivals may leapfrog to the next generation of technology, leaving the would-be monopolist at the bottom of an obsolete learning curve. Most importantly, there could be rivalry to pre-empt the market. There could, in the simplest terms, be a race to be first in the market and obtain the advantages of incumbency (first-mover advantages) described above. This rivalry may exhaust all the potential profit inherent in successful pre-emption. A firm participating in these races for market niches will win with some with profit to spare, win some and exhaust its potential profit in so doing, and lose some. In the final analysis, it will earn, on average, a normal rate of return commensurate with the risk involved.

The foregoing establishes a private interest in racing for and pre-empting market niches. This strategy is most likely to prove profitable in industries characterized by experience curves. The role for industrial policy has yet to be established. Given the profit opportunities that it offers, why does entry into markets characterized by dynamic cost advantages have to be encouraged by the government?

The answer to this question is provided in a major study of industrial policy written for this Royal Commission by Richard Harris (volume 13 of the research series). Like any good economist, Professor Harris looks for the externality. Why is the social return to the pre-emption of international markets for high-technology products greater than the private return?

The reason, according to Harris, is that part of the benefits of successful market pre-emption accrue to labour rather than to capital: "In an open economy framework, the main social return to R&D is in the form of supernormal profits on equity, but a great deal of it may be in the form of higher wages to domestic labour" (1985, p. 101).

The externality here is again a labour externality. Workers capture part of the profit from successful pre-emption and therefore the private rate of return on what Harris calls Schumpeterian competition is less than the social return. In Harris's view, there are two reasons why labour may capture part of these "Schumpeterian rents."

The first is that the supply schedule of labour to the Schumpeterian firm or industry may be upward-sloping. This implies that unique capabilities are required of workers in this industry. Failing this, the supply of labour to the industry will be infinitely elastic at a wage which compensates for the cost of skill acquisition and for physical and financial risk.

Harris's second argument is that:

> In most Schumpeterian industries, workers acquire on-the-job skills and experience which makes them more productive within the firm than in alternative employment. At the same time, this makes them more productive than a new worker to the firm's work force. . . . The relationship between the firm and its workers can be described as a situation of bilateral monopoly. . . . the monopoly power of the firm is transferred to some extent to its workers. (p. 102)

Harris's argument that industrial policies should be designed to encourage technology-intensive firms and industries derives largely from his view that the returns from successful pre-emption of world markets for these goods and services accrue in part to domestic workers.

Most criticism of arguments for targeting are of the operational variety, arguing that while it is theoretically attractive, it is impractical. Questions can also be raised at the theoretical level regarding the existence of both the labour externality and ex ante excess profits (Schumpeterian rents).

With respect to the externality argument, note first that if, as the quotation above suggests, the skills acquired by the workers are specific to the firm — the workers cannot threaten to take them elsewhere and do not have much in the way of bargaining power. In the event that they do, this would normally be reflected in the initial supply price of labour.

Second, if the skills acquired by the workers are transferable, then a standard infant-industry situation results. If workers and firms are unable to take account of the benefits they confer on each other by contractual means, the usual argument for subsidization applies. This does not, at this stage, imply any special treatment for technology-intensive firms. Special support for technology-intensive industries would be justified if the transferable learning were greater in these sectors. An example might be the number of new technology-intensive companies formed by former employees of Bell-Northern Research.

Third, the fact that technology-intensive production is characterized by a learning curve does not necessarily imply that workers in such industries acquire more-than-normal additional skills during their employment. Learning could inhere entirely in the organization — that is, in the form of better production arrangements and practices. In this event, there is no externality.

Fourth, if workers are mobile internationally or if, as has become common practice, production is moved abroad early in the product cycle, the externality becomes external to the domestic economy and the argument for special support is correspondingly weakened. With respect to the potential rents or excess profits to be earned by participating in Schumpeterian competition, it has already been argued that, on average, Schumpeterian competitors will just cover their opportunity cost. It is true that successful pioneers in various industries have earned huge profits. This is the same as observing that the rate of return on a winning lottery ticket is very high. The question is why a firm would expect to earn an excess return, on average, from its efforts to pre-empt market niches and why, if it did expect an excess return, this did not attract even more rivals.

It may be that there are a limited number of firms big enough to participate in Schumpeterian competition. Indeed, Harris's case for targetting specific firms is based on the necessity of building up Canadian firms to the size at which they can engage in Schumpeterian competition. This argument may have some validity, although first-mover advantages can be competed away by as few as two rivals and the rivalry for world market pre-emption would certainly involve more rivals than that. Moreover, for what it is worth, the existing empirical literature has never shown much in the way of advantages from sheer size.

Finally, the arguments applying to the private return also apply to the social return from Schumpeterian competition. Support of Schumpeterian firms by the national governments of all industrialized countries would have the effect of driving down the expected social return from participating in this rivalry to the point at which this endeavour offers no advantages over any other use of national resources.

While this discussion concentrates on the theoretical arguments for targetting adduced by Harris, other rigorous arguments for targetting have recently emerged. The most prominent of these is by Spencer and Brander (1983). Their theory and others which are even more recent are discussed by Spence (1984) and Krugman (1984).

Targetting in Operation

If targetting is to be practiced, it must be determined:

- which firms or groups of firms should receive support;
- how the firms to be supported should be determined; and
- what type of support is to be provided.

Harris (1985) makes a number of suggestions in this regard:

> First, the policy should be targetted specifically at small to medium size domestic firms in technologically progressive industries where the benefits are likely to emerge and the barriers to entry in export markets are greatest. Second, it should provide support to the firm in its early phase of development either prior to getting into the export market or shortly thereafter. Third, programs should be targetted at firms rather than industries, or at individual R&D projects. . . . Two types of policies seem like obvious candidates: support of R&D through tax, subsidy, loan guarantees, or procurement policies; and explicit underwriting of lower cost loans in the capital market to foster the development of these types of firms. (p. 138)

Additional administrative criteria include:

- not supporting industries already partly through the product cycle;
- not intervening directly to promote mergers and rationalization;
- not providing export subsidies;
- terminating support if firms prove unable to penetrate export markets; and
- terminating support when firms are operating successfully in export markets.

An aspect of targetting, then, is to support what Steed (1982) calls threshold firms in high-technology industries. There remains the question of how a threshold firm might be defined and which threshold firms should receive support. There must be a choice, because the logic of pre-emption and the learning curve specifies that volume must be built up in the domestic market. Hence, the government must actively discourage domestic firms from racing to pre-empt the same market niche. Thus the essence of targetting is choosing, favouring some firms and actively discouraging others.

Steed attempts to define specifically the type of firms which should receive support. He defines a threshold firm as "a Canadian-owned enterprise with 100 to 2499 employees in Canada that provides 100 or more jobs at one or several establishments classified according to its (their) main product as belonging to one of the more technology-intensive sectors" (p. 47). Steed then divides his threshold firms into "sleepers" (below-average profits) and "thrusters" (above-average profits). In the machinery sector, for example, there are nine "threshold thrusters" (p. 81).

Threshold firms are also divided into "speedsters" and "laggards," which are the top and bottom 25 percent of firms ranked according to employment growth, respectively (p. 89). Assuming that the "thrusters" and the "speedsters" are not identical, Steed implicitly defines a target group of something under nine Canadian-owned machinery producers with above-average profits and high employment growth, which he might consider worthy of special assistance.

Members of this group would be offered assistance tailored to their specific needs. Steed argues that while some of these firms do not want assistance and past attempts to provide assistance have not been particularly successful, this can be remedied by an assistance mechanism that is "more responsive" (p. 140).

The measures from which each of the target firms might choose include training, export incentives, R&D grants, "more competitive loans," research centres, tooling development grants, joint venture arrangements, foreign technology surveillance, procurement favouritism, export consortia arrangements, and overseas market appraisals (pp. 141–42).

Similar measures including firm-specific R&D subsidies, promotion of high-tech joint ventures and mergers, and the subsidization of equity capital for technology-intensive firms are advocated by the Science Council (1979, 1981, 1984).

Implementation Problems and Experience

The targetting mechanism suggested in the previous section involves support of small, high-profit, fast-growing firms in industries characterized by a high rate of technical progress and a high rate of growth of world demand.

Some of the potential problems with targetting become apparent when the selection criteria are examined. Other things being equal, it is better to have a position in a fast-growing market with entry barriers than in a slow-growth easy-entry market. The point is that this is hardly proprietary knowledge. The potential profit characteristics of various markets will generally be known to others besides Canadians. The number of rivals for a particular market niche will reflect its potential profitability. This will tend to equalize the expected returns from participating in the rivalry for individual markets.

With respect to the choice criteria at the firm level, assisting firms with the highest growth and profit rates has nothing to do with picking a winner in the investment sense. Realization of an excess return in the latter sense implies investment in a firm with unrecognized potential, which — to use Steed's terms — would require further scrutiny of the "sleepers" and "laggards."

The ability to pick winners in the investment sense is perhaps not the issue. Harris would argue that the important thing is to encourage firms which demonstrate a potential for growth to a sufficient size to participate in Schumpeterian competition from a Canadian base. Whether the profit potential (private return) has been fully capitalized or not is irrelevant.

This is only partly correct, as consideration of the next choice criterion reveals. Steed would confine assistance to Canadian-owned firms.

Presumably, the reason is that a Canadian-owned firm is more likely to exploit world market niches from a Canadian base, allowing Canadian workers to share in the excess profits involved. This raises three issues.

First, it is not necessarily true that a foreign-owned threshold firm, having achieved success, is more likely to leave Canada than a domestically owned firm. Indeed, Daly and McCharles (1983) determine from a series of interviews that managers of smaller Canadian-owned firms showed no reluctance to move their production facilities abroad.

Second, if facilities are moved abroad, the rationale for government support disappears. Thus, from a public policy point of view, picking winners involves much more than picking products which can be sold profitably. The products must be manufactured (at least initially) and improved locally, this activity must improve the skills of the local labour force, and this new learning must not be readily transferable to other countries.

Third, foreign ownership matters either if foreign-owned firms are more likely to accept Canadian R&D and financial support and exploit the results elsewhere, or if the foreign-owned firm happens to be an established multinational. As suggested in the preceding section, an established multinational such as Pratt and Whitney or Bell Helicopter will sell high-technology jobs to the Canadian or any other government at a price which may or may not leave that government with any surplus.

This brings us to the industrial policy analogue of buying an undervalued stock. The government wishes to purchase high-technology jobs at the lowest possible price. The argument for supporting threshold firms in their efforts to grow to the size necessary to participate in Schumpeterian competition is that this may be less costly than dealing with the established firms. This implies that the Canadian authorities can recognize the potential in a Canadian firm before other governments can, which seems reasonable, but also that the government and the threshold firms can make a binding arrangement (to exploit new technologies from a Canadian base), which seems less reasonable.

Some other problems that will burden the targetting process include, first, the problem of terminating assistance. Harris proposes that assistance be terminated once world markets have been penetrated or once it becomes apparent that this will never happen. Trebilcock (1985b) argues that the support of a particular firm creates an interest group which may be able to lobby for continuing assistance regardless of merit. Moreover, it is not clear that a government could terminate assistance even to a successful firm. Presumably the learning externality is an ongoing phenomenon. The subsidies spent to build the firm up to Schumpeterian size are sunk. The now-successful Schumpeterian competitor can demand continuing support and the government must either provide it or lose the benefits of future learning.

There is also the problem of the firm selection mechanism. Unlike the case of basic and generic applied research, which can be guided by objective peer group oversight, the selection of Schumpeterian competitors is likely to be all but crippled by opportunism. As Nelson (1982) argues, considerable proprietary wealth rides on the outcome of the selection process. Where, then, does one find an informed yet objective opinion?

In his analysis of firm-specific subsidies (investment grants), Usher (1983) cites further problems with targetted support. First, it is costly to administer — administration costs are estimated to be roughly 23.1 cents per dollar transferred (p. 67).[6] Second, firm-specific support is more vulnerable to rent seeking (chap. VI). Finally, firm-specific subsidies may not result in a net increase in the activity the government seeks to encourage. This is the much-discussed incrementality problem.

As Usher and others note, subsidized investment projects may not be incremental to the firm, in that they would be undertaken in any case. Society then simply loses the cost of making the transfer. Harris and Steed recommend subsidizing firms rather than projects. This obviates project-rearrangement problems but does not ensure firm-level incrementality. The latter depends on the existence of a menu of extra-marginal investment projects that would be undertaken only with the inducement of a subsidy.

Supported projects may be incremental to the firm but not to the market, because supported firms may simply crowd out competitors. To advocates of targetting, this is not a problem. Indeed, it is what is supposed to happen. However, this is not, as Usher suggests, necessarily a question of an inefficient firm crowding out an efficient one. Those favouring targetting would maintain that if the targetting is properly done, a larger learning externality will be crowding out a smaller one.[7] Whether targetting decisions can ever be so well informed as to make this distinction, however, must be regarded as doubtful.

It should also be noted that industrial policy, whether targetted or untargetted, rearranges the pattern of production. Something must be crowded out. It may be investment in the same market or in a different market, or it may be consumption. General R&D support, for example, will lead to the expansion of the more R&D-intensive industries at the expense of the less R&D-intensive.

The basic question is, or should be, whether the social return (including learning and other externalities) on the supported activity exceeds the social return on the crowded-out activity. It is generally assumed that as a consequence of the taxation of capital income, the marginal return on investment exceeds the return on consumption. Given this distortion, crowding out consumption is socially beneficial. No such presumption can be made regarding the crowding out of investment.

Palda (1985) and others argue that technological intensity must be defined in much broader terms than Steed, Scott and others do. It turns out that the naive measures of technological intensity (R&D intensity) tell us about the same thing as the more sophisticated measures (see the study by McFetridge and Corvari in volume 3 of the Commission series). What is not known, however, is whether any of these measures are related to the kind of worker-appropriated learning necessary to rationalize industrial policy intervention.

Experience with targetting has been evaluated by a number of authors including George (1983), Nelson (1982), Krugman (1983, 1984) and Scott (1984). George (1983, pp. 31–34) describes a targetting exercise carried out by the federal government in 1981. The study began with 12,000 product classes in 144 industries and eliminated those with the following characteristics:

- industries outside of secondary manufacturing;
- industries that used "old" processes or were known to be declining because of changes in technology;
- industries in which government involvement was already significant;
- industries in which imports were less than the overall industrial average; and
- industries with 1977–79 growth rates of less than 10 percent.

The remaining 20 industries were broken down into 735 sub-industries and again subjected to the 1977–79 growth-rate test. The survivors of that test (less 11 others removed for other reasons) totalled 69 sub-industries producing 642 commodities. These were subjected to the same screening process as the industries. This left 102 commodities, of which the following had the highest import intensities (George, 1983, p. 33):

- computer equipment not elsewhere specified, parts of;
- electronic equipment components;
- loader, front end integrator, excavator, wheel type;
- drilling machinery, oil well rotary type, parts;
- semi-conductors, not elsewhere specified;
- integrated circuits;
- combines, agricultural parts and accessories;
- computer equipment, not elsewhere specified; and
- plates, carbon steel, not elsewhere specified, 60"–100" wide, cut length.

The detail presented here may be tedious but it is essential. It has been suggested that winning sectors, firms or products can be selected as a matter of routine. There is some humour in a list of winners such as the one reproduced above, which includes combines, agricultural parts and accessories, and front-end loaders. But to find some bad investments (ex post) in someone's list of winners does not necessarily discredit either the method or the goal.

What raises serious doubts are the details of the method and the application. The individuals deriving this list may not have found their career paths altered, regardless of how well the industries did that they chose. More importantly, they used data that were outdated (1977–79 growth rates for winners chosen in 1981). They used data grouped for statistical purposes which may have had no relationship at all to products that actually offer an opportunity. They used selection criteria which bore no discernible relationship to what might normally be deemed a winner.

In this case, the emphasis was on import substitution. As George notes (p. 34), a high import intensity may indicate that domestic producers are already losers. It may also be the case that the high-import-intensity products observed were simply the result of intra-industry trade in which some products in an industry are exported and some are imported — that is, a consequence of specialization. This strategy of picking winners would move Canadian industry away from this specialization.

Although market growth is discussed above, it should be reiterated that relying on market growth data — even recent data — does have an "after the fact" element to it. Picking a winner in a commercial context usually involves anticipating market growth, rather than waiting for it to happen and to be recorded and analyzed, and then proposing entry. This is also true of the strategy of pre-empting a market niche, which cannot be achieved simply by waiting for statistical evidence on market growth. The true winners will revitalize (or "demature" — to use the term coined by Abernathy et al., 1983) a declining market. Winning firms may struggle for years pioneering — that is, essentially creating — a market. Choosing winning products from past growth rates calculated from the census of manufactures is not only not a good method, it may well mean heading in entirely the wrong direction.

Nelson (1982) provides a comprehensive assessment of alternative support strategies in a U.S. context. He concludes for a number of reasons, some of which are given above, that the U.S. effort in the applied generic research area has been effective while the effort in the proprietary-commercial area has not:

> The lesson here is a general one. . . . There are many other studied cases, most of these European, in which government has tried to identify and support particular products that it was hoped would ultimately prove to be commercial success. While there are a few successes, the batting average has been very low, except when the government in question has been willing to subsidize or require the procurement of the completed product as well as the R&D on it.

This should not be surprising. In many of the industries in which this has been attempted (in Europe), the private companies also were investing in R&D, and the government was in a position either of duplicating private effort, subsidizing that effort and probably therefore replacing private R&D monies, or investing in a design that the private companies had decided to leave alone. (p. 469)

George (1983) surveys the industrial policies of ten nations, and finds that three — Ireland, France and Japan — profess to follow a strategy of targetting winning industries, firms or projects. The other seven — Britain, Norway, Sweden, West Germany, the Netherlands, Italy and Canada — profess to follow the opposite course and employ either general incentives or no incentives. Of the professed targetters, Ireland turns out to follow a strategy of labelling as a winner any firm it is able to attract (p. 20). France attempts to pick winners by using a statistical method to discern winning sectors (p. 35). The most recent list of chosen winners includes the usual suspects — telecommunications, aviation and space, underwater technology, new engineering technology, bio-technology, nuclear energy, robotics and machine tools and energy utilization (p. 36).

With respect to the French experience, Scott (1984) concludes:

Successful targeting seems to depend more on a broad commitment to productivity and competitiveness than on technical analyses of which industries to promote and which to exit. France has practiced targeting almost as long as Japan, beginning with similar concepts based on wartime rationing and using similar control mechanisms including credit controls and administrative guidance. And, like Japanese firms, large French firms basically accepted that government should consult with industry and give guidance from time to time. For a variety of reasons, the French results have been modest. There has been a much lower priority given to international competitiveness both at the political level and among key bureaucrats. . . . Savings were targeted disproportionately toward losers because they were political problems, and toward housing . . . (pp. 49–50)

Lecraw (1985) echoes these sentiments, arguing that despite their pro-fessions to the contrary, the French have never fully carried through a targetting exercise (plans are announced only to be dropped later) and that the attention received by a sector has more to do with salvaging declining regions or building up French industrial prestige than with the existence of high-yield investments. The willingness to abandon or at least avoid social support for losers is crucial. To support everybody is to support nobody.

The success of the Japanese economy is indisputable. There is also general agreement that industrial targetting is not only preached but practised in Japan. The evolution of Japanese industrial structure toward more technology-intensive products has been widely documented (see

Chandler and Trebilcock, 1985; D'Cruz and Fleck, 1985; McMillan, 1984; and Scott, 1984; among others). The Japanese have also shown no reluctance to abandon losing industries (aluminum, petrochemicals, shipbuilding, and so on), provided that they are outside the agricultural sector.

It might be argued on the basis of this evidence that targetting can enhance the national income if it is done correctly, and that Canadians should look to Japan to see how to do it correctly.

Many books have been written espousing different views about what constitutes the essence of Japanese industrial policy. This issue cannot be adjudicated here. Two observations by McMillan might meet with the approval of other experts and are useful in the present context. First, Japanese targetting does not involve picking national champions:

> While the Japanese plan, they are fiercely market oriented. There is little sympathy for the view usually found in Europe of picking a single industrial champion for each sector: the Japanese approach is like a stable of race horses with many champions competing in each sector. (p. 90)

Second, neither the plan nor, for that matter, government departments are central to targetting. Rather, it is the information generated and exchanged in the planning process itself which is crucial:

> Contrary to what the anti-planners think, Japanese planners put far less emphasis on a plan than on a process. The vision is forward-directed but the impact is one of using the plan to interpret the past. The planning process obviously brings an enormous statistical and information gathering apparatus into play, but this process of constant dialogue serves an educational purpose of widening choices and increasing analytical depth. (p. 63)

A similar view comes from the OECD (1983a):

> In the 1970s Japanese technology reached the leading edge of innovation in many industrial activities. Future technological and economic developments, which will crucially affect Japanese industry, are much less predictable. It is therefore not surprising that MITI no longer provides direct guidance to industry. Instead, so-called "Visions" are being prepared to which Japanese industry and also labour, consumers and academics contribute, and which Japanese firms may use as background information in their planning and investment programs. They are not meant to act as a binding framework for the decision-making of individual enterprises, and allow for active and dynamic domestic and international markets. It also appears consistent with these changes that the Japanese Government *now encourages new and promising industrial activities by helping to develop basic and horizontal technologies rather than directly promoting specific industries.* (p. 51, emphasis added)

Ouchi (1984, pp. 109–18) provides a vignette about the Japanese very large scale integrated circuit (VLSI) project which is also instructive. In 1975, Japanese companies, being well behind the United States in the development of a 64K RAM (random access computer memory) decided, in consultation with MITI (Ministry of International Trade and Industry) on a joint research project to catch up. Five companies and the government-owned Electro-Technical Laboratory supported the research, which took four years. Another company was excluded from the consortium and proceeded on its own. The government financial contribution came to $132 million of the $308 million project cost. This contribution took the form of a loan repayable out of any attributable profits earned by the five companies over the 1983–88 period. The project was limited to basic research to which all five supporting companies had equal access.

Of interest here are the joint investigation of the merits of investing in this technology; confinement of the collaboration to basic research; the provisions for rivalry at the commercial stage; and the relatively modest nature of the government contribution. Over this same period, according to Palda's calculation, the government of Canada spent $451.3 million for R&D on the CANDU reactor, which was already commercially dubious.

This leads to a possible conclusion that Japanese targetting is, first of all, a collective information-gathering and interpretation process which helps individual firms make investment decisions and guides the government in allocating support. Second, emphasis is placed not on firms or even on commercial product classes but on broad technological areas, the advancement of which receives government support.

Another view of the Japanese economic record is that it has indeed been outstanding but that this has nothing to do with targetting. Krugman (1983, 1984) takes this view. He argues that the ultimate criterion of success must be social and private rates of return. He notes that by the latter standard, the Japanese targetting of the steel industry has been a signal failure and that — other impressions to the contrary notwithstanding — the jury is still out on semiconductors (1983, pp. 46–7).

This brief examination of the experience with targetting is that as far as the Atlantic industrial countries are concerned, it either has not been tried or has not worked. It has been tried after a fashion in Japan, and Japan is said to be the model for Korea, Singapore, Taiwan and Hong Kong. Whether targetting has contributed to Japanese economic success is a matter of dispute. Whatever its contribution, in recent years it has not involved the centralized selection of national champions.

This is not to dismiss Japanese industrial policy. The policy apparatus for the assembly, exchange and use of detailed market intelligence by business and government merits Canadian attention. Most important is the Japanese commitment to competitiveness. How is it sustained in the face of repeated onslaughts by losers desirous of protection?

Alternatives to Targetting

Both advocates and opponents of targetting agree that two policy pre-conditions for economic success are the maintenance of appropriate aggregate or generic incentives (see the subsection on industrial policy perspective) and the ability to avoid providing continuing support of economic losers. This begs the question (discussed further below) of whether it is any easier to target losers and avoid entanglement with them than it is to target winners.

The disagreement comes over whether there are potential gains from attempting to identify and provide special support to winners and whether any potential gains are likely to be realized in democratic market economies as they are or as they could reasonably be expected to be. The problem is as much one of political economy as it is of economics. Unfortunately, most of the industrial policy literature focusses on targetting criteria and instruments. Treatment of political implications is generally confined to exhortations to the authorities to show more political will or to develop a commitment to competitiveness. There is little in the way of advice as to how the authorities might go about resisting the embrace of the losers. The Trebilcock monograph (1985b) is an exception in this regard. It is considered in detail in the next section.

Does a policy alternative exist to targetting winners? There remains the usual externality (inappropriability) case for supporting basic and applied generic research. Nelson (1982) argues that this is what governments do best in the area of high technology. There are some estimates of very high rates of return on agricultural research in the United States and Canada (see McFetridge and Corvari, 1985). It is hard to believe that the same is not true of forestry.

Support of applied research in the natural resource sector, on such matters as dryland farming or faster-growing species of trees, has the additional virtue that it does not rely on the slender reed of pre-emption and the learning curve to yield rents. Given world prices, technological improvements specific to the Canadian resource sector would increase the rents to and thus the value of our forests, farm lands and minerals.

There are also the usual arguments — including imperfections in the market for human capital — for supporting education. As the Wright Commission (Task Force on Federal Policies and Programs for Technology Development, 1984) has argued, there is considerable scope for improvement of the contribution made by the university system to technological education and diffusion.

With respect to industrial innovation — that is, proprietary technologies — the policy alternative is non-targetted support. A better term might be self-selecting support. An example would be R&D tax credits. The value of tax credit support awarded to a firm depends simply on the amount of R&D it does. There is targetting in the sense that only firms which do R&D benefit from the credit. There is no targetting from the government end, at least within the R&D-incentive sector. Tax credits have the virtue of being market led. As Harris argues, however, tax credits may not be sufficient to build up small firms to the point at which they can engage in Schumpeterian competition.

Much of the opposition to R&D tax incentives has been based on their alleged windfall component and their lack of value to firms with no taxable income. With regard to the windfall element in the R&D tax credit, Jeffrey Bernstein, in his Commission study in volume 3, reports that the elasticity of R&D expenditures with respect to tax benefits received is approximately one. For every dollar foregone by the government, approximately one additional dollar is spent on industrial R&D.[8]

As far as start-ups are concerned, access to tax incentives can be improved by making them refundable by the government (as the IRDIA[9] incentive was) or salable (as the SRTC[10] was).

Positive Adjustment

Adjustment Policy and Industrial Policy

As the discussion in the preceding section suggests, the targetting debate has centred on the likelihood that industrial policy can improve upon the market allocation of resources to new or so-called sunrise activities. The advocates of targetting maintain that an improvement is achievable.

The purpose of positive adjustment policies is somewhat different. Advocates of positive adjustment proceed from the general premise that, left to itself, the market mechanism is effective in extricating resources from declining (sunset) industries. The problem they see is that the market mechanism is not allowed to work. Positive adjustment policies are advocated either to neutralize or to remove impediment to market processes. The goal is thus one of restoring the normal capacity of market economies to adjust to changing circumstances.

The OECD (1983a) puts the argument this way:

It is not only the adjustment requirements which have been too great or which came too abruptly but also a diminished capacity and/or willingness of the economy and society in the industrialized countries to respond positively to them, which makes present economic difficulties so troublesome to resolve. Socioeconomic rigidities which may further endanger the adaptability of the industrial countries in the 1980s include particular features of labour and capital markets, increasing direct and indirect government involvement in the economy, rigidifying effects of lumpy, capital intensive technology, large scale investments and also some revival of protectionism in international trade. (p. 7)

In the view of the OECD, this lack of adaptability derives from four sources:

First [they reflect] attitudes and institutional developments which evolved during the period of uninterrupted high levels of employment and which were slow to change during the entirely different circumstances of the 1970s. Second, they reflect the rapid growth of the public sector and of social programmes and regulations which, however desirable in themselves, have sometimes had unintended adverse side effects on incentives to work, save and invest. Third, they derive from attempts by governments to alleviate the social consequences of structural change by preserving given production and employment structures. Fourth, and most importantly, slow growth itself makes structural adjustment more difficult. (pp. 7–8)

The proposition that there has been a decline in the willingness of the members of democratic societies to adjust to new circumstances has been widely discussed (see, for example, Courchene, 1980; Green, 1984; Olson, 1982; and Thurow, 1981). Some commentators, Scott (1984) for example, lay the blame on the welfare state. Others, such as McCallum and Blais (1985), would dispute this explanation.

I cannot adjudicate the question of whether there has been a decline in the willingness and ability of democratic, industrial economies to adjust to new circumstances. I begin here with the presumption that the purpose of adjustment policy is to facilitate adjustment by " . . . enhancing the flexibility and resilience of markets in the face of change" (OECD, 1983a, p. 8). I then proceed to evaluate industrial policy by that standard.

Thus, the central question for this section is whether industrial policy as defined in this paper (as the direct support of specific firms or industries) is an important component in a positive adjustment program.

As already noted in the discussion on the goals of industrial policy, adjustment assistance measures can be rationalized in equity (ethical), efficiency, or political terms. Trebilcock's monograph examines these three rationales and finds that both ethical and efficiency considerations militate in favour of assisting individuals rather than firms or industries while political considerations often favour assistance to firms or industries. He sees the essential task as one of designing institutions that give the greatest weight to ethical and efficiency considerations, implicitly minimizing the use of industrial policy.

In a less detailed analysis, Richardson (1985) reaches much the same conclusion. Thurow (1981) puts the general view regarding the ideal adjustment policy succinctly, arguing that it should: "provide economic security for individuals without providing economic security for failing institutions" (p. 95).

In general, the consensus is that governments can best facilitate adjustment by:

• maintaining a stable macroeconomic environment and appropriate work, saving and investment incentives;[11]

- removing barriers to adjustment; and
- assisting individuals faced with serious unanticipated adjustment problems.

This agenda does not contain much in the way of a role for what has become known as "proactive" industrial policy. What is the reason for this outcome? Is it subject to question?

The case for individual or labour-market-centred adjustment policies turns on efficiency and ethical considerations. The efficiency question is — as always — how, if at all, can the market be made to work better? The answer is that while relatively little can be done to improve the workings of the market for physical capital, the market for human capital (skills and knowledge) has significant defects that might be remedied by public policy.

Human capital is not fungible. It is difficult to borrow against it or to subdivide it and sell portions. It is therefore more difficult to finance the accumulation of human capital (knowledge and skill acquisition) than is the case with physical capital. It is also more difficult to diversify away the risk associated with an investment in human capital.

This type of reasoning leads to the widely accepted proposition that government intervention can improve upon the market by assisting individuals in the financing of human capital acquisition and by insuring (implicitly at least) a portion of the return on human capital. This, in turn, implies some type of subsidization of the training, education and mobility costs incurred by individuals. This extends to retraining, re-education and relocation costs and in this sense involves adjustment policy.

Insuring human capital is somewhat more complex. This issue has been considered in some detail by Boyer (1984). The risk associated with human capital is potentially insurable in that the incomes of different individuals and occupations will be less than perfectly correlated over time. The question is why it falls to the government to provide this type of insurance.

The provision of insurance on human capital will burdened by problems of severe moral hazard and adverse selection. Individuals will be less diligent in maintaining their incomes (that is, in doing their jobs well) if these incomes are insured. Individuals intending to take advantage of the insurance to run down their human capital will be the ones to take it out.

For these reasons, regardless of who provides it, human capital insurance would be very limited in its coverage and would entail severe loss control restrictions. It might, as Boyer suggests, involve a dentist, for example, being able to insure against declines in the price of dental services in general but not against a decline in his or her market share. It would also involve measures that would limit both the length of time an individual spends as a claimant and the probability of being a repeat claimant. This may be one reason why many adjustment policy experts insist that payments to victims of changing economic circumstances be contingent on their taking steps to improve their own situation.[12]

As with medical insurance, there may be a case for compulsory human capital insurance under which individuals would be eligible for temporary income support when they lose their jobs or a significant part of the income from their human capital through no fault of their own. This would again be termed adjustment assistance.

Similar assistance is not targeted to physical capital because there are not the same institutional barriers either to financing its accumulation or to diversifying away the risk associated with investments in it. Considering the issue of trade-related adjustment assistance, David Richardson, in his Commission study in volume 12, puts the case as follows:

> With respect to firms in distinction from their workers, the case for trade related adjustment programs seems weak on exactly these grounds. . . .
> Capital markets are national and international; labour markets are local. Risk-taking owners of capital are presumably better informed than workers about prospects for international change, and also about finding more lucrative employment of their resources by moving to other industries. They therefore have more opportunities to diversify than workers. Firms are supported (or confronted) by financial intermediaries with multinational scope or contacts who are presumably even better informed about international and inter-industry prospects. Except perhaps for gargantuan high-risk endeavours with long start-up periods and economically disen-franchised future beneficiaries, one can argue that financial markets assess more or less correctly the relative productivities of alternative firms and projects. Therefore government programs to encourage modernization and product diversification by trade-pressured firms would seem most often to indenture workers to an institutional shell that was revealed by the market to be comparatively unsuccessful . (If it had been a successful firm, moderni-zation and diversification would presumably have been profitable for it without special government encouragement). There seem to be few eco-nomic reasons for preserving institutions, especially unsuccessful ones, in contrast to preserving the skills and well-being of individuals. So it would seem more productive to allow firms to die rather than to modernize or diversify. After death, diversification does take place, but on an individual basis by employees of the dead firm — into new skills, new responsibilities and relatively more successful institutional shells (firms). (pp. 177–78)

This leaves relatively little room for a proactive industrial policy. There are, of course, the industrial policy aspects of removing barriers to adjustment — that is, of getting out of the way. These are considered below in the discussion of reducing barriers to adjustment. There are also those who suggest that industrial policy can improve upon the market adjustment process and that there is a place for both industrial and labour market policies in a positive adjustment program. Arguments to this effect are considered next.

With respect to labour market policies themselves, lengthy discussions of how effective they have been and how they might be improved are provided in Commission papers by Michael Trebilcock (volume 8), Matthew Robertson and Alex Grey (volume 12), Jonathan Kesselman (volume 1), Jean-Michel Cousineau (volume 1), and John Vanderkamp (volume 64).

Positive Adjustment and Proactive Industrial Policy

The purpose of this section is to investigate arguments that positive adjustments require an industrial policy of more than just staying out of the way.

As has been suggested in previous discussions, paying off losers who might otherwise be able to block beneficial economic change facilitates adjustment. This payoff can take many forms and may include support of declining firms or industries. The point here is that firms may serve as agents through which payments to workers are channelled. It is important to note that directing payments to firms is not necessarily the same as providing adjustment assistance to capital. The firm may be simply a convenient administrative device.

The firm or industry suffers from some important disadvantages as an administrative device for conveying assistance to workers. In the contemporary jargon, it lacks transparency.[13] This means that when adjustment assistance is provided in the form of subsidization or protection of firms or industries, both the cost (more properly the amount of the transfer) and the quid pro quo are hidden. Indeed, Trebilcock (1985b) argues that this lack of transparency makes firm and industry support ideal for forestalling rather than facilitating adjustment.[14]

It is certainly difficult to see how adjustment has been facilitated anywhere in the Canadian economy by the billion-odd dollars which Devco has lost mining coal in Cape Breton during the last ten years.[15] The same is true of the two billion dollars burned up by Canadair or the billion dollars that De Havilland has lost, and is also true of the bailouts catalogued by Trebilcock (1985a).

The basic point here is that while firm or industry support may, on occasion, be a convenient way of assisting the adjustment of a particular group of workers, this is more than outweighed by its potential for encouraging adjustment-inhibiting arrangements. The implication is that ` positive adjustment is best served by forswearing proactive industrial policies.

There is more to firm- or industry-specific support than simple administrative convenience. Several externality arguments merit attention.

It is trite to point out that economic adjustment is not costless. Glen Jenkins and his associates (see, for example, Jenkins and Montmarquette, 1979) have pioneered the measurement of adjustment costs. While it has not been true of the cases studied by Jenkins, it is possible that, on occasion, the cost of making an economic change such as reducing tariffs or eliminating quotas outweighs the benefits of doing so. Governments should be aware of this.

Given the public policy environment, however, I would expect economic actors to weigh the costs and benefits of engaging in new activities as opposed to continuing the old ones. They will make the correct decision unless there is an externality — that is, unless the social costs and benefits of adjustment fail to correspond with the private ones.

Consider, as an example, the case of a manufacturer of vacuum tubes faced with the introduction of the transistor. Demand and sales fall. What is the adjustment decision? The owners of the plant will want to keep it running as long as it earns quasi-rents — that is, as long as its earnings exceed those in its next best alternative. The workers would find it in their interest to accept pay cuts up to the amount they would lose by having to seek work elsewhere. This would include wages lost while searching for new employment, the cost of the search itself, the cost of moving to new employment, and the value of any human capital (skills) which are specific to the job. If plant revenues cover the opportunity costs of labour and capital, it will be in the interests of all concerned to keep the plant running until the specific human and physical capital involved has been depreciated. Thus, while adjustment costs exist, they are internalized and adjustment decisions are efficient.

An externality can arise if, for example, laid-off workers are eligible for unemployment insurance. Since UI reduces the amount they lose by having to seek work elsewhere, the concessions they would be willing to make to keep the plant operating would also be less. Hence the plant may close even though on a social opportunity cost basis it should have remained open. This would also happen if wage concessions are prohibited by nationwide union contracts or if they run afoul of minimum wage legislation. Harris, Lewis and Purvis (1982) suggest that the plant might also close if workers are unable to make wage concessions which are viewed as binding by the employer.

This line of reasoning gives us the so-called labour externality which was discussed in the section on the goals of industrial policy. It is the basis upon which governments "bid for jobs" by subsidizing the firms which provide them. As far as this externality is concerned, it does not matter whether the jobs are acquired by attracting a new business or by keeping an old one going.

The disagreement between this line of reasoning and the recommendations of Trebilcock, Richardson and others that adjustment assistance should go to workers only is less than it may appear. The maximum subsidy here is equal to the wage concessions the workers would make but, for some reason, cannot. There is no subsidy to capital. Indeed, this subsidy could be paid to the workers who could — if they can act collectively — either use it to keep the plant open or allow the plant to close and use it elsewhere.

In appraising this rationale for adjustment assistance, it should be recognized that it is not aimed at improving the market so much as neutralizing the distorting effects of other public policies (unemployment insurance, minimum wages, and so on). While this may appear to make sense in the short run, the long-run consequences call it into question. First, while it might be difficult to arrange wage concessions, the anticipation by employees that these concessions will be made on their behalf by the government ensures that concessions will never be made. This is also true of the bankruptcy-reorganization process in general. The possibility that the government might intervene creates circumstances under which the government must intervene.

There is a further problem in identifying firms that are truly failing, since all firms have an incentive to threaten to discharge workers and qualify for subsidization. Indeed, firms and workers have an incentive to cooperate in this type of opportunism vis-à-vis the government.

In the longer run, the supply price of labour to industries qualifying for these subsidies will decline and the industries themselves will expand. Adjustment problems will get bigger rather than smaller.

Another form of adjustment externality is thought to arise from congestion of the job search process. When firms lay off workers, they do not take account of the effect of these layoffs on the job opportunities of workers who are already unemployed. One suggested solution is to subsidize firms to avoid, postpone or stagger layoffs (see Trebilcock, 1985a). The maximum amount of the subsidy would equal the "damages" in terms of longer unemployment spells for the other laid-off workers which are avoided as a consequence.

There are also serious problems with this form of intervention. Paying firms to avoid or stagger layoffs to avoid congestion in labour markets is like reducing entry into the Atlantic fisheries by paying people not to fish. Government ultimately ends up paying a lot of people.

Trebilcock also suggests a layoff "tax" — perhaps in the form of a prenotification requirement. The problem with either a layoff tax or a subsidy is that potential labour market congestion costs will already be reflected in the supply price of labour in a given labour market. If there are potential gains from staggered layoffs or prenotification arrangements, then these will be a matter for bargaining between individual firms and workers. Prenotification can be had, if desired, in return for a lower wage. Yet there is still an externality here. The acceptance of prenotification by firm A reduces the supply price of labour to firm B regardless of its layoff policy. This implies that there is something to be gained from collective layoff arrangements, perhaps sponsored and enforced by government. Although there is a potential role for the state here, it does not lie in the realm of industrial policy.

Another externality is derived from the existence of transferable on-the-job learning, which is the basis for infant-industry subsidies and apparently for the targetting of winners by the state. This argument is been discussed in detail above in the section on targetting theory.

For the purposes of this section, it is necessary only to note that firms in so-called sunset industries may be able to pre-empt market niches based on their learning curve. There is no reason, in principle, why this could not happen in the footwear or textile industries as well as in microelectronics. Indeed, Abernathy et al. (1983) suggest that the goal of North American firms and governments should be to "de-mature" hitherto static technology industries — that is, to turn them into dynamic, learning-curve industries in which they can again compete against low-wage countries.

At one level, this amounts merely to a restatement of the difficulties of targetting. It is, in fact, slightly more. It is almost never the case that a declining firm or industry approaches government for protection or support on the basis of the kind of arguments made here. That is, support is requested not to ease the exit of labour from the industry but to give the firm or industry "a little support" so that it can become a winner. Governments which purport to pick and support winners may have a difficult time resisting requests for support by apparent losers.

This brings up two common arguments for firm-specific support in an adjustment context — the breathing space argument and the foreign targetting argument.

The breathing space rationale is simply one of providing "temporary" support while a firm or an industry restructures or reorganizes. This type of support is an established component of Canadian adjustment policy.[16] While a request for "breathing space" might and perhaps should influence a bank manager, it has no special implications for public policy. The externalities discussed above may provide a rationale for assistance. Representations to the effect that difficulties are temporary do not.

The foreign targetting issue is more difficult. It has been discussed at length by Krugman (1983, 1984) and by Trebilcock. At issue again is the learning curve case in which a foreign producer builds volume and a permanent cost advantage over domestic rivals on the basis of subsidized or protected sales. Insofar as the targetted industry is concerned, responding in kind to foreign targetting results in low rates of return for all concerned. This may be preferable, however, to a foreign monopoly of the industry. It may also convey the signal to foreigners that targetting will bring retaliation and forestall further attempts at it.

There is nothing to be gained by responding to foreign subsidization of exports in industries that are not characterized by a learning curve. If foreigners wish to supply Canada at a loss, this is Canada's gain. Subsequent attempts to monopolize will be frustrated by re-entry of competitors both in Canada and elsewhere. On the other hand, governments would not want to renounce firm and industry support as a strategic weapon against foreign targetting in learning-curve industries. Whether this issue is of much practical or, for that matter, theoretical significance remains to be seen.

The various arguments for a proactive industrial policy as part of a positive adjustment strategy lead to the conclusion that if governments bid for jobs on the basis of the so-called labour externality, there is as much to be gained from keeping a firm from closing as there is from attracting a new one. This assumes, of course, that the declining firm can "deliver" the jobs, which may not always be true. Moreover, support which is limited to the labour externality will typically be quite modest and will not be sufficient to keep most failing firms afloat. Finally, the labour externality argument is short run in nature. Taken to the limit, very few firms in the economy will not qualify or seek to qualify for some subsidy.

In general, then, I have to agree with Trebilcock (1985a, 1985b) that the arguments for adjustment support for firms and industries are far from compelling. The question that remains is how democratic governments can avoid granting this support — especially in its more insidious forms such as tariff and quota protection and loan guarantees.[17]

The Japanese appear to have had more success than most countries in withholding support from declining firms and industries. Part of the reason may lie in the policy formation apparatus which allows contending interest groups to confront one another in the context of the best available information on their respective economic prospects. Another explanation lies in the characteristics of the Japanese economy and the high aggregate growth rates which it has experienced. These tend to make adjustment easier. Many workers are transferred across industries while remaining within the same industrial group and retaining their seniority. These transfers do not often involve a significant geographic relocation.[18]

Insofar as policy itself is concerned, the only device Japan makes use of which is not generally employed in North America is the capacity contraction cartel, the alleged virtues of which are discussed in the next subsection.

Reducing Barriers to Adjustment

The analysis to this point has failed to find much in the way of a role for proactive industrial policy as a device for improving the adjustment capacity of the market. There is perhaps more to be said for getting out of the way — that is, for eliminating or neutralizing the adjustment-inhibiting effects of various regulatory policies.

The OECD (1983a) cites four areas in which regulatory intervention has historically occurred:

First there are policies to keep competition active and vigorous by measures to prohibit or control anticompetitive market structures or market behavior. Second, governments may regulate economic activities where competition cannot be sustained because conditions create a natural monopoly. Third, governments may regulate business conduct and conditions of entry into particular activities for the purpose of protecting customers and suppliers from the consequences of imperfect knowledge or inferior bargaining power. Fourth, regulation of business activity may be directed toward the reconciliation of private and social costs — particularly in the field of environmental protection. (p. 37)

In each case, the OECD perceives that however well intended the regulation, there are potentially removable adjustment-inhibiting side effects:

The common essential problem which emerges with regard to dynamic adjustment is that the policies directed towards enhancing social welfare through correcting certain shortcomings in the operation of markets may also impose rigidities on market structures and on the behaviour of enterprises. Such rigidities can frequently be avoided if policy makers take into account that many regulations have negative side effects on the functioning of markets and on the long-term adjustment capability of market participants. (p. 37)

The purpose of this subsection is to investigate the extent to which various forms of regulation have inhibited the adjustment process in Canada.

With respect to competition policy, it is difficult to believe that Canadian efforts in this area have inhibited market processes in any way. Canadian policy has not posed a material barrier to mergers, to the operation of large firms, or to cooperation in export markets. Until the *Aetna* and *Atlantic Sugar* decisions of the mid-1970s, Canadian law could be said to have prohibited industry-wide cartelization of domestic markets (see McFetridge and Wong, 1981).

As noted above, the Japanese have made use of cartels to coordinate capacity reductions in declining industries, such as shipbuilding, aluminum, petrochemicals and cement. Harris's Commission monograph argues that cartelization may prevent strategic behaviour with respect to capacity cuts by individual firms. In response, it might be argued that unlike the case of capacity expansion, where pre-emptive expansion is an obvious possibility, the possibilities for gaining on the decline side are limited. Exit must occur when quasi-rents fall to zero. The producers with the newest facilities will remain.

While cartelization might assist the exit process in some isolated instances, it does not appear to offer sufficient advantages to warrant moving cartelization from its present status of per se illegality. The last few years have seen drastic cuts in petroleum-refining capacity carried out with apparent efficiency under the intense scrutiny of competition policy authorities alert to the possibility of cartelization. It is difficult to think of an instance in Canada where a capacity-cutting cartel might have been beneficial. It may be conjectured that the principal problem has not been industry rivalry but the pressure of various governments to keep plants open.

With respect to regulation, two areas merit comment. The first is the regulation (the screening and, in some cases, prohibition) of foreign investment. It is hard to say what Canadians get from the control of foreign investment, other than pride of ownership. The best of recent investigations into the matter indicate that foreign investment leads to faster acquisition of new technologies, with possible spillovers to Canadian firms, and does not result in suboptimal plant scales and the low productivity that goes with them.[19]

The case study of the large appliance industry by Harold Crookell, in this volume, demonstrates how ownership restrictions can seriously inhibit if not entirely frustrate the adjustment process. In the large electrical appliance industry, the government attempted to promote rationalization of production and increase Canadian ownership at the same time. Crookell finds that this stalled the adjustment process and ultimately did not increase Canadian ownership. There is much to be said for altering the screening process to exclude from review the transfer of a Canadian affiliate from one foreign owner to another.

It should also be noted in passing that the incidence of the cost of the "benefits to Canada" which are extracted from foreigners by the Foreign Investment Review Agency has never seriously been studied. There is reason to believe that the cost of the commitments extracted by FIRA serves to reduce the price foreigners offer for Canadian businesses they are acquiring. In this event, the "benefits" negotiated by FIRA are, in effect, paid for by Canadian entrepreneurs wishing to sell their businesses. This is hardly an incentive for them or others with similar skills and inclinations to turn around and build up new ones.

The second regulatory issue relates to what Richard Schultz and Alan Alexandroff, in their Commission monograph, call "planning regulation" — known in the regulatory literature as public finance regulation. This involves complex sets of entry and output restrictions that are used to create monopoly profits in some activities which are then used to finance others.

The financial, telecommunications and air transportation industries are all subjects of detailed federal regulatory planning. Schultz and Alexandroff argue that this type of regulation necessarily evolves in the direction of increasing complexity, politicization and concomitant inter-governmental (interprovincial or federal-provincial) conflict. In their view, this will end in regulatory and perhaps corporate paralysis. These authors argue for a retreat from planning regulation to a less interventionist policing or promoting regulation. This would amount to an abandonment of entry and output controls but not of safety and related regulation.

As Keith Acheson and John Chant point out in their survey papers in this volume, entry controls can be functional and it would be a mistake to advocate their abandonment in all cases. There will, however, be cases — the transportation, telecommunications and financial sectors are clearly among them — in which the cost of enforcement, including the political conflict involved, overwhelms any potential benefits.

A positive adjustment strategy would also include policies to reduce non-regulatory barriers to entry. Two are often suggested. The first is in the area of competition policy and relates to entry-deterring behavior by so-called dominant firms. The possibility of strategic entry deterrence has been widely discussed. Indeed, it is the basis of industrial targetting. In this regard, targetting by guaranteeing certain markets to chosen instruments or national champions can inhibit adjustment.

While I would recommend that the government not serve as an accessory to strategic entry deterrence, I would also add that it should also not devote much in the way of effort to control it. As McFetridge and Wong (forthcoming, 1985) argue in a detailed study of the matter, any law against strategic entry deterrence would be extremely costly to enforce and would probably not be worthwhile.

The second barrier to entry is the familiar issue of the imperfect capital markets barrier. This issue has received detailed study in recent years and no doubt will receive more.[20] In some areas, such as debt financing, there does not appear to be a problem. In others, such as equity financing, there may be problems which are amenable to a reduction in entry restrictions (such as, into the brokerage and underwriting function).

Conclusion

The analysis in this paper leads to some simple conclusions.

- There is little to be gained in the long run from firm-specific assistance or targetting.
- The principal focus of adjustment policy should be on the labour market.
- Adjustment can be facilitated by reducing regulatory barriers to entry in a number of sectors and by reducing controls on changes in ownership.

- While interprovincial industrial policy rivalry has not been a serious problem, a reduction in firm-specific support and regulatory control of certain industries would help to reduce the potential for future conflict.
- Pressure to assist losing firms may be reduced if they are filtered through advisory committees composed of contending interest groups.
- The joint collection and analysis of data relevant to investment decisions by the business, academic and other communities and government is a feature of the Japanese industrial investment process which merits further scrutiny from all segments of the Canadian economic community.

Notes

This study was completed in March 1985.

1. See the excellent discussions and bibliographies provided in Commission studies by André Blais (volume 45), and by Reuven Brenner and Léon Courville, Marsha Chandler and Michael Trebilcock, and Donald Lecraw, all in volume 5 of the research series.
2. The study these authors cite relates to the United States.
3. Obviously, so-called market arrangements have some element of state participation, even if it is only the enforcement of property rights. Similarly, "government intervention" can employ market incentives to varying degrees.
4. The Kirby Report (Task Force on Atlantic Fisheries, 1982) documents the effect of subsidized entry into fish processing on existing processing plants. Officials of the Anti-Dumping Tribunal have indicated that in their experience, this type of occurrence is not uncommon.
5. Proponents of targeting call these the "income elasticity criterion" and the "technical progress criterion." See Scott (1984, p. 22).
6. Usher (1983) also calculates the cost of raising money by taxation, which is relevant if one is concerned about whether government should provide support rather than how this support should be provided.
7. This argument does not apply to such industries such as the tourist (restaurant, hotel) industry, where the argument for support is simply the excess of wage rates over the opportunity cost of labour. In most urban centres, support of new entrants can be expected to crowd out incumbents, with no increase in external benefits and a strong likelihood of replacing more efficient with less efficient firms.
8. The issue is not entirely settled. Mansfield and Switzer (1984), for example, report that on the basis of survey evidence, tax elasticities are well below one. On the other hand, see Usher (1983, pp. 90–93).
9. The Industrial Research and Development Incentives Act was in effect between 1967 and 1976.
10. The Special R&D Tax Credit was introduced in 1983 and modified in 1984.
11. See the section on industrial policy perspectives and OECD (1985a, pp. 24–34). It should again be emphasized that there is no consensus as to the net effect of the welfare state in toto on adaptability. The net incentive effects of individual welfare measures must be examined.
12. The issue of contingent adjustment assistance remains unsettled. In principle, a lump sum insurance settlement should not reduce an individual's incentive to find a new career. Many experts, Glen Jenkins, for example (in conversation with the author), recommend large cash settlements to victims of economic change, such as textile workers. Trebilcock (1985b) argues that these settlements will not be lump sum, that the victims will be able to lobby for more. He suggests that the only way to break up the

political coalition which can extract continuing assistance is to require geographic or occupational movement as a condition of assistance. Why any lobby group would accept dispersal except in return for assistance with a higher present value remains an unresolved question.

13. See OECD (1983b).

14. This follows from the general proposition that because firm support can be provided by various regulatory means and off-budget expenditures, it is ideal for rent-seeking. In essence, the amount of the wealth transfer and perhaps its very existence are hidden from those who must pay it but not from those who receive it.

15. Accumulated losses plus capital grants.

16. See the paper by the Department of Regional Industrial Expansion, in volume 12, on domestic adjustment to trade policy changes and external shocks.

17. These forms of support are deemed by many to be insidious because of their lack of transparency and conditionality.

18. See "Land of the Setting Sun," *The Economist* (June 30, 1984), p. 57.

19. See McFetridge and Corvari (1985) and McFetridge (1985) for references. For a partial dissent, see Bishop and Crookell (1985) and the Science Council of Canada (1984).

20. See Economic Council of Canada (1982) and Gagnon and Papillon (1984).

Bibliography

Abernathy, William J., Kim B. Clark, and Alan M. Kantrow. 1983. *Industrial Renaissance*. New York: Basic Books.

Acheson, K. 1985. "Economic Regulation in Canada: A Survey." In *Canadian Industrial Policy in Action*, volume 4 of the research studies prepared for the Royal Commission on the Economic Union and Development Prospects for Canada. Toronto: University of Toronto Press.

Alberta. 1984. *Proposals for an Industrial and Science Strategy for Albertans 1985 to 1990*. Edmonton: Government of Alberta.

Baldwin, J.R. 1982. "Federal Regulation and Public Policy in the Canadian Petroleum Industry 1958–1975." *Journal of Business Administration* 13 (1): 57–97.

Bernstein, J.I. 1985. "Research and Development, Patents, and Grant and Tax Policies in Canada." In *Technological Change in Canadian Industry*, volume 3 of the research studies prepared for the Royal Commission on the Economic Union and Development Prospects for Canada. Toronto: University of Toronto Press.

Bishop, P., and H. Crookell. 1985. "Specialization and Foreign Investment in Canada." In *Canadian Industry in Transition*, volume 2 of the research studies prepared for the Royal Commission on the Economic Union and Development Prospects for Canada. Toronto: University of Toronto Press.

Blais, A. 1985. *The Political Sociology of Industrial Policy*. Volume 45 of the research studies prepared for the Royal Commission on the Economic Union and Development Prospects for Canada. Toronto: University of Toronto Press.

Bliss, M. 1982. "The Evolution of Industrial Policies in Canada: An Historical Survey." Discussion Paper 218. Ottawa: Economic Council of Canada.

Boadway, R.W., and W.S. Clarke. 1985. "The Government Budget, the Accumulation of Capital, and Long-Run Welfare." In *Fiscal and Monetary Policy*, volume 21 of the research studies prepared for the Royal Commission on the Economic Union and Development Prospects for Canada. Toronto: University of Toronto Press.

Boyer, M. 1984. "Information, Risk and Public Policy." Study prepared for the Royal Commission on the Economic Union and Development Prospects for Canada.

Brenner, R., and L. Courville. 1985. "Industrial Strategy: Inferring What It Really Is." In *Economics of Industrial Policy and Strategy*, volume 5 of the research studies prepared for the Royal Commission on the Economic Union and Development Prospects for Canada. Toronto: University of Toronto Press.

Canada. 1982. Task Force on Atlantic Fisheries. *Navigating Troubled Waters* (Kirby Report). Ottawa: Minister of Supply and Services Canada.

Canada. 1984. Task Force on Federal Policies and Programs for Technology Development. *A Report to the Honourable Edward C. Lumley, Minister of State for Science and Technology.* Ottawa: Minister of Supply and Services Canada.

Chandler, M., and M.J. Trebilcock. 1985. "Comparative Survey of Industrial Policies in Selected OECD Countries." In *Economics of Industrial Policy and Strategy*, volume 5 of the research studies prepared for the Royal Commission on the Economic Union and Development Prospects for Canada. Toronto: University of Toronto Press.

Chant, J.F. 1985. "An Agenda for Research on Financial Markets." In *Canadian Industrial Policy in Action*, volume 4 of the research studies prepared for the Royal Commission on the Economic Union and Development Prospects for Canada. Toronto: University of Toronto Press.

Cheung, S. 1973. "The Fable of the Bees: An Economic Investigation." *Journal of Law and Economics* 16 (April): 11–34.

Conklin, D. 1984. "Subsidy Facts." Toronto: Ontario Economic Council. Mimeographed.

Courchene, T.J. 1980. "Towards a Protected Society." *Canadian Journal of Economics* 13 (November): 568–77.

Cousineau, J.-M. 1985. "Unemployment Insurance and Labour Market Adjustments." In *Income Distribution and Economic Security in Canada*, volume 1 of the research studies prepared for the Royal Commission on the Economic Union and Development Prospects for Canada. Toronto: University of Toronto Press.

Crookell, H. 1985. "The Impact of Government Intervention on the Major Appliance Industry in Canada." In *Canadian Industrial Policy in Action*, volume 4 of the research studies prepared for the Royal Commission on the Economic Union and Development Prospects for Canada. Toronto: University of Toronto Press.

Daly, D.J., and S. Globerman. 1976. *Tariff and Science Policies: Applications of a Model of Nationalism.* Toronto: University of Toronto Press.

Daly, D.J., and D.C. McCharles. 1983. "Canadian Manufactured Exports: Constraints and Opportunities." Toronto: York University. Mimeographed.

Davenport, P., C. Green, W.J. Milne, R. Saunders, and W. Watson. 1983. *Industrial Policy in Quebec and Ontario.* Discussion Paper Series. Toronto: Ontario Economic Council.

D'Cruz, J.R., and J.D. Fleck. 1985. *Canada Can Compete: Strategic Management of the Canadian Industrial Portfolio.* Montreal: Institute for Research on Public Policy.

Department of Regional Industrial Expansion. 1985. "Experience in Canada with Adjustment Policies." In *Domestic Policies and the International Economic Environment*, volume 12 of the research studies prepared for the Royal Commission on the Economic Union and Development Prospects for Canada. Toronto: University of Toronto Press.

Economic Council of Canada. 1982. *Intervention and Efficiency.* Ottawa: Minister of Supply and Services Canada.

Faucher, P., A. Blais, and R. Young. 1983. "L'Aide financière directe au secteur manufacturier au Québec et en Ontario 1960–1980." *Journal of Canadian Studies* 18 (Spring): 54–78.

Gagnon, J., and B. Papillon. 1984. *Financial Risk, Rate of Return of Canadian Firms, and Implications for Government Intervention.* Study prepared for the Economic Council of Canada. Ottawa: Minister of Supply and Services Canada.

George, R. 1983. *Targeting High-Growth Industry.* Montreal: Institute for Research on Public Policy.

Green, C. 1984. *Industrial Policy: The Fixities Hypothesis.* Toronto: Ontario Economic Council.

Grossman, L. 1984. *Economic Transformation: Technological Innovation and Diffusion in Ontario.* Toronto: Ministry of Treasury and Economics.

Harris, R.G. 1985. *Trade, Industrial Policy and International Competition.* Volume 13 of the research studies prepared for the Royal Commission on the Economic Union and Development Prospects for Canada. Toronto: University of Toronto Press.

Harris, R., and D. Cox. 1983. *Trade, Industrial Policy and Canadian Manufacturing.* Toronto: Ontario Economic Council.

Harris, R.G., F.D. Lewis, and D.D. Purvis. 1982. "Economic Adjustment and Public Policy in Canada." Kingston: Queen's University, Department of Economics. Mimeographed.

Jenkin, M. 1983. *The Challenge of Diversity: Industrial Policy in the Canadian Federation.* Science Council of Canada Background Study 50. Ottawa: Minister of Supply and Services Canada.

Jenkins G., and C. Montmarquette. 1979. "Estimating the Private and Social Opportunity Cost of Displaced Workers." *Review of Economics and Statistics* 61 (August): 342–53.

Kesselman, J.R. 1985. "Comprehensive Income Security for Canadian Workers." In *Income Distribution and Economic Security in Canada*, volume 1 of the research studies prepared for the Royal Commission on the Economic Union and Development Prospects for Canada. Toronto: University of Toronto Press.

Krugman, P.R. 1983. "Targeted Industrial Policies: Theory and Evidence." Paper presented to a Symposium on Industrial Change and Public Policy, sponsored by the Federal Reserve Bank of Kansas City, Jackson Hole, Wyoming.

————. 1984. "The U.S. Response to Foreign Industrial Targeting." *Brookings Papers on Economic Activity* 1: 77–121.

Lecraw, D.J. 1985. "Industrial Policy in the United States: A Survey." In *Economics of Industrial Policy and Strategy*, volume 5 of the research studies prepared for the Royal Commission on the Economic Union and Development Prospects for Canada. Toronto: University of Toronto Press.

Mansfield, E., 1985. "Technological Change and the International Diffusion of Technology: A Survey of Findings." In *Technological Change in Canadian Industry*, volume 3 of the research studies prepared for the Royal Commission on the Economic Union and Development Prospects for Canada. Toronto: University of Toronto Press.

Mansfield, E., and L. Switzer. 1984. "The Effects of R&D Tax Credits in Canada." Philadelphia: University of Pennsylvania, Department of Economics. Mimeographed.

Maule, C. 1984. "Does Canada Have an Industrial Strategy?" Ottawa: Carleton University, Department of Economics. Mimeographed.

McCallum, J., and A. Blais. 1985. "Government, Special Interest Groups and Economic Growth." In *Responses to Economic Change*, volume 27 of the research studies prepared for the Royal Commission on the Economic Union and Development Prospects for Canada. Toronto: University of Toronto Press.

McFetridge, D.G. 1985. "The Economics of Industrial Structure: An Overview." In *Canadian Industry in Transition*, volume 2 of the research studies prepared for the Royal Commission on the Economic Union and Development Prospects for Canada. Toronto: University of Toronto Press.

McFetridge, D.G., and R.J. Corvari. 1985. "Technology Diffusion: A Survey of Canadian Evidence and the Public Policy Issues." In *Technological Change in Canadian Industry*, volume 3 of the research studies prepared for the Royal Commission on the Economic Union and Development Prospects for Canada. Toronto: University of Toronto Press.

McFetridge, D.G., and S. Wong. 1981. "Agreements to Lessen Competition After Atlantic Sugar." *Canadian Business Law Journal* 5 (September): 329–45.

————. 1985. "Predatory Pricing in Canada: The Law and the Economics." *Canadian Bar Review* (forthcoming).

McMillan, C.J. 1984. *The Japanese Industrial System.* Berlin: de Gruyter.

Nelson, R.R. 1982. *Government and Technical Progress.* New York: Pergamon.

Olson, M. 1982. *The Rise and Decline of Nations.* New Haven: Yale University Press.

Organization for Economic Co-operation and Development. 1983a. *Positive Adjustment Policies.* Paris: OECD.

————. 1983b. *Transparency for Positive Adjustment.* Paris: OECD.

Ouchi, W.G. 1984. *The M-Form Society.* Reading: Addison-Wesley.

Palda, K. 1985. *A Canadian Industrial Policy Toward Innovation.* Vancouver: Fraser Institute.

Richardson, J.D. 1985. "Factor Market Adjustment Policies in Response to External Shocks." In *Domestic Policies and the International Economic Environment*, volume 12 of the research studies prepared for the Royal Commission on the Economic Union and Development Prospects for Canada. Toronto: University of Toronto Press.

Robertson, M., and A. Grey. 1985. "Trade-Related Worker Adjustment Polices: The Canadian Experience." In *Domestic Policies and the International Economic Environment*, volume 12 of the research studies prepared for the Royal Commission on the Economic Union and Development Prospects for Canada. Toronto: University of Toronto Press.

Schultz, R., and A. Alexandroff. 1985. *Economic Regulation and the Federal System*. Volume 42 of the research studies prepared for the Royal Commission on the Economic Union and Development Prospects for Canada. Toronto: University of Toronto Press.

Science Council of Canada. 1979. *Forging the Links: A Technology Policy for Canada*. Report No. 29. Ottawa: Minister of Supply and Services Canada.

————. 1981. *Hard Times Hard Choices*. Ottawa: Minister of Supply and Services Canada.

————. 1984. *Canadian Industrial Development: Some Policy Directions*. Report 37. Ottawa: Minister of Supply and Services Canada.

Scott, B. 1984. "National Strategies: Key to International Competition." Boston: Harvard Business School. Mimeographed.

Spence, M. 1984. "The Industrial Organization and Competitive Advantage in Multinational Industries." *American Economic Review* 74 (May): 356–60.

Spencer, B., and J. Brander. 1983. "International R&D Rivalry and Industrial Strategy." *Review of Economic Studies* 50: 707–22.

Steed, G. 1982. *Threshold Firms: Backing Canada's Winners*. Science Council of Canada Background Study 48. Ottawa: Minister of Supply and Services Canada.

Thurow, L.C. 1981. *The Zero Sum Society*. New York: Penguin.

Trebilcock, M.J. 1985a. "The Political Economy of Business Bail-Outs in Canada." In *Domestic Policies and the International Economic Environment*, volume 12 of the research studies prepared for the Royal Commission on the Economic Union and Development Prospects for Canada. Toronto: University of Toronto Press.

————. 1985b. *The Political Economy of Economic Adjustment*. Volume 8 of the research studies prepared for the Royal Commission on the Economic Union and Development Prospects for Canada. Toronto: University of Toronto Press.

Trebilcock, M., J.R. Prichard, T. Courchene, and J. Whalley, eds. 1983. *Federalism and the Canadian Economic Union*. Toronto: Ontario Economic Council.

Tupper, A. 1985. "Federalism and the Politics of Industrial Policy." In *Canadian Industrial Policy*, volume 44 of the research studies prepared for the Royal Commission on the Economic Union and Development Prospects for Canada. Toronto: University of Toronto Press.

Usher, D. 1983. "The Benefits and Costs of Firm-Specific Investment Grants: A Study of Five Federal Programs." Discussion Paper 511. Kingston: Queen's University, Department of Economics.

Vanderkamp, J. 1985. "The Efficiency of the Interregional Adjustment Process." In *Disparities and Interregional Adjustment*, volume 64 of the research studies prepared for the Royal Commission on the Economic Union and Development Prospects for Canada. Toronto: University of Toronto Press.

Walker, M., ed. 1984. *Focus on Alberta's Industrial and Science Strategy Proposals*. Vancouver: Fraser Institute.

Watson, W. 1983. *A Primer on the Economics of Industrial Policy*. Toronto: Ontario Economic Council.

Whalley, J. 1983. "Induced Distortions of Interprovincial Activity: An Overview of the Issues." In *Federalism and the Canadian Economic Union*, edited by M.J. Trebilcock, J.R.S. Prichard, T.J. Courchene and John Whalley. Toronto: University of Toronto Press.

2

The Impact of Government Intervention on the Major Appliance Industry in Canada

HAROLD CROOKELL

Impending tariff decline is fostering a shift in Canada's industrial policy toward improved productivity and international competitiveness. Federal government commitment to the Tokyo Round of the GATT negotiations constitutes for Canada a partial dismantling of the protection that has attracted so much industry investment in the past, and the question being asked is how existing manufacturers can be streamlined to cope with stronger competition from abroad. The answer in theory is that they must specialize and trade. Specialization is expected to provide focus for R&D effort to advance technology, and trade is expected to result in greater scale economies and opportunities to compete in new markets. But even in theory, some industries are expected to fail to make the transition to international competitiveness because of relative factor cost disadvantages. These industries will become targets for government assistance, not primarily to prop them up — although that is sometimes done, but to provide adjustment assistance in the form of retraining so that workers can transfer to other industries with growing labour demands, assuming there are some.

This report examines Canada's major appliance industry as an illustration of these transition issues. It is an industry with high employment levels, which has experienced some government attention and intervention in the past. It is not a high-tech industry, and over the past six years it has not been a growth industry either. In fact, an econometric study done in 1981 for the Department of Industry, Trade and Commerce suggested that the major appliance industry was among the least likely to survive tariff cuts. At the same time, government has encouraged the industry to restructure and rationalize on the assumption it can adjust successfully. These conflicts make it an interesting proxy for study and the ready availability of industry data makes the task a manageable one.

We turn first to an examination of the industry between 1977 and 1982. The focus is on employment, competition, productivity and international trade. The report then examines specific incidents of government intervention in the industry, beginning with the 1976 decision to block the takeover of the Westinghouse appliance division by White Consolidated Industries (WCI), and including federal designation of the industry for assistance under the Industry and Labour Adjustment Program (ILAP) through which the government helped Inglis to buy Admiral. It concludes with some reflections on the problem of conflicting government objectives — specifically, the objectives of greater Canadian ownership, improved industry structure and performance, and fairer regional distribution of economic activity. The relative importance of these issues to Canada in the long run seems almost inversely proportional to their power to galvanize political action in the short term. This is an important problem for Canada. Many other mature industries face the same difficulties. It is not enough to look to the high-tech industries to pull us out of our economic difficulties. Maturity is payoff time to yesterday's innovations. We cannot linger there too long, but neither can we afford to diminish or lose the payoff through inappropriate policies. Too many jobs are involved.

The Major Appliance Industry, 1976–82

The major appliance industry is characterized by mature products with high market saturation levels, manufactured by established production processes which are very scale sensitive — i.e., unit production costs are lowered as plant size increases. It is in many ways characteristic of Canadian secondary industry as a whole. Because it has produced largely for the Canadian market behind protective tariffs, it has not achieved cost competitiveness with its U.S. counterpart; and because much of it has been foreign-owned, an efficiency shake-out has always been difficult to orchestrate.

These general industry conditions were first identified in Canada by English in 1964 and expanded on three years later by Eastman and Stykolt. In fact, the major appliance industry was studied in 1970 by Quirin, Wilson et al. on the economies of scale model, with results very similar to those reported in this study. Caves established in 1975 that Canadian manufacturers tended to produce more products per plant than U.S. manufacturers. Daly took the issue of scale economies further in 1979 in a study which addressed non-production scale economies as well as those related to factory costs. While these studies have been important for Canada and germane to a review of the major appliance industry, they appear to have been predicated on the wish that Canadian industry were not structured as it is. Hence, while the theory has been around for some twenty years, firms have only recently begun to specialize in earnest (Bishop and Crookell, 1983). The reason, of course, is that the structural changes needed to secure the scale economies required a lower Canadian dollar along with the motivation of a weak domestic market. Furthermore, specialization in production can have adverse effects on marketing (Crookell, 1968), some of which are discussed later in this paper.

With the exception of dishwashers and microwave ovens, major appliances are increasingly purchased as replacement items. In times of economic recession, replacement purchases are often deferred beyond the 18-year average life that has been the experience in the industry. Replacement can be accelerated, on the other hand, by the development of desirable new features, but few major innovations have been introduced since the self-cleaning oven.

This is not to imply that the industry has been static. Over the last six years there have been major changes in industry structure that presage important competitive adjustments for the future. These changes have been the disappearance of most small appliance manufacturers and the emergence of three giant, full-line competitors, one of which may have difficulty surviving profitably. The most dramatic incidents were the formation of Camco in 1976 from the major appliance divisions of Canadian General Electric (CGE), General Steel Ware (GSW) and Westinghouse, and the acquisition of Admiral by Inglis in 1982. The federal government was an active player in both moves and is on record as supporting mergers that will improve industry productivity through greater scale economies. The government's position is given added urgency by the fact that import tariffs on major appliances are scheduled to drop from the present level of 20 percent to 12.5 percent by 1988. Productivity improvements are seen as necessary to prevent excessive import competition as tariffs decline. The casualty in this grand stratagem is the small, "inefficient" Canadian appliance producer. A world of giants is emerging and the small firms have been or will be devoured or crushed unless they are very nimble indeed.

The last six years have seen a significant reversal in the traditional growth pattern of major appliances sales in Canada. The core products — refrigerators, electric ranges, automatic washers and electric dryers — have all experienced sales declines. From 1976 to 1982, unit sales in these products dropped in aggregate by 30 percent. Of this, 27 percent occurred between 1980 and 1982 (see Table 2-1), demonstrating how recent and severe the reversal is. These core products have all achieved effective market saturation, so sales are a function of replacement needs (about 75 percent) and new household formations (about 25 percent). Despite the slowdown in housing starts in Canada, the builder market for appliances did not decline as severely as the retail

TABLE 2-1 Canadian Sales of Major Appliances (thousands of units)

	1976	1978	1980	1982	% change 1976–82	% change 1980–82
Core Products						
Refrigerators	561	616	542	372	−34	−31
Electric Ranges	491	508	430	315	−36	−27
Automatic Washers	461	473	474	359	−22	−24
Electric Washers	394	389	375	277	−30	−26
Average	1907	1986	1821	1323	−31	−27
Freezers	362	318	341	278	−23	−18
Dishwashers	61	291	308	215	−18	−30
Microwaves	65	98	147	252	+288	+71

Source: Major Appliance Forecast 1983. Canadian Appliance Manufacturers Association (CAMA).

replacement market. Clearly, consumers were making their appliances last longer.

Unfortunately for the industry, the prices at which appliances were sold between 1976 and 1981 failed to keep pace with the rate of inflation. Table 2-2 shows the relationship between the major appliance selling price index and the general consumer price index over the six-year period. There was a 48 percent price increase between 1976 and 1981, which means that appliance sales in dollars increased in spite of the decline in units sold. However, costs rose more sharply still, as the general index of all prices moved up by 59 percent during the same period. Had it not been for improvements in productivity, corporate profits would have declined substantially. They did not, as Table 2-3 illustrates. Industry executives attributed this largely to productivity improvements made possible by restructuring.

TABLE 2-2 Appliance Prices Compared to Consumer Price Index

	Aggregate Employment	Consumer Price Index	Appliance Price Index	CPI 1976 = 100	API 1976 = 100
1982		350.5		176.3	
1981	6,902	316.3	209.8	159.1	148.0
1980	9,106	281.2	183.1	141.4	129.1
1979	9,199	255.3	166.8	128.4	117.6
1978	12,806	233.9	157.7	117.7	111.2
1977	11,170	214.7	148.1	108.0	104.4
1976	11,888	198.8	141.8	100.0	100.0

Source: Statistics Canada Catalogues 62–001, 62–011.

One bright spot for Canadian appliance manufacturers was that imports secured a smaller percentage of the Canadian market. Hence, although the market in Canada was declining, Canadian producers held on to more of it. Import penetration in core products plus dishwashers and microwaves declined from 25 percent of Canadian sales in 1976 to

TABLE 2-3 Industry Trends, 1977–82
(based on the three leading
competitors, Camco, Inglis, WCI)

		1982	1981	1980	1979	1978	1977
Sales	– Actual	690	660	600	564	516	478
(1977 = 100)	– Index	144	138	126	118	108	100
Consumer price index (1977 = 100)		163	147	131	119	109	100
Return on net assets[a]		18.8	15.7	10.0	14.1	15.1	6.7
Return on equity[b]		13.8	10.2	5.8	13.7	15.7	3.1

Source: Calculated from company annual reports.
a. Return on net assets = net income before interest and taxes divided by working capital
         + net fixed assets
b. Return on equity = net income after tax, divided by total equity

19 percent in 1982, meaning that the decline in unit sales in Canada from Canadian production was smaller than the sales decline itself. This was widely attributed to the decline in value of the Canadian dollar, particularly against the U.S. dollar. At the same time, there was a significant increase in refrigerator and freezer exports from Canada between 1978 and 1981 (declining in 1982), but no corresponding increase in exports of other appliance products. The bottom line is that Canadian appliance manufacturers have not suffered as great a decline in their output as the market has experienced in its sales, but they have been under a price/cost squeeze which has pressed them toward greater productivity.

Before we look at how these events have affected the major firms in the industry, it is useful to point out that imports of parts are frequently higher in dollar value than imports of finished products. It is the deficit in parts trade that keeps the industry in a net trade deficit position similar to the automotive industry. In general, technological advances have been largely in the parts, and the Canadian appliance industry has not been a leader in technology. Instead it has followed the practice of importing product designs from the United States either through licensing or parent linkage, and then importing needed parts from those who supply their licensors or parents. This is why import penetration in newer products (i.e., dishwashers and microwaves) is so much higher than import penetration in mature products. In this connection, industry sources indicate an increase in component sourcing by U.S. appliance producers using points of supply in the Far East. There is a concern that leadership in the process technology for manufacturing appliances may shift away from the United States, as it has with automobiles. It is doubtful, however, that this will extend beyond selected components to affect assembly activity itself. Shipping costs on finished appliance products are high and assembly is fairly labour intensive; few governments will be pleased to see the related jobs go offshore.

The Key Competitors

The key participants in the Canadian appliance industry are (a) the big three full-time manufacturers — Camco, Inglis and White Consolidated Inc. (WCI) — whose comparative financial performances are shown in Table 2-4; (b) the smaller specialized firms — Wood and General Freezer in freezers and Keeprite in air conditioners; and (c) the importers, of whom the best known are Maytag, Amana and Hobart (which also does some manufacturing in Canada). Data on the importers are difficult to obtain, but importers are generally known in the industry for "top of the line" strategies involving high product quality, selective distribution, and higher than average prices. Other imports, primarily from Europe and Japan, take the form of small appliances, below the size customarily purchased by Canadian households.

TABLE 2-4 Comparative Financial Performances

	1982	1981	1979	1977
Sales growth index				
Camco	124	123	109	100
Inglis	181	163	126	100
WCI	154	147	132	100
Fixed asset growth index				
Camco	86	89	94	100
Inglis	n.a.	104	92	100
WCI	134	130	122	100
Return on equity[a] (%)				
Camco	18.9	12.9	23.4	(4.3)
Inglis	11.8	9.2	11.9	4.8
WCI	10.6	8.4	4.5	3.5
Return on assets[b] (%)				
Camco	21.5	18.9	16.9	6.4
Inglis	19.8	15.5	15.6	7.8
WCI	15.1	13.0	7.5	4.5
Net income: sales (%)				
Camco	2.0	1.1	1.8	− .2
Inglis	2.3	1.8	2.7	1.1
WCI	3.4	2.5	1.7	1.8
Income from operations: sales (%)				
Camco	5.3	4.7	4.9	1.5
Inglis	6.4	4.1	5.2	2.8
WCI	5.5	4.5	3.1	2.5

Source: Calculated from company annual reports.
a. Return on equity = net income after taxes divided by total equity.
b. Return on assets = income from operations (before interest and income tax) divided by
   total equity plus long-term debt.
n.a. = not available

Wood and Keeprite are the only major Canadian-owned participants in the industry. Both are specialized. Neither firm releases financial data for public review. Wood has a very good reputation in the industry. They produce about half the freezers sold in Canada and export to a number of markets. Their factory is well equipped for efficient production and they have been relatively quick to adopt advanced process technology. The result is a strong leadership position in freezers, their chosen area of specialization, and some attempt to get into small refrigerators. They seem to have taken over Danby for this purpose. Their main competition in freezers comes from General Freezer and WCI. Inglis and Camco are not in direct competition. The Wood strategy of competing through product specialization is one that has proved effective in the present industry structure and appears to be in no immediate danger. Keeprite has followed a similar strategy with air conditioners.

Camco

Camco was formed in 1976 by a merger between the appliance divisions of CGE and GSW, and the subsequent acquisition of Westinghouse Canada's appliance division. Sales were $267 million in 1977, its first full operating year, and rose to $441 million by 1982 — a much more modest growth rate than either of its two main competitors and well below the consumer price index and the major appliance selling price index (see Table 2-2). The slow growth of Camco was certainly not expected. When the federal government blocked WCI from acquiring the Westinghouse appliance division in 1976, it gave Camco a chance to come together, with substantial Canadian ownership (40 percent equity and 50 percent voting), and hold a large market share (between 35 and 40 percent). The expectation was that with the market share Camco would improve its productivity through rationalization of output, lower its costs and prices, and become inexorably the market leader. This has not happened, in part because Camco has had to contend with a tough competitive thrust by WCI for the market share originally held by Westinghouse.

More significantly, however, the opportunity for production rationalization appears in general not to have been seized. An examination of Camco's balance sheets from 1977 to 1981 shows no major expenditure on fixed assets. Executives at CGE estimate that capital expenditures in the region of $50 million are needed to handle the rationalization and modernization of Camco's inherited facilities. If this were carried out, each product could be manufactured in a single location with modern, special-purpose equipment geared to long continuous runs. Camco has, in fact, achieved rationalization in some products but has not invested in the new special-purpose equipment needed to secure the scale economies made possible by that rationalization. The main cause has been internal friction, but this was resolved in 1983 by a takeover of Camco by CGE. The company now appears poised to move forward.

At present Camco sells a full line of appliances except for freezers under its own brand names, and a limited line under private brands. Brand names include Hotpoint, with which much of the Westinghouse market share had been retained, GE, and a group of GSW names such as Moffat, McClary, Beatty and Easy. Microwave ovens are sold under both the GE and Litton-GSW brands, giving Camco a very strong position in that market. Despite some evident slippage in general market share over the past five years, Camco's financial performance has not been bad. Operating income before interest and taxes was up in 1981 to $18.6 million, or 5.7 percent of sales, and net return on equity stood at 12.9 percent despite a debt/equity ratio of 2.53. Still, in aggregate, the level of debt would probably be of great concern to the bank were it not for the assumption of CGE backing for Camco. Interest expense has declined from $13.25 million with earnings coverage of only 1.4 in 1981, to $8.43 million with coverage of 2.1 in 1982.

Inglis

Before Inglis bought out Admiral in 1981, it was already the fastest growing company in the appliance industry. Its income statements and balance sheets over the past five years show an annual growth rate of 16 percent in sales, a sustained but modest level of profitability, and debt/equity ratio of only .4 prior to the acquisition. Income from operations in 1981 stood at $8.25 million, some 4.1 percent of sales, compared to which interest expense of $2.5 million had a coverage of 3.4 times. Results for 1982 are complicated by treatment of the acquisition.

The real strength of Inglis lies in its ownership structure. Whirlpool Corporation of Benton Harbour, Michigan holds 43 percent of the equity in Inglis and provides a strong source of technology and product design. Furthermore, Whirlpool is the key supplier of major appliances to Sears-Roebuck, and Sears-Roebuck owns over 70 percent of Simpson-Sears, which in turn owns 20 percent of Inglis. It is not surprising therefore that Inglis has the Simpson-Sears appliance business quite securely locked in. This is a very considerable account to have. Industry sources estimate Simpson-Sears' market share in major appliance retailing to be between 23 and 28 percent of industry sales. Inglis, however, did not supply all of it because they were not a full-line manufacturer. Inglis did not produce ranges or freezers and until 1981 could not compete against D&M's imported dishwashers (D&M supplied Sears-Roebuck with dishwashers and were reputed to be the most efficient dishwasher manufacturer in the United States). The decline of the Canadian dollar has altered the competitive logistics, however, and the battle for Simpson-Sears' dishwasher business is now on. Inglis currently produces close to 50 percent of the Simpson-Sears dishwashers sold in Canada.

By reputation, the product strength of Inglis is in its automatic washers and dryers. The company's refrigerators and dishwashers are fighting for market share, and it is staying out of freezers. Inglis was not in the business of producing ranges until May 1982, when the purchase of Admiral was completed with federal financial help. Admiral had a strong position in ranges which Inglis has now inherited. If Inglis can hold on to the Admiral market share, the company's sales by 1983 may equal those of Camco. Admiral had sales of $130 million in 1979. Furthermore, Inglis is not participating in the microwave oven business, which is fairly lucrative for Camco, so for other products the aggregate Inglis market share may be higher than Camco's.

WCI Canada

When the Foreign Investment Review Agency (FIRA) denied WCI the opportunity to buy out the appliance division of Westinghouse Canada, it literally robbed the company of its established growth strategy. WCI grew originally by acquisition, both in Canada and the United States. In fact, its array of regional brands, including Franklin, Gibson, Hupp and Roy, along with its better known Kelvinator, Frigidaire and White-Westinghouse brands, had come about largely as an accidental by-product of its acquisition strategy in the United States. The presence of FIRA blocked the acquisition strategy in Canada after 1975. Certainly, if WCI could not get approval to buy out Westinghouse, which was foreign owned, it was unlikely to get approval for any other takeovers in Canada. The alternative route for WCI growth was to win market share from Camco and Inglis. But winning market share is problematic at best in a scale-sensitive industry in which your chief competitors are both three times your size and there has been no industry growth since 1975. Furthermore, in 1982 WCI lost its stencil brand range business with Inglis because of the latter's acquisition of Admiral. Nevertheless, 1982 sales were marginally higher than 1981, but not by as much as the rate of inflation.

The company is doing a good job of hanging in. By concentrating on very tight operations management, it has managed to maintain its market share in the industry and to do it profitably. The company has a secure source of technology in the United States via its Westinghouse and other acquisitions. Its sales have grown from $88 million in 1977 to $130 million in 1981 and $136 million in 1982, an average annual growth rate of 12 percent. This rate is more or less in concert with the inflation rate but better than the general increase in appliance prices. Income from operations in 1982 stood at 5.5 percent of sales, up from 4.5 percent the previous year. Interest charges were a modest $253,000, covered 29 times, due to a very low debt/equity ratio. Return on equity has ranged between 5 and 8 percent over the past five years, and reached 11 percent in 1982.

The company's reputation in the industry is as mixed as its brand identity. It is seen as a good competitor in ranges, refrigerators and freezers but not so strong in laundry equipment or dishwashers. The company has a strong private label position with Eatons and the Bay and is a manufacturer of Beaumark. (Beaumark is the private label name introduced by the Bay when it acquired Simpsons. Production of Beaumark is handled primarily by Camco and WCI.) To do well in the private label segment requires strong production efficiency, which is generally associated with scale and specialization. WCI does not have the scale to specialize effectively. The company's good performance over the past five years is a testament to its tight operations management and also reflects the company's investment commitment over that period. Fixed assets have grown much faster than those of competitors, indicating a commitment to modernization of production facilities.

The Appliance Industry and International Competitiveness

Three years ago, U.S. appliance manufacturers were producing established products like refrigerators and washing machines at costs about 20 percent below those of Canadian manufacturers. With newer products like dishwashers, the gap was closer to 35 percent. Explanations for the gap centred on the size of the U.S. market, the greater level of corporate concentration there, and the smaller number of products in a given factory compared to Canada. With the Canadian dollar dropping below US$0.80, the situation in 1984 is that major appliance costs are about equivalent in core products in both countries, while the United States has about a 15 percent edge in new products. But because of the much higher U.S. commitment to process technology, the cost differential between Canada and the United States is widening at about 1 percent a year. This estimate is provided by industry executives and reflects a higher ratio of R&D to sales in the parent companies. Large-scale specialized facilities in the United States undoubtedly provide clearer focus and greater opportunity to improve productivity. It is likely that this 1-percent-a-year productivity differential would disappear if firms were to rationalize on a north-south basis. However, if rationalization proceeds within Canada the differential will not disappear unless the Canadian firms match their parents' commitment to process technology. When we introduce the tariff (20 percent on most products but 15 percent on dishwashers, declining to 12.5 percent by 1988), the competitive position alters. One final ingredient is that Canadian producers could lower their costs by about 15 percent overall if they invested to secure the gains already available because of rationalization within each firm. The situation is shown in Table 2-5.

The precision implied by numbers like these is not found in the real world. There are all kinds of aberrations. For example, because so few Canadian homes use gas ranges, no Canadian manufacturer makes them. Canadian output of electric ranges is much more than 10 percent of U.S. output. In general, U.S. electric ranges do not meet the specifications of the Canadian Standards Association, with the result that few are imported into Canada. For refrigerators, about 25 percent of materials requirements are imported, mostly from outside the United States. For dishwashers, the figure is about 45 percent, mostly from within the United States. Indeed in core products, some U.S. producers are buying components offshore, usually from the Far East or South America. Few refrigerator compressors are made in Canada or the United States anymore. There is a lot of untidiness in the real world that defies generalization.

What the figures do suggest is that Canada is relatively safe from cost-based imports of core products at present but faces a stronger import threat from newer products like dishwashers. At the same time, Canadian producers are not in a position to export but could be so in core products if the firms invested to seize the scale advantages open to them. However, that competitive edge will erode over the years unless Canadian producers also invest in or license process technology and learn to match year-to-year productivity gains with their U.S. competitors. From this perspective, the needs of the industry are for encouragement to:

- move to a position where there are only two manufacturers of each major appliance in Canada, either through greater concentration in the industry or through a variety of north-south rationalization arrangements by the firms;
- invest in new equipment (accelerated capital cost allowance for tax purposes); and
- spend on process technology (inflated R&D write-off for tax purposes).

TABLE 2-5 Comparative Appliance Costs — Canada Versus United States

	Core Product	New Product
Assumed cost of production in Canada	100	100
Estimated cost of production in US$ (in Cdn dollars, $.80)	100	85
Tariff rate 1982 (20% and 15%)	20	13
Tariff rate 1988 (12.5%)	12	10
Landed cost of U.S. product 1982	120	98
Landed cost of U.S. product 1988[a]	107	90
Potential cost in Canada (if firms invested to modernize and rationalize production)	85	85

a. Assuming an exchange rate still at .80 and a widening of cost competitiveness at 1% a year for five years.

Canadian tax treatment for R&D and capital expenditures is already reportedly better than that in the United States, and one might well ask just how much better it needs to be. At the same time, to confront an industry with the challenge to emerge from decades of protection and transform itself into international competitiveness is an enormously complex and costly affair. It is sometimes spoken about with little recognition of the cost of implementation. The intent of the incentives suggested above is to encourage the transition and perhaps accelerate it. From this perspective, the incentives need not be permanent and could take a different form. But to expect the industry to accomplish the transition to international competitiveness without incentives is to underestimate the magnitude of the challenge. Specialization is easier said than done.

It is perhaps useful here to touch on one of the dilemmas of specialization that is not often talked about in the public policy debate. It concerns the marketing side of business activity, which is seldom featured in public policy. The dilemma arises because scale economies in an industry like major appliances are built on market share; market share is sustained by brand proliferation; and brand proliferation is threatened by specialization. If all Camco refrigerators are produced in a single location, it gets more difficult to sustain brand differentiation. A Hotpoint becomes like a GE or a GSW. The channels of distribution are affected. There is a risk of losing market share and with it some of the gains to scale and specialization. So firms are likely in any event to move more slowly toward specialization than industry observers may wish.

We turn now to a review of major government actions over the past six years in relation to the major appliance industry.

Government Actions

The Westinghouse Case

The first and best known incident of government intervention in the industry was the rejection by FIRA (and Cabinet) of WCI's bid to take over the major appliance division of Westinghouse in 1976. Some history is perhaps in order. Westinghouse was really the prime mover. It was losing a lot of money on its major appliance division in the United States and actively looked for a way out. White Consolidated Industries (WCI) ended up the buyer. The Canadian appliance division was part of the package as long as satisfactory terms could be arranged with Westinghouse's Canadian board of directors, and as long as FIRA approved.

The selling price to WCI was 20 percent below the book value of the appliance division's assets, reflecting the heavy loss position in the United States. In Canada, however, Westinghouse not only was making money on appliances but held around 16 percent of the market, a much higher share than the company held in the United States. Furthermore, 25 percent of Westinghouse Canada shares were held by Canadians and a majority of the company's directors were Canadian. In view of these conditions, Westinghouse offered to pay its Canadian subsidiary a disproportionate share of the proceeds of the overall sale. The amount agreed on was $42 million, some $8 million above book value.

At this point FIRA entered the arena and turned down WCI's application to take over Westinghouse's appliance business in Canada. Shortly thereafter WCI was invited by the Minister of Industry, Trade and Commerce to apply again to FIRA and was promised a swift decision. WCI did re-apply but as things turned out the decision was neither swift nor positive. It was rumoured that Cabinet overturned a positive FIRA recommendation. In any case, the takeover was blocked and the decision was widely criticized in the U.S. media. The criticisms were at three levels. First, the takeover of one foreign-owned firm by another did not increase foreign ownership in Canada and should not have involved FIRA at all. Second, WCI had made all the assurances FIRA had asked it for and was denied anyway. And third, no explanation was given for the denial.

Behind the scenes was GSW, the only Canadian-owned full-line major appliance manufacturer, with an offer to buy Westinghouse's appliance division in Canada at the book value price of $34 million, a price clearly less acceptable to Westinghouse. Furthermore, GSW did not have the capacity to raise $34 million but had obtained a government loan guarantee to facilitate its bid from Industry, Trade and Commerce — the same government department that supervised FIRA. After FIRA's rejection of the first WCI bid, Westinghouse opened negotiations with GSW, but the negotiations stalled when it became clear that GSW would not be able to secure access to Westinghouse's technology, parts supply or trade name. Westinghouse Canada finally withdrew from the negotiations because it could not meet GSW's terms. Then WCI was invited to re-apply to FIRA, but while the second application was under consideration GSW formed a joint venture with CGE, called Camco, and announced its willingness to buy Westinghouse without the technology and parts supply conditions, but for a price of $28 million. With this offer on the table, the WCI bid was rejected again, FIRA approval criteria notwithstanding. To be sure, GSW marshalled support for its bid from the Ontario Government, the United Electrical Union, and the Committee for an Independent Canada, but there was more to it than just pressure. The underlying argument was rooted in industry structure.

In 1976, the major appliance industry comprised six full-line manufacturers, each with between 12 and 16 percent of the market. It was a stable oligopoly, consisting of Admiral, CGE, GSW, Inglis, WCI and Westinghouse. Because production costs in the industry are quite sensitive to scale, a merger between WCI and Westinghouse would create the opportunity to put severe price pressure on the other four. The company least able to stand that pressure was GSW, which was heavily in debt, only marginally profitable, and without a parent. Hence the question before FIRA on the first pass was whether to support a continued Canadian presence in the industry. The decision was to do so. The question on the second pass was different, however. GSW and CGE had already merged their appliance divisions and Camco would have been roughly the same size as WCI and Westinghouse combined. Continued Canadian participation in the industry seemed assured. Camco had access to GE technology and GE brand names. Furthermore, two equal-sized competitors would keep each other on their toes. When the second decision went against WCI and the battle for the Westinghouse market share was over, Camco came away with just under 40 percent of the total market. WCI, Inglis and Admiral were each below 16 percent. The scene was set for Camco to rationalize its operations and dominate the industry. The outlook for the other three was not promising.

But the opportunity created by Camco was not, in fact, seized. Five years later, Inglis had grown in market share, Camco had shrunk a little, WCI was holding its own and Admiral was on the ropes, but for a strange set of reasons. We examine the Inglis-Admiral situation next, but first we must ask why Camco did not seize the opportunity open to it between 1976 and 1982. The simple answer is that it was not obliged to. There was no competitive pressure in the marketplace forcing it to do so — just an opportunity. If Cabinet had approved a White takeover of Westinghouse after GSW merged its appliance operations with CGE, the two resulting companies would probably have provided the competitive pressure to move the industry forward in productivity much faster.

It appears that the Cabinet was more concerned about ownership and structure than about competition. When the decline of the Canadian dollar reduced U.S. competition, there was simply not enough pressure to make Camco move. The presence of an opportunity galvanizes managerial action less swiftly than the pressure of competition. We turn later to some of the internal reasons why Camco did not move sooner to seize the opportunity presented through government-aided restructuring. But the simple answer is that Camco did not have to, and therefore, for various reasons, did not do so.

The Inglis-Admiral Acquisition

Inglis and Admiral were the two major competitors not involved in the Westinghouse transaction. They were close observers because each has significant foreign ownership. Admiral was soon to find itself in a similar position to Westinghouse. Its parent company had been acquired by the conglomerate North American Rockwell, which in 1979 decided to get out of major appliances. The U.S. assets of Admiral were sold to Magic

Chef, but the Canadian assets were not part of the transaction. Rockwell had clearly learned from the Westinghouse experience with FIRA. Admiral in Canada was deliberately kept liquid and offered for sale in Canada. It was picked up by Montreal conglomerate York Lambton, controlled by Sogebry which in turn was controlled by group Bienvenu of Quebec. What followed was a reverse takeover of Admiral by the smaller and money-losing York Lambton. The takeover price was about $35 million, which York Lambton reportedly paid for with money borrowed from the Mercantile Bank and the National Bank of Canada. Part of the financing package involved the sale of 20 percent of Admiral to SDIQ (a Quebec government industrial expansion agency) for $5 million. Before the sale to SDIQ was finalized, however, York Lambton paid itself a dividend of $25 million from the resources left in Admiral. Furthermore, Admiral was required to buy out BFG Industries Ltd., a troubled appliance manufacturer based in St.Bruno, Quebec, and owned by York Lambton. The price of $5.7 million was reportedly much more than BFG's worth as a going concern. This group of transactions taken together enabled York Lambton to discharge its debt obligations for the purchase of Admiral, but Admiral itself was left with a stripped treasury and weakened management at a time of looming recession. In good times Admiral might have survived the radical surgery of 1979, although concerns about the ongoing flow of product technology were unresolved. As it happened, good times were not characteristic of economic conditions in Canada as the 1980s began, and Admiral found itself without the resources it needed to weather the storms. It had borrowed to buy BFG and again within a matter of months to buy the Speed Queen appliance division of McGraw-Edison for between $6 and $8 million. As interest rates rose during 1980 and 1981, and demand for appliances weakened, Admiral was forced into bankruptcy.

When the bankruptcy came, two relatively small plants in Quebec were affected — the old BFG plant in St.Bruno which had closed the previous year and another plan in Montmagny. Admiral executives had reportedly wanted to close both of these plants and switch production to the main plant in Mississauga, which was running well below capacity. York Lambton executives had disagreed. In fact, when Admiral's Ottawa plant was closed down in 1979, York Lambton transferred production to Montmagny instead of Mississauga, where Admiral had reportedly planned to move it. The fact that these two Quebec plants were affected by the Admiral bankruptcy seemed to galvanize political will in Ottawa to encourage a takeover of Admiral by Inglis and to secure FIRA approval.

In June 1982, the Department of Industry, Trade and Commerce announced a $15-million assistance package for the industry. Public pronouncements associated the assistance with plans to restructure the industry for greater productivity and an improved balance of trade. The Inglis purchase of Admiral had already been concluded, but with a promise of government assistance, part of which ultimately came out of the $15-million fund. A sum of $4 million was involved, of which $3 million came from the federal government and $1 million from the Ontario Development Corporation. Of the $3 million, $1.8 million was given as an interest-free loan from the $15-million fund. Among the terms of the package was an agreement to keep the Montmagny plant operating.

The advantage to Inglis in buying Admiral was to become a full-line manufacturer. Admiral had a strong brand image in electrical ranges, a product which Inglis did not manufacture but which it sold on a stencil basis from WCI. Admiral was also expected to give a boost to Inglis' refrigerator business. In fact, if Inglis succeeded in holding on to most of Admiral's market share, its sales in 1983 would equal Camco's sales, excluding microwaves which Inglis does not produce. Thus Inglis could challenge Camco in the quest for scale economies and productivity.

The view of Camco and WCI on the Inglis takeover of Admiral was understandably negative. The entire industry was operating below capacity and it was difficult for WCI and Camco executives to see the benefit of keeping the Admiral plants open. Why not simply let Admiral die and allow the remaining competitors to compete for its share in the marketplace? Higher plant capacity would improve the productivity of the entire industry. However, if Inglis had chosen to buy Admiral without government help, that would have been accepted. It was the government assistance that caused the irritation. The view of the firms was that the entire $15-million program was put in place because of the political potency of the dilemma in Quebec. It seemed paradoxical that a government committed to industry restructuring and productivity improvement would pay to keep small-scale plants functioning. If the key message from the first intervention was that ownership was more important than productivity, the message from this second intervention was that location was also more important than productivity.

The Inglis acquisition of Admiral appears to have had a major impact on Camco and also indirectly on WCI. From WCI's standpoint, there is literally nobody left to buy in the appliance industry in Canada, and the company is left with sales of less than half of either Camco or Inglis. If Camco and Inglis move aggressively to rationalize their production arrangements and modernize their plants, WCI will be hard-pressed to compete. The possibility of one more takeover is not out of the question. For Camco the option of waiting it out may no longer be tenable. The threat of an equivalent-sized Inglis seems to have generated some action. It is to the evolution and growth of Camco that we now turn.

Camco — Getting Along in a Joint Venture

When CGE and GSW merged their appliance divisions, CGE ended up with 60 percent of the invested capital in Camco. However, in order to provide evidence of significant Canadian ownership, the voting shares of Camco were divided equally between the two partners. Significant managerial decisions, including investment decisions, required approval from the board of directors, which was chaired by the head of GSW. The chief executive officer came from CGE. By this arrangement, CGE was to supply the hands-on management and technology and GSW was to provide strategic direction through its power on the board to block or redirect management's plans.

When Camco acquired Westinghouse's appliance division, it inherited the task of reconciling three markedly different managerial styles. Pain and friction were inevitable, as ultimately was the emergence of a dominant style that was acceptable to CGE, which had the responsibility to make it work. Making it work, in turn, strained the partnership. Within a few years the strains were a matter of public record. While the causes were many, the central effect was to stall the investment needed to achieve the higher productivity made possible by the merger. According to the public record, it was GSW that blocked new investment. A brief glance at Camco's financial statements from 1977 to 1982 shows negligible fixed asset investment over the six-year period, whereas competitors, particularly WCI, were more aggressive. The situation came to a head when CGE offered to buy out GSW for $21.6 million — a seemingly generous price — but FIRA blocked the bid. Subsequently CGE moved in the courts to dissolve the Camco partnership on grounds of irreconcilable differences. The matter was recently settled out of court in a quiet and ingenious way which hints at the kind of difficulties being faced.

Stepping back for a moment and looking at the partnership, we have CGE, an established and well financed firm with an eye fixed five or ten years into the future, and GSW, a small young firm with an eye on meeting the payroll. Since Camco was formed, no dividends have been paid. Profits have been modest and have been reinvested in working capital and latterly in long-term debt reduction. The debt/equity ratio is weak. CGE has announced a need to invest up to $50 million to modernize and restructure Camco. While CGE sees Camco leading the industry and competing in the U.S. market in five to ten years, GSW must see it at times as a permanent cash drain. Who would want to invest $50 million in a declining and barely profitable industry? It depends on one's vision, and CGE and GSW have different perspectives and time horizons.

In the out-of-court settlement, the share structure of Camco was reorganized with 15 percent of the common shares offered to the public — 9 percent from CGE and 6 percent from GSW — and a dividend of $1.3 million was declared prior to the reorganization. By this arrangement, GSW will receive cash in the amount of $520,000 in dividends and approximately $4.8 million from the sale of its shares and CGE will receive 50 percent more. In addition, GSW will receive $4 million from Camco for its trademarks and technology. After the transaction, GSW will hold 34 percent of Camco's shares and CGE 51 percent, and these will also represent their voting rights. GSW's position is protected by an agreement on a formula for distributing a proportion of annual profits as a dividend and by the opportunity to sell more of its share should it wish to do so. The old separation of voting shares has disappeared. CGE now controls Camco although the head of GSW remains chairman of Camco's board. The takeover has been quietly approved by FIRA and Cabinet. Camco, the national champion, is now a foreign-owned firm. A majority of Cabinet presumably feels that this arrangement best serves Canada's interests. This is a very different mood than prevailed in Cabinet in 1976 when WCI was blocked from buying out Westinghouse.

Speculating briefly on why an agreement was possible between GSW and CGE in 1983, one cannot help but be led back to the competitive threat posed by Inglis after its acquisition of Admiral. For the first time since Camco was formed, the protagonists faced strong competitive pressure. Further loss of market share seemed inevitable unless problems were resolved in a way that permitted Camco to pursue a more aggressive strategy. The announced agreement certainly cleared the way. It also left WCI in a more vulnerable position. As the much smaller competitor in a scale-sensitive industry, WCI has survived through lean management, low overheads and substantial investment in modernization. If Inglis and Camco now move to modernize and rationalize their production facilities, the higher productivity from their greater scale economies may make WCI a high cost competitor. Since WCI has a substantial share of private brand business which is very price sensitive, the longer-term outlook for the company in Canada is not encouraging without a change in its structural arrangements.

Appraising Government's Interventions

In the mid-1970s Canada had a major appliance industry with six full-line competitors sharing a market too small to permit optimal scale economies to any one of them. A mixture of tariff protection and foreign ownership permitted them to earn profits in spite of this inefficiency. Now the industry is down to three full-line competitors, one decidedly smaller than the other two, and tariffs are declining, opening the industry to more foreign competition. Furthermore, the industry's trade balance has improved, largely through aggressive displacement of imports by domestic manufacturers. Whatever else we say about Canada's major appliance industry, it is in a better position now than it was in 1975. And it appears to be poised for a major step forward in productivity and international competitiveness. If this remarkable transformation could be attributed mainly to government intervention, one would be obliged to acknowledge a measure of federal omniscience. It seems, however, that the main factor in improved performance has been the decline in value of the Canadian dollar. This has allowed Canadian manufacturers to capture a larger share of the Canadian market, which in turn has compensated to a degree for the decline in the size of the market itself. The structural shake-out in the industry seems to have occurred largely because of the general decline in industry sales. Government has influenced the result, but not in the way intended and not necessarily for the good of the industry.

If we review briefly the specific points of intervention by government and attempt to trace the results, we have the following.

First Rejection of the WCI Bid for Westinghouse.

Objective   To help Canadian-owned GSW survive and prosper among its U.S.–owned competitors.

Results   GSW was unable to negotiate a Westinghouse takeover because it required more from the transaction than a foreign subsidiary can normally deliver (e.g., technology, trade name, parts supply). When a subsidiary division is organized on the miniature replica model and the parent moves out of the business in question, the subsidiary is cut adrift without a guarantee of parts supply or ongoing technology. In addition, the issue of trade name introduces complex international legal issues. It was simply impossible for Westinghouse Canada to provide GSW with all it required to make a takeover worthwhile. Part of the problem was that GSW did not have strong in-house competence in technology and needed time to build it up. But the larger problem was whether GSW would be able to hold on to the Westinghouse market share if the trade name did not go with the acquisition. Put simply, if WCI got use of the Westinghouse name and GSW got control of the Westinghouse sales force, who would hold the dealers? Who would get the Westinghouse market share? Who would get the potential scale economies?

As a result, the government's intervention to block WCI and open the way for GSW to buy Westinghouse was ineffective, government loan guarantees notwithstanding. The impact on Westinghouse was $8 million less in the offer price. Westinghouse was understandably upset. The final outcome was a government request to WCI to submit a second application to FIRA; certainly not the outcome envisaged when the intervention was first undertaken.

Second Rejection of the WCI Bid for Westinghouse.

Objective   To create a national champion in the major appliance industry with a dominant market share and a significant Canadian ownership.

Result   GWS, having already merged appliance divisions with CGE to form Camco, was able to acquire Westinghouse for $28 million. This second intervention left Westinghouse with no other approved buyer and a very costly alternative if it chose to stay in the business without its parent. WCI got the Westinghouse name and Camco got the Westinghouse sales force. When the dust settled Camco held on to most of the Westinghouse market share and secured a dominant position in the industry. The GE name and reputation were important elements in Camco's success.

This intervention succeeded in its objective, though at some cost both to Westinghouse and WCI. However, the expected downstream benefits did not materialize. The expected investment in modernization and rationalization did not take place. Industry productivity did not improve. International competitiveness improved only because the Canadian dollar declined. The intervention had created an opportunity but not the competitive pressure to ensure that it was seized. Furthermore, the opportunity required a sizable investment at a time of shrinking demand and high interest rates, and GSW had pressing resource limitations.

In retrospect, and there are many advantages to writing in retrospect, industry productivity would probably have improved faster if there had been no intervention. Given the GSW–CGE merger, if WCI had been allowed to buy Westinghouse, two large competitors of similar size would have emerged and each would probably have kept pressure on the other to reduce costs. Industry productivity and consumer benefit would have been enhanced. Would things really have turned out that way? With the benefit of hindsight, I think so. But might I be wrong? Is it possible that this way Canada would have ended up with three strong competitors in an industry capable of sustaining only two at optimal scale? And if it had, how much would it matter?

The point is that to criticize the intervention, one has to assume the same measure of omniscience assumed in the first place by the intervenors. That events turned out differently from their expectations is not so much a criticism of their intellects as a reminder of their humanity and the innate difficulty of predicting behaviour in a free society. It is a reminder that needs to be made more often.

Encouraging the Purchase of Admiral by Inglis.

Objectives   To keep a Quebec plant open and provide a strong, full-time competitor for Camco.

Result   Keeping the Quebec plants open was a specific condition written into the subsidy agreement and has consequently been carried out to this point. Inglis, by acquiring Admiral, has become a full-line manufacturer with output levels for most products similar to Camco.

Soon after the acquisition, Camco in fact resolved its internal difficulties. It now appears ready to handle stronger competition. The main objectives of this intervention, if they are correctly stated, have been achieved.

It is worth noting, however, that had it not been for FIRA's blockage of WCI in the first place, Admiral would probably not have gone through such a tortuous experience. When Admiral first came up for sale the firms capable of running it — Inglis, WCI and Camco — were not willing to bid against a Canadian-owned company. They felt FIRA had made its position clear in the Westinghouse case. Hence Inglis was only willing to bid when Admiral faced bankruptcy, and then only with federal government encouragement and an indication that FIRA approval would be no problem, as was indeed the case.

WCI and Camco executives were both upset at federal behaviour over Admiral — Camco because of the emergence of a strong competitor and WCI because Inglis was treated so much better by FIRA than it had been. Both were upset that federal funds were used to strengthen one competitor at the expense of the other two. They felt that Admiral should have been allowed to die, and its market share divided among the remaining three companies on the basis of free market competition. On this basis, both Camco and WCI would probably have ended up with some increased output and employment in their existing Quebec plants. But perhaps the most consequential concern expressed was that the prime political objective — to keep the Montmagny plant open — seemed at odds with the stated policy of restructuring the industry for greater international competitiveness.

In the final analysis, the government found it necessary to announce a $15-million program to assist the major appliance industry. Depressed industry conditions were cited as the main reason for the program. Industry conditions were certainly depressed, but so were conditions in many other industries at the time. The firms saw the program as the government's way of providing funds to others to match the Inglis loans and grants. For its own protection, government set as criteria for handing out the money:

• that it be invested in projects to improve productivity;
• that increased exports or reduced imports result from the projects; and
• that it be invested in projects with marginal profitability that would not have been undertaken without government help.

At first glance, the criteria seem prohibitive and designed primarily to protect those administering the program. However, by dint of ingenuity and liberal interpretation, some funds have now been made available to other firms in the industry. Nevertheless, the view left behind is that Ottawa responds best in times of crisis and on matters of regional significance. Well managed firms striving to achieve international competitiveness do not press the sensitive political nerves that galvanize intervention. To get federal largess requires a hand-to-mouth organization adept at crisis management and government relations. Most executives in the industry understand this and resent it.

Blocking the Takeover of Camco by CGE.

Objective   To maintain a measure of Canadian ownership in the industry.

Result   CGE took GSW to court to terminate the Camco partnership. Irreconcilable differences were cited as grounds for termination. Specifically, CGE claimed GSW had blocked approval of investment needed to modernize and restructure Camco. From CGE's perspective, FIRA's rejection placed ownership ahead of investment and productivity.

An out-of-court settlement was agreed to recently in which the shares of Camco were reclassified and sold to the public by both CGE and GSW in such a way as to leave CGE with 51 percent of the voting shares. It is possible that FIRA approval was not required for this move, but certainly Camco has now become a foreign-owned firm subject to FIRA regulation in any future acquisition.

The objective in blocking the CGE takeover of GSW has not been achieved. Ironically, CGE may be pleased. The last two years have been very difficult for most manufacturers in Canada, and CGE has not escaped the recession. Under its original proposal, rejected by FIRA, CGE would have paid GSW $21.6 million and would then have had to find additional funds for modernizing Camco. Under the new, apparently acceptable, format, CGE receives a dividend from Camco of $780,000 plus $7.2 million from the proceeds of sale of 900,000 shares, and acquires majority voting control. In the economic climate of 1983, CGE may well prefer this new arrangement to the costly takeover rejected by FIRA.

One further thing is clarified by the Camco saga. Joint ventures between Canadian and foreign-owned firms do not necessarily act more in the Canadian interest than wholly foreign-owned firms. This is a lesson many other countries have already learned. Furthermore, joint ventures — like marriages — cannot be kept together by compulsion if the partners are not getting along. Joint venture success requires clear and agreed objectives and an allocation of tasks between partners that facilitates managerial decisiveness.

Coping with Conflicting Objectives

It is one thing to discover that intervention sometimes fails to achieve its purpose, or that it does but the purpose turns out to be less beneficial than anticipated. It is quite another to find conflicting objectives behind the intervention — to be more specific, to find that the conditions which galvanize political will are different from the conditions that give rise to the formulation of industry policy. In the major appliance industry, the stated policy was to improve productivity and international competitiveness in light of declining tariffs. Preceding sections have dealt with ways of achieving this. On the other hand, the political will to act was galvanized by other matters, specifically by issues of regional distribution and Canadian ownership. That these issues conflicted directly with established policy did not seem to matter at the time. When in doubt, it seemed political imperatives prevailed. Long-term policies to build and nurture the international competitiveness of the industry lacked any short-term political constituency. They could not be brought to pass as long as the instruments of government assistance and intervention were politically controlled.

Executives in the major appliance industry — and in other industries too — feel very deeply about this issue. When government assistance is administered through specific corporate applications, rather than through adjustments in the tax system, the process becomes politicized in dysfunctional ways. Rigid and unworkable criteria are put forward with an eye to political defensibility. Grants are awarded publicly by ministers with an eye to personal visibility. Regional matters exert more influence because they correspond to political jurisdictions. A case in point was the attempt to persuade Volkswagen to build its parts plant in Winnipeg, Windsor, Montreal or the Maritimes, rather than the economically preferred Barrie, with offers to cover the higher transportation burden through grants, as though government spending had no effect on costs in Canada. But regional priorities are not the only objective of government intervention. Canadian ownership and jobs are two others. They tend to conflict. In general, government handles the conflict by giving primary attention to Canadian ownership in times of affluence and to jobs in times of recession. In the past, it has somehow been assumed that the national interest would be given precedence over specific regional or political interests — not that other interests were unimportant, but that they would be woven into a fabric based on the national interest. Of late, this has not been happening. In fact, the reverse has been happening. Narrower interests have prevailed over national interests. The politicization of government assistance seems to be one of the causes.

Taking the major appliance industry as an example, the national interest might be defined as "improving the industry's productivity and international competitiveness." This is the overriding interest because failure to achieve it in a world of falling tariffs will result in a progressive loss of export opportunities, and indeed a progressive loss of our own market to importers — in other words, a loss of jobs and economic activity to Canada as a whole. Unless this national interest is attended to with fundamental long-term commitment from business and government, other interests cannot in the long term be attended to at all. Trying to maintain Canadian ownership in a decaying Camco or to keep a small Quebec appliance plant open may be important politically but must not take precedence over the national interest. The problem is that pursuit of the national interest has no strong political constituency, whereas the lesser interests have. Therefore, the more government assistance to industry becomes politicized, the more attention and money will be diverted away from the national interest into issues with higher political visibility. This process has been going on for some time in Canada, as though international competitiveness were not really important. It has been an insular, inward-looking process. One would think Canada had never signed the Tokyo Round accords, that tariffs were not dropping, that we could remain protected from outside assault. The time has come for a reappraisal.

For the appliance industry in Canada, the most practical strategy for the medium term is to seize the productivity gains available by rationalizing and modernizing. According to industry sources, costs could be cut by an estimated 15 percent. There should be greater commitment to building in-house competence in process technology so as to arrest the year-to-year erosion of our productivity when compared to the United States. Finally, the industry would be better positioned in terms of efficiency if each major appliance product were manufactured in Canada by only two firms.

Pursuit of this medium-term strategy would benefit from transitional incentives encouraging R&D and capital investment. Tax treatment of R&D and capital investment is relatively generous in Canada, but transition to international competitiveness would be costly. It would also benefit from an international view of competition policy, with less opposition to industry concentration in conditions where international trade provides the necessary market discipline. Furthermore, from the perspective of this study, market discipline through freer trade is more likely to get results in terms of productivity gains than are incentives coupled with continued protection.

What the industry does not need is direct government intervention to divert the industry from the pursuit of productivity to the pursuit of regionalism. This is not to suggest that regional priorities are not important. In Canada they are. But each of the three major competitors has production in both Ontario and Quebec. When they rationalize, there is no reason to suppose that one area must suffer at the expense of others. Camco, for example, has already closed its factory in Weston and may soon close its London facility as well. The production of refrigerators and ranges is to be consolidated in the former Westinghouse plant at Hamilton. At the same time dishwasher production will be consolidated with the production of washers and dryers in the former CGE plant in

Montreal. Firms can give attention to regional employment issues themselves, and have clear political incentive to do so. Furthermore, they can do it with an eye firmly fixed on productivity.

The lessons to be learned from government involvement in the major appliance industry over the past six years are important ones for Canada. The need for creative business-government cooperation in pursuit of national economic interests is increasing because of declining tariffs and tough competition from abroad. However, in the major appliance industry, the needed cooperation has not materialized and the blame has to be placed largely on government, which has intervened in the industry not primarily in pursuit of national economic welfare but with narrower, more parochial interests in view. This intervention has probably set the industry back five years in its pursuit of improved productivity. Needed investment has been stalled and development of in-house skills in technology has been seriously impeded because government has intervened to fulfill political objectives unrelated to economic efficiency and sometimes in conflict with it. The government has taken Industry and Labour Adjustment Program (ILAP) funds designed to provide for industry retraining and has put them to use to keep less efficient small plants in regionally sensitive areas from closing down. Firms have had difficulty reconciling the interventions with stated administrative policy for the industry. Hesitation and uncertainty have resulted. It used to be thought that government could be relied on more than firms to act in the national interest. The experience of the major appliance industry negates this view. Not only does the national interest lack a short-term political constituency, but in general the cost of bad decisions is not borne by government.

Whether these circumstances call for more intelligent intervention or less intervention and a return to market forces to guide the economy we leave to others. The one thing that is clear is that no matter how the economy is to be guided, the process must relate more to international competitive conditions than to internal political preferences. Firms naturally will develop their own opinion of what constitutes the national interest and what constitutes their own. But reduced protection at home and fierce competition for foreign markets should bring about an alignment of those interests on the one hand, and a desire for positive business-government cooperation on the other.

Note

This paper was completed in June 1984.

Bibliography

Bishop, Paul M., and H. Crookell. 1983. "Specialization and Foreign Investment in Canada." Ottawa: Department of Finance.

Canada. Department of Industry, Trade and Commerce. Trade and Structural Analysis Directorate. 1981. "The Impact of the Multilateral Trade Negotiations on Industrial Adjustment." Ottawa: The Department.

Caves, Richard E. 1975. *Diversification, Foreign Investment and Scale in North American Manufacturing Industries*. Ottawa: Economic Council of Canada.

Crookell, H. 1968. "The Marketing Implications of Free Trade Between Canada and the U.S." *Business Quarterly* 33 (Autumn): 22–31.

Daly, D.J. 1979. *Canada's Comparative Advantage*. Ottawa: Economic Council of Canada.

Eastman, H.C., and S. Stykolt. 1967. *The Tariff and Competition in Canada*. Toronto: Macmillan.

English, Edward H. 1964. *Industrial Structure in Canada's International Competitive Position*. Montreal: Private Planning Association of Canada.

Quirin, G.D., T.A. Wilson, and R.M. Sultan. 1970. *The Canadian Appliance Industry*. Vol.1. Study prepared for the Department of Industry, Trade and Commerce. Toronto: University of Toronto.

3

Crown Corporations and Economic Efficiency

SANDFORD F. BORINS
BARRY E.C. BOOTHMAN

The rapid growth of Crown corporations and other government-controlled enterprises in recent years, the magnitude of some of their investments, and in some cases the large losses they have suffered have attracted substantial public attention and led to considerable debate. Much of this debate has been ideological in nature, concerned with the appropriate balance between the public and private sectors in business. This paper is an attempt to clarify that debate by surveying the academic literature, both theoretical and empirical, regarding the economic efficiency of Crown corporations. By economic efficiency, we refer to the traditional criteria by which economists have evaluated the performance of firms in the private sector. Does a given Crown corporation earn a rate of return on capital which is equivalent to the "normal" rate of return in the economy and/or in its own industry? Are the costs of production incurred by the Crown corporation equal to the feasible minimum average costs of production? Is the Crown corporation adopting new technology rapidly enough that its costs will remain at the feasible minimum level over time? If the Crown corporation has "social objectives" or "social responsibilities" in addition to its business objectives, does it carry them out at the feasible minimum cost?

Government-controlled enterprises are those companies over which ultimate formal authority is retained by the state. A government may exercise such authority if it totally owns a firm or has a significant share of its equity. In a strict sense, this should mean an absolute majority, more than 50 percent, but in many cases a de facto ability to control corporate operations can exist with a much smaller ownership share. Government-controlled enterprises often are referred to as "public enterprises," "public corporations," or "public firms," while private firms are private sector companies whose equity is closely held by a few individuals or is traded publicly in markets.

Government-controlled enterprises in Canada have included wholly owned corporations, Crown corporations, enterprises with ownership jointly shared by two or more governments, and enterprises with mixed public and private ownership. This paper is concerned primarily with Crown corporations and not with the other types of public enterprise. By Crown corporations, we mean those firms which clearly meet the characteristics of that organizational genre which has been set out in federal and provincial legislation — wholly owned corporations, either directly or indirectly, which have been *formally designated as agents of the Crown* for the attainment of public policy objectives, and for whose liabilities the state itself is both immediately and directly liable (see Gracey, 1978; Lambert, 1979).

Given our concern with economic efficiency, the attention of this paper is restricted to those Crown corporations which, as a result of either their establishment or their evolution, have as one of their central objectives the pursuit of commercial success or profit. As business enterprises, they produce economic goods or provide services for sale at prices intended to wholly or largely cover costs. However, nearly half of all the Crown corporations which have been created by the federal and provincial governments in Canada cannot be characterized properly as commercially oriented organizations. The corporate form often has been employed to supply numerous public services to governments or to the public at large. These services include: industrial and scientific research facilities, foreign and monetary policy assistance, advisory or academic research activities, municipal and educational finance support, and regulatory or marketing services (see Langford and Huffman, 1983; Vining and Botterell, 1983). Some firms, such as SYSCO and the Cape Breton Development Corporation, have been established primarily to provide economic support and employment for declining industries or regions. Politicians often have been less concerned about the operating losses which may be incurred by those firms than about the social disruption which would result from a termination of their activities.

In order to discuss the economic efficiency of Crown corporations, it is necessary to have some standard of comparison by which efficiency can be defined, such as the relative costs of producing certain outputs. Therefore, public and private firms must be assessed on a like-with-like basis. An appropriate standard would be the comparison of Crown corporations and private firms which produce the same goods or services. In some instances, such as Canadian National and Canadian Pacific, public and private firms may be in competition with one another. In other instances, such as the provincial hydro or telephone utilities, similar input costs and technology permit a comparison of their efficiency at producing similar outputs.

On this topic, as in many areas of applied economics, there has been a serious imbalance in the literature. Hypotheses and theories about public enterprise behaviour and its determinants have proliferated, and they have often been presented in normative or prescriptive terms. Verifications of these propositions through detailed empirical analysis and studies of actual rather than optimal corporate practices represent a much smaller segment of the literature. In many countries with extensive public ownership, particularly in Western Europe and the United Kingdom, government-controlled enterprises often have taken the form of national monopolies and have not had to compete directly against domestic private firms (see Monsen and Walters, 1984). Researchers seeking to develop meaningful comparisons have been compelled to focus upon a smaller number of countries where public and private firms coexist in several sectors. Most of this empirical work relates to North America, Australia and Switzerland. Moreover, although historians and political scientists have long considered extensive use of public enterprise to be a fundamental element of the development of Canada, until the mid-1970s there was little systematic study of Canadian public corporations either in terms of their effectiveness in achieving public policy objectives or in terms of the economic efficiency of their operations.

Most of the research on public firms carried out in Canada and abroad has dealt with relatively mature and capital-intensive industries such as airlines, railroads, and electrical or telephone utilities. Among the industrialized nations, government-controlled enterprises have traditionally played a significant or dominant role in those sectors. During the last two decades, however, these enterprises have also become very important in other areas such as resource exploration and development, manufacturing, technological research and innovation, and financial services (see Langford and Huffman, 1983; Vining and Botterell, 1983). The literature is particularly weak with respect to government firms which have been involved with venture capitalism, with businesses in the early stages of the product life cycle, or with other commercial activities carried out within turbulent and uncertain environments.

These methodological constraints and deficiencies in the literature limit the sample of firms which can be surveyed in this paper. The available research indicates whether Crown corporations have been inherently more inefficient than private firms within several industries, but the narrowness of our sample generally restricts us to those contexts where Crown corporations could be expected to perform well relative to their private sector counterparts. The 1983 sales, assets and employment of most of the corporations discussed in this paper are shown in Table 3-1. These corporations account for more than half of the revenues and nearly two-thirds of the assets of all federal and provincial Crown corporations (Statistics Canada, 1982, 1983, 1984). This sample, nonetheless, should be contrasted against the broader "universe" of Canadian public corporations.

Langford and Huffman (1983) identified 119 corporations in which the federal government had a direct interest as of 1981. There were 81 corporations wholly owned by the government, 20 with joint or mixed ownership, and 18 in which the government had a sponsorship or continuing membership role. These enterprises in turn had an interest in 210 subsidiaries (more than 50 percent ownership) and 124 associated companies (less than 50 percent ownership). Only 56 of the 81 wholly owned corporations had been formally designated as Crown corporations under federal legislation. Vining and Botterell (1983) identified 233 provincial Crown corporations existing as of 1982. There are no publicly available estimates of the number of mixed or joint enterprises, subsidiaries, and associated companies in which provincial governments may have an interest. In 1983, the *Financial Post* listing of the 500 largest non-financial corporations in Canada included 31 Crown corporations, 5 mixed or joint enterprises, and 9 other firms in which significant minority positions were owned by Canadian governments or their agents.

Although a large number of public firms have been created, a relatively small group of enterprises account for most of the earnings and investments. The ten largest non-financial corporations account for about one-third of the assets and sightly more than half of the revenues of all corporations controlled by the government of Canada. Thirteen electrical utilities account for nearly two-thirds of the assets and about 40 percent of the revenues of all provincial Crown corporations (Statistics Canada, 1983, 1984).

In the case of federal Crown corporations, approximately 20 percent of total assets and 30 percent of revenues are associated with transport firms. Another 34 percent of the assets and over 50 percent of aggregate revenues involve federal Crown corporations engaged in trade, mining and manufacturing (Statistics Canada, 1983, pp. 14–17). Electricity has accounted for the largest share of the investments and earnings of provincial Crown corporations. Another 34 percent of the revenues and a mere 6 percent of the assets of provincial Crown corporations are accounted for by firms in the trade, mining and manufacturing sectors (Statistics Canada, 1984, pp. 30–31, 34–37). At both levels of government, most of the balance is accounted for by firms in real estate, insurance or financial services.

Almost all of the literature relevant to a discussion of the behaviour and efficiency of Canadian Crown corporations has been written in the last fifteen years. The earlier literature simply did not address these issues in any depth. A basic overview of the literature on Canadian Crown corporations reveals several fundamental themes.

TABLE 3-1 Sales, Assets, Employment of Major Public Corporations Discussed in this Paper, 1983

Financial Post Rank	Corporation	Sales	Assets	Employment
Transportation				
12	Canadian National Railways	$ 4,625.1	$ 6,789.8	63,496
35	Air Canada	2,298.5	2,190.6	21,584
124	VIA Rail	624.5	652.4	3,474
Electric Utilities				
19	Ontario Hydro	3,805.1	12,193.9	31,233
20	Hydro Quebec	3,656.0	23,199.0	18,975
54	B.C. Hydro	1,528.4	8,910.0	8,667
107	Saskatchewan Power	704.9	2,356.0	3,105
134	New Brunswick Power	545.6	2,743.5	2,600
168	Manitoba Hydro-Electric	414.7	2,884.5	3,680
181	Nova Scotia Power	373.3	1,241.7	2,521
264	Newfoundland and Labrador Hydro-Electric	242.8	1,962.5	1,306
Steel				
151	Sidbec	475.3	824.8	3,693
309	Ipsco	192.8	330.9	1,730
Oil				
15	Petro-Canada	4,123.8	8,239.0	6,601
Telecommunications				
90	Alberta Government Telephone	892.8	2,311.0	11,924
199	Saskatchewan Telecommunications	326.1	873.5	4,440
227	Manitoba Telephone	284.4	763.7	4,547
Total		$25,114.1	$88,955.2	193,536

Source: Maclean-Hunter Ltd. *The Financial Post 500*, May 26, 1984, pp. 70–109.

From the early writings of Innis (1930) and Creighton (1936) to the more recent reinterpretations of Aitken (1959, 1964) and Naylor (1972, 1973), Canadian economic historians have attempted to provide an overview of how the Canadian state, through numerous policy instruments including Crown corporations, has sought to overcome the physical obstacles imposed by geography and create an integrated transportation network for a staple-oriented economy. Intellectual historians (Lower, 1958; Morton, 1963, 1972; Horowitz, 1967; Bliss, 1971, 1973; Hardin, 1974) have attempted to show how the ideologies and value systems of Canadian society, at either the elite or mass level, have been supportive of this public intervention. There have been a number of descriptive and "official" histories of Crown corporations such as Canadian National (Fournier, 1935; Stevens, 1966), Ontario Hydro (Dennison, 1960), Air Canada (Ashley, 1963), and Eldorado Nuclear (Bothwell, 1984). Insights into the problems encountered by the executives of Crown corporations also can be garnered from the memoirs of Gordon McGregor (1980) and the biographies of Donald Gordon (Schull, 1979) and John Grierson (Evans, 1984).

Political scientists have traditionally concerned themselves with the relationship of public enterprises to the formal structure of government. Thus, they have tended to outline the key aspects of control and accountability legislation and some of the legal characteristics of Crown corporations as instruments of public policy. Examples of books or articles along these lines include Balls (1953), Hodgetts (1953, 1970), Blakeney (1954), Musolf (1959), Ashley and Smails (1965), Gracey (1978), and Langford (1979).

Interests in Crown corporations on the part of Canadian political scientists mushroomed in the wake of several well-publicized and embarrassing scandals during the mid-1970s involving several federal corporations (Air Canada, Atomic Energy of Canada Limited, and Polysar) and after deficiencies in federal legislation for the control and accountability of Crown corporations were outlined by the Public Accounts Committee of the House of Commons, the Privy Council Office (1977), and two royal commissions (Estey, 1975; Lambert, 1979). This research has taken three lines: (a) attempts to document and map the actual size, growth, sectoral composition and functions of public enterprise in Canada (Tupper and Doern, 1981; Langford and Huffman, 1983; Vining and Botterell, 1983); (b) attempts to outline alternative regimes for increasing the accountability of Crown corporations (Langford, 1980, 1982; MacLean, 1981); and (c) case studies of individual Crown corporations (Gordon, 1981; Tupper and Doern, 1981; Prichard, 1983). In terms of the objectives of this paper, the case studies are particularly interesting since some of them examine efficiency issues. These will be discussed in some detail below.

The outline of the paper will therefore be as follows. The next section surveys the theoretical literature that reflects upon the economic efficiency of public corporations, particularly as compared with the alternative of private ownership. This review discusses the initial orientation of researchers toward explanations of how public enterprise could be used to enhance allocative efficiency within society, and then concentrates on three major streams of thought in the contemporary literature about the determinants of performance of public firms. The following section examines the empirical studies of Crown corporations and private enterprise. The final section attempts to draw conclusions from the review of the literature, in terms of both the agenda for future research and recommendations for government policy makers designing accountability and control mechanisms.

Theoretical Interpretations of the Economic Efficiency of Crown Corporations

Until the 1960s, economic research on government enterprise centred primarily on how the provision of various public services by the state could be financed with minimal distortion of the allocation of national resources. Little attention was given to the study of the public services themselves, the methods by which they were to be supplied, or the behaviour of the relevant public agencies. These issues tended to be addressed indirectly, as part of broader explanations of why some goods should be provided by the public sector.

Economists traditionally have acknowledged that public enterprise may be employed in three types of circumstances:

• The state should be responsible for the supply of certain "public goods" (e.g. defence, education, public order) which are necessarily supplied simultaneously to very large groups of consumers. The very nature of a public good is such that if one individual in a defined group is supplied with a service, all others in the group will also be supplied with it. Since the provision of a public good will not be contingent upon the amount an individual is willing to pay for it and no individual can be excluded from enjoying its benefits, the rational user will conceal and systematically undervalue his preferences for such goods. The cumulative distortion caused by these actions will result in market mechanisms incorrectly gauging the prices which should be paid, and the shortfall in revenue must be made up by taxation and subsidization.

- Some industries (hydroelectric power, water supply, urban transport) are characterized by tendencies toward natural monopoly. If unconstrained by direct regulation, a private producer could maximize profits and distort income distribution significantly by reducing output and raising prices.
- Private firms based in declining industries may cut output and employment despite the disruptions which those decisions could impose upon local economies. Extensive subsidization and controls on production, at the very least, may be required to allow a gradual reduction of those activities.

A massive literature has developed around the theme of how these problems could be avoided by having these activities supplied by the public sector. Studies on this theme include Shepherd (1965), Turvey (1968, 1971), Reed (1973), and Rees (1976). These writers have drawn heavily upon public finance and taxation theory, and have been similarly concerned with the development of optimal solutions and appropriate prescriptions for public policy. They have argued that public corporations will build more capacity, employ more labour, and sell more output at lower prices than comparable private firms in the three situations above, provided that decision-making is guided solely by the criterion of economic efficiency. Public enterprise investments and pricing policies should be guided by the analysis of marginal costs and outputs, social cost-benefit studies where spillover effects may occur, and the use of optimal modes of cash flow discounting.

Several problems with this approach emerged by the early 1970s. First, the overwhelming thrust of the literature took the form of highly objective constructs for the maximization of allocative efficiency. While the arguments retained an intellectual and theoretical elegance, they often left unclear how the principles were to be implemented in day-to-day corporate operations. The development of optimal investment and pricing policies requires a thorough understanding of all relevant transactions in an economy, and accordingly there have been major difficulties in achieving reliable cost and benefit projections. In mixed economies some key industries will remain privately owned, and researchers increasingly had to develop "second-best" solutions which would compensate for the impact of these "uncontrolled" sectors (see Rees, 1976; Lintner, 1981).

Moreover, virtually all of this analysis focussed upon public firms that were monopolies or were based in totally nationalized industries. Largely overlooked were those corporations that competed against private firms. Finally, while the approach indicated some of the logic underlying collective intervention in the economy, the mode of that intervention was rarely discussed in any detail. Why, after all, should a state choose a public corporation as a policy instrument instead of subsidizing or directly regulating private enterprise or using departments and other types of public agencies?

The concern with allocative efficiency has not subsided among contemporary researchers. Rather, it has been complemented and partially subsumed by a growing interest in the actual behaviour and economic performance of public enterprise. Three streams of thought have emerged in the recent literature. These streams are interrelated and not mutually exclusive, but the proponents of each differ significantly with respect to the determinants and aspects of organizational behaviour which are emphasized.

- Property rights theory stresses the importance of ownership characteristics and relationships to factor markets, and argues accordingly that private enterprise must be inherently more efficient than government enterprise.
- Political market theory looks at public corporations as government entities whose decisions and policies are externally controlled by coalitions of voters who use political power to achieve their own objectives.
- Managerial research incorporates some of the insights provided by the other two streams but stresses that the formation of corporate strategies and policies is the responsibility of the managers of public firms, who must respond to the pressures emanating from both the economic and political environments of their firms while attempting to achieve their own goals for enterprise survival and autonomy.

Property Rights Theory

The property rights approach was initially formulated by A.A. Alchian, an economist of the "Chicago" tradition in the 1960s, and has been extensively elaborated by numerous authors (see De Alessi, 1980; Borcherding, 1983). The focus of their attention has been the implications of different attributes of ownership and of the influence of the capital market, or absence thereof, for managerial behaviour. Different property rights structures present decision makers with different cost/ reward or incentive structures and will affect the choices of managers and the output of firms in systematic ways.

Individual managers, whether employed in public or private firms, are assumed to seek the maximization of their own utility rather than that of the organization or its owners. Their utility will consist of both pecuniary benefits (salaries, bonuses) and non-pecuniary income (security of tenure, managerial perquisites, shirking of work, empire-building). Where they are unable to alter their pecuniary income, rational managers will seek to maximize their utility by increasing non-pecuniary income, even though this will raise the costs of production and reduce the residual income which would ultimately accrue to the owners. Moreover, monitoring company performance and preventing inefficiencies will take considerable time and effort, and impose significant costs upon owners and managers.

In small firms, where owners often are managers, the owners/managers will have strong incentives to carry out these activities, since any inefficiencies will immediately reduce their pecuniary income. Where control of private firms is concentrated among a few investors, monitoring costs will be small in comparison to the size of the benefits which the owners could receive by preventing "unreasonable" declines in productivity. Among large private firms with widely dispersed ownership, however, the connection between owners and managers is generally weaker and the incentives and the ability to monitor performance are therefore reduced. As the number of investors increases, the benefits of ownership begin to assume the characteristics of a public good, and each individual owner has a smaller incentive to assume the costs of policing managerial behaviour. The dispersal of ownership also makes it more difficult to mobilize a coalition of investors capable of directly intervening and changing managerial behaviour.

Proponents of property rights theory argue that several institutional factors enable joint stock companies to avoid these tendencies. First, capital markets serve as formal mechanisms through which individual investors can signal the level of their confidence in management policies. Sales of shares represent indications of dissatisfaction with a firm's performance. Lower share prices thus provide indirect pressure for managers to make appropriate changes and, in extreme cases, can encourage a takeover and the introduction of a new and more effective management team. Investors will have to incur transaction fees and share premiums, but these costs would be low relative to the costs associated with attempting direct intervention through annual meetings.

Second, the existence of a market for ownership rights reduces the monitoring and policing costs which would have to be borne by individual investors. The capital market, by evaluating the price of a firm's shares, provides an objective standard for comparing the managerial performance of different firms. The market capitalizes expectations about the future performance of a company, which provides the owners with an indication of how outsiders with an incentive to be informed evaluate the firm's management. This tendency is reinforced by legislative requirements for standard reporting and independent audits of financial statements. The capital market permits the possibility of realizing comparative advantages through the specialization of shareholding. Individuals with a special interest or expertise in certain types of companies are likely to identify poor performers or decisions quickly. The capital market may also be used to give managers a direct financial interest in the efficient management of a company by means of stock options or other profit-sharing devices as part of a compensation package. This tends to encourage a coincidence of interests between owners and managers.

Third, intensive competition for executive positions, both from the lower managerial ranks of a firm and from potential managers in the labour market, may serve as an additional constraint. The confidence of owners in managers also will be reflected in the quality of executives hired and the level of compensation which they receive. Owners thus may be able to transfer to managers some of the higher costs of production which are associated with anticipated inefficient administration.

This incentive structure can be contrasted with the incentive structure facing the managers of a public enterprise. Ownership of a public corporation is axiomatically broader than for private firms, and all citizens who pay taxes can be considered shareholders. Like private sector investors, they should have an interest in maximizing the profits of the public firm, but the pecuniary share for each citizen is quite small. There is no organized capital market through which equity in a government enterprise can be traded or information about inefficiency can be easily disseminated. In real terms, citizens can terminate their ownership rights only through two high-cost strategies: either by leaving the country, since ownership is based upon residency, or by attempting to have the public firm abolished.

The taxpayer-owners of a public firm possess no direct supervisory power over its managers. Any influence they exert must come through the intermediation of politicians, who may have their own interests in the public enterprise's performance and policies, as will be discussed later in this paper. The costs of intervening via the political market by influencing politicians are likely to be higher than the costs of operating through the capital market. Given higher monitoring and policing costs and the smaller benefits accruing from ownership, individual citizens would be likely to assume a passive role with respect to government enterprise practices.

This attenuation of property rights has several consequences. The supply of goods and services by public firms would be characterized by poorer efficiency and lower profits than for private firms. The managers of public firms will have more scope for enhancing non-pecuniary income and for pursuing policies in accord with their own objectives and welfare, not necessarily with those of taxpayers. They will be inclined to use investment and financing techniques that enable them to divert a disproportionate share of collective resources to those ends.

Property rights theory can be seen as a response to the position presented by Berle and Means (1932) and their intellectual descendants, notably J.K. Galbraith (1973). The modern corporation, they have contended, is characterized by a wide dispersal of ownership and market power as the basis of competitive advantages. Real control of large private firms will therefore be exercised by their managers, who will be just as likely as public sector managers to reduce the efficiency of their corporations in the search for non-monetary rewards.

Proponents of the property rights approach make several responses to this perspective. They assert that while the private capital market is not perfect, it at least ensures a higher degree of efficiency than the political market will provide for public enterprise. Ultimately there is the possibility of a takeover bid, which might not be too difficult in a company with widely diffused ownership. They have claimed that the existing empirical data do not support the arguments raised by writers like Berle and Means or Galbraith.

The logic of property rights theory has been extended by drawing upon the transactions cost approach to economic organization. Coase (1937) and Williamson (1975) note that production and exchanges of goods and services involve formal and informal contractual arrangements that may be carried out within firms rather than through markets. Significant costs may be incurred in establishing and maintaining those arrangements due to: bounded rationality (the inability of individuals to absorb and comprehend all of the issues relevant to ensuring stable economic behaviour); opportunism (the manipulation of information or power by one party to the detriment of others); and information asymmetries (variations in the data about current and future events which are available to different parties). Large private corporations emerge as firms internalize within their boundaries the transactions and activities which will be affected by these problems. By substituting internal authoritative commands for the use of the price mechanism or complex negotiations in markets, they are able to achieve a superior and less costly mode of organizing production and transmitting information.

Property rights theorists contend that these types of problems often are not as critical for many of the goods or services supplied by the public sector as they can be for private firms. In addition, governments may arbitrarily select cumbersome policy instruments, such as public corporations or regulatory agencies, with little regard to options which would fulfill collective goals at lower costs. At the heart of the analyses made by the theory's proponents, therefore, is the idea that many of the goods and services provided by government agencies could be supplied less expensively by contracting them out to private sector firms (Borcherding, 1983, pp. 152–163).

The discussion of public enterprise by the advocates of property rights theory is unfortunately imprecise in its definition of public enterprise. The theory has as its definition of government enterprise any activity undertaken by the government which is not financed by the trading of equity on capital markets. However, there are many varieties of public or quasi-public ownership which could involve various monitoring regimes within the public sector, various ways of issuing debt or equity to the private sector on the capital market, various incentive systems for public sector managers, and various degrees of competition with private sector firms. The use of the capital market for either equity or debt exposes government enterprise to the very monitoring that property rights theorists think is so important. A government may be able to give orders unilaterally to a wholly owned corporation, but the diffusion of ownership in joint and mixed enterprises changes the rules of the game. Consultations among shareholders must take place before management policies can be changed. Managers also may be able to employ alternative financing techniques and patterns of investment which will enhance their autonomy from shareholder control (see Eckel and Vining, 1982). It is interesting to note that Borcherding (1983, p. 169), near the end of his admirably thorough survey of the property rights literature and the empirical research, states: "Until now I have not attempted to draw distinctions between bureaus, Crown corporations (or independent agencies), and mixed enterprises, though the descriptive literature's comparisons are extensive."

In their reviews of the literature, De Alessi (1980) and Borcherding (1983) have adduced support for the theory from the available empirical evidence. However, from a methodological perspective, many of their illustrations do not provide clear tests of its central hypotheses. Much of the research cited consists of comparisons of private sector firms that are subject to the pressures of market competition (such as competition for government contracts) with government departments which have legally sanctioned monopolies. Most of these studies deal with public services, such as firefighting (Ahlbrandt, 1973), garbage collection (Savas, 1977a, 1977b, 1980; Pomerehne and Frey, 1977; Kitchen, 1976; Kemper and Quigley, 1976), and processing of medical insurance data (Frech, 1976, 1980). Most but not all of these studies find that the private sector does these jobs with substantially lower costs than government bureaus. Unfortunately, except for Kitchen, who found comparable cost levels, none of these studies use Canadian data, nor do they involve comparisons between private sector firms and Crown corporations, which have a greater degree of independence and a stronger commercial orientation than the traditional government departments. These studies also do not differentiate the effects of market structure from the effects of ownership. As observed earlier, good empirical work should compare public corporations with private sector firms which operate in similar market conditions.

Whether capital markets constitute an effective constraint upon managerial behaviour is an empirical issue, and the available research has produced very mixed results, at best. Several studies undertaken in the United States and Great Britain have reported statistically significant but quite modest results indicating that management-controlled firms earn lower profits than firms in which there is not a clear separation of ownership from management (Monsen, Chiu and Cooley, 1968;

Boudreaux, 1973; Stano, 1976; McEachern, 1978). No significant differences, however, have been found by numerous other authors including Elliott (1972), Sorenson (1974), Ware (1975), and Herman (1981). In examining the relationship between corporate objectives and the nature of the compensation paid to managers, researchers have found that profit maximization is not as important as overall growth or sales maximization (see Marris, 1964; Ciscel, 1974; Meeks and Whittington, 1975; Boyes and Schlagenhauf, 1979). These studies, however, use pre-tax income as a measure and ignore stock options, dividends and capital gains — factors that may amount to more than half of the compensation received by senior executives. Studies which use more precise definitions of true income have tended to reach the contrary conclusion (see Larner, 1970; Masson, 1971; Smyth, Boyes and Peseau, 1975). Thus, financial compensation may encourage a coincidence between owner interests and managerial actions, but the available evidence does not permit firm conclusions to be drawn.

Political Market Theory

A second stream in the contemporary literature may be characterized as political market theory. It incorporates insights which have been generated in two areas of economic research: (a) the nature of collective choice in democracies, classic statements of which include Downs (1957), Buchanan and Tullock (1962), and Olson (1965); and (b) the theory of economic regulation, particularly as presented by Posner (1971) and Stigler (1971). This work is distinguished by an emphasis upon the dynamics of political systems and upon external control as key determinants of the behaviour of public corporations and other government agencies. Since Crown corporations are established and owned by the state, citizens and politicians will attempt to influence their policies via the political process. This may be contrasted with private sector firms which, by virtue of their ownership, are somewhat less vulnerable to political input into management decisions. For example, Crown corporations may be influenced by numerous devices including Orders-in-Council, ministerial directives or simply ministerial "suasion" or pressure. On the other hand, changing the behaviour of a privately owned firm may require the formal enactment of legislation, a much more complex, time-consuming and public process. Furthermore, the enactment of legislation can create particular difficulties for policy makers, since corporations other than the original target almost undoubtedly will be affected.

Governments are conceived of as forms of markets which make and impose rules (especially with respect to the creation or alteration of property rights), and which can provide services to client groups. Most government policies will have effects upon the distribution of income and wealth;

and the costs and benefits of public policies will be distributed unequally across the elements of a society. Collective decision-making also is assumed to be characterized not by an altruistic pursuit of the "public interest" and the maximization of social welfare, but by the adversarial efforts of groups and individuals seeking to maximize their own welfare, and by the constant resolution of these conflicting interests.

Through a barter process, citizens bid with votes, or with resources which can be utilized to influence votes (such as campaign contributions), to receive policies which will benefit them. Individual politicians or groups of politicians organized into parties attempt to maximize their political support through promises to supply certain policies. Clearly, the political market will distribute more benefits to those citizens whose demands are highest and who are swing voters — that is, to voters who can bid the most in terms of political support for the policies they favour or whose support is essential for election.

Political markets are characterized by high information and monitoring costs. In many instances, voters have small per capita stakes in various issues, and accordingly have little incentive to gather additional information. The process is characterized by free-rider problems. The benefits of government activities will be received by numerous individuals who do not contribute to the coalitions designed to bring about the benefits, thus reinforcing the difficulties of forming coalitions. Voting occurs infrequently and is complicated by the problem of "full-line forcing." When a voter attempts to decide which politician or party to support, the choice must be made between packages of actual and promised policies (platforms). In order to secure a given policy, a voter must be prepared to support a party that is likely to implement or retain many other policies, some of which may be quite unattractive to the voter. These policies may not be important to most citizens, but they will be to the affected interest groups.

It also will be costly for a party to construct a coalition of support. Not only must potential supporters secure the information that will enable them to perceive their own interests, but the party must then mobilize its members to contribute appropriate resources for its candidates, while encouraging other voters to support — or at least not actively oppose — them. The strength of the incentives to back a political party will be a function of the per capita interests of citizens in its policies, and the central concern of the party will be to construct a package of policies which, relative to those of its opponents, will appeal to influential or swing voters. However, for several reasons the costs of organizing and retaining support tend to grow faster than a coalition's numerical size. As the size of the opposition parties decreases, the per capita stakes of their supporters increase, compelling them to fight more energetically. The problems of preventing free-riders from benefitting from the party's policies become more difficult to police as party support grows. In order to avoid offending the disparate elements of a large coalition, a party will find it necessary to maintain an ambiguous stance about some issues. Individual voters may therefore become uncertain about the party's actual support for particular policies or the costs of some promises.

Given these general characteristics, the coalitions of interests which use the political market effectively will be those that can mobilize effectively. This could happen because: the number of beneficiaries is small but the benefits to each are large; a coalition of interests can invent ways of excluding non-members from receiving benefits; or a coalition is able to affect political outcomes, either through contributions of resources or because its members are willing to behave as one-issue voters. One of the key postulates of political market theory, therefore, is that special interests will often triumph over the broad mass of voters. Well organized, narrowly defined interest groups will be able to influence politicians to produce outcomes which serve their interests, while the costs are imposed upon large, ill defined and poorly organized groups for whose members the per capita losses are very small.

Trebilcock, Prichard, Hartle and Dewees (1982) have noted that the legal or institutional characteristics of the various types of governing instruments (regulatory agencies, Crown corporations, departmental bureaucracies) create different kinds of technical and political costs for policy makers. A political party may not select the most technically efficient instrument, or the least coercive, but will choose the one which can best enhance its coalition of support. A Crown corporation can be more flexible than most instruments and requires less formal modes of monitoring and control, because it operates outside of the hierarchies and regulations of government departments. Politicians will perceive the public enterprise as an attractive instrument where policy formation entails considerable novelty or uncertainty (due to changes in environmental conditions or technology), and where government policies must be marginally adjusted on a continuing basis. By establishing a Crown corporation, a political party is able to give supporters a tangible and dramatic symbol of its commitment to a particular cause or set of values.

At the same time, responsibility for much of the development of detailed policy positions is delegated to corporate executives and thereby effectively excluded from direct public scrutiny and debate. A Crown corporation can provide a government with a low-visibility, selective and incremental means of modifying or reversing policy decisions, minimizing the costs associated with more public or formal methods of announcing policies and errors of judgment. By combining in the mandate of a Crown corporation a set of objectives and activities, some of which may not be financially self-sustaining, politicians can achieve political gains from cross-subsidization or indirect taxation. The costs of such practices will have low visibility to the bearers since they will not appear in the public accounts. When the state provides financial support to a public corporation, the assistance often can be rationalized to potential critics as essential for the genuine business purposes of the firm, or as a means of ensuring the enterprise's long-term profitability and survival.

Models of the influence of the political market upon the policies of public enterprises are few in number but have been presented in studies of the supply of electricity (Peltzman, 1971) and urban transportation (Pashigian, 1976; Cooter and Topakian, 1980). These have been based upon U.S. municipal administration, where there are close links between public managers and politicians, and have been concerned with the use of government enterprise to enhance re-election prospects. These writers have noted that any departure from a profit-maximizing price structure by a public firm will present an individual with a net gain if the rise in the tax bill as a citizen-owner is less than the savings made as a consumer. The sum total of all such net gains over the population of taxpayers cannot be positive, but there may be a larger group of gainers than losers. When the demand for a product or service varies significantly among the population, a price reduction will present heavy users with major economic gains. If this group is numerous, then the increase in voter support resulting from these benefits will be greater than any losses among those who must pay taxes but only consume small amounts.

Proponents of this approach suggest that the costs of supplying different consumers will not be reflected in the price structure of a public enterprise to the same degree as in that of a private sector firm. Two consumers may have similar demand characteristics for a product or service, but may present different costs to a supplier because of location. A public firm may choose to treat them alike and charge similar prices since each has equal voting power. For example, a uniform tariff rate may be adopted, rather than one which is based upon length of trip. Prices may be structured to cross-subsidize use by certain politically influential interests at the expense of other less well-organized, less influential consumer groups. There may be a downward price bias from profit-maximizing levels in order to enhance the overall benefits accruing to users, but non-voting users who live outside the jurisdiction could be expected to pay higher prices than the taxpayer-owners.

Several other implications may be observed. Workers for public firms probably will be organized, either through their own unions or through broader organizations, and will attempt to exert pressure upon politicians for higher wages and greater job security than would be the case for comparable private firms. Politicians will want to use public corporations to support — or at least attempt to prevent them from undercutting — various government priorities. For example, ministers of the environment will want public firms to behave in environmentally sound ways; ministers of Indian affairs and northern development will want them to create employment opportunities for Native people; ministers responsible for the status of women will want them to promote women to senior positions; and so forth. As well as being expected to adhere to the objectives of entrenched programs, politicians will subject government firms to a constant stream of new goals and concerns. For instance, the "six and five" program was implemented by requiring not only government departments, but also Crown corporations and regulated firms, to follow its guidelines. In all cases, the frequency and degree of external intervention in the activities of government corporations will be greater than that experienced by private firms, and their economic performance may consequently suffer. Indeed, the very existence of a public corporation and its accessibility to external control may serve to diminish social pressure on private sector firms.

Most of the empirical work developed by proponents of political market theory relates to direct regulation, and many of the hypotheses about public enterprise behaviour are based upon casual empiricism. Peltzman (1971), Pashigian (1976), and Cooter and Topakian (1980) have inferred directional support for the theory's propositions from their examinations of public enterprise in the United States, but they have not demonstrated a *direct* relationship between patterns of electoral activity and the distribution of costs and benefits among consumer groups. Most of the results generated by these studies have not been statistically significant and the sensitivity of the cost and price data often leaves the outcomes open to alternate explanations.

Managerial Research

The locus of attention in managerial research, in contrast to research on property rights and political market theory, is on the process of public enterprise management itself and the pivotal role played by executives in the formation of the strategies and policies of their corporations. The most recent of the three streams of research, it has drawn upon elements of a broad research tradition in organizational sociology and political science. This work has been based upon many of the insights which were originally presented in the behavioural theory of the firm by the "Carnegie" school (March and Simon, 1958; Cyert and March, 1963), and which have been elaborated in studies of decision-making in public and private enterprise by Braybrooke and Lindblom (1963), Allison (1971), and Quinn (1980).

From the perspective of organizational theory, an organization is not so much a concrete entity as a process of mobilizing support around certain types of activities. Any organization is buffeted by a disparate array of stakeholders who affect or are affected by its actions, behaviour and policies. These stakeholders include all of the internal and external interest groups, actors, claimants, and institutions which can exert a portation, and venture capital. While the sectoral composition of CDC's investments has evolved over time to include investments in the life sciences and office information sectors, there is at least some evidence that investments in some of these sectors might have been in pursuit of public policy rather than profitability goals.

Even allowing for the sectoral composition of CDC's investments, however, the company has done poorly. Boardman and Vining calculate the average rate of return on equity in the sectors in which the CDC has investment and weight these sectoral rates of return by their respective shares in the CDC's portfolio. As Table 6-1 indicates, the CDC's average rate of return was less than half the return on this shadow portfolio over the 1977–82 period. Thus, the CDC's poor financial performance is due more to a poor choice of investments within sectors than to a poor or perhaps politically constrained choice of sectors.

TABLE 6-1 **Average Return on Shareholders' Equity, 1977–82**

Company	Rate of Return
	(percent)
CDC	5.1
Brascan	8.4
Power Corporation	14.8
CP Enterprises	18.0
TSE 300 Management Companies	10.5
CDC Mirror Portfolio	10.5

Source: A. Boardman and A. Vining, "An Evaluation of Canada Development Corporation," mimeographed (Vancouver: University of British Columbia, Faculty of Commerce and Administration, 1984).

Boardman (1984, p. 10) and Boardman and Vining (1984, Table 6) note that the price-earnings ratio of CDC was 3:1 in 1980 and 2:1 in 1981, compared with 7.6:1 and 6.0:1, respectively, for the TSE 300 management companies' composite. This difference may reflect one or all of the following:

- lack of confidence on the part of the market regarding the CDC's future acquisition strategy and the skill with which it will be pursued;
- lack of confidence in the future income potential of current CDC investments; and
- the expectation that the government will extract more political services (perhaps in the form of bailouts) from the CDC, for which the latter will not be compensated.

Two conclusions follow from these price-earnings data. First, an argument made for a government equity presence is that it somehow reassures investors and reduces the market supply price of capital. Obviously, the opposite has been true of CDC. Second, the CDC may provide an illustration (admittedly only one illustration) of why the capital market cannot discipline the management of a mixed enterprise. A corporation with a price-earnings ratio as low as the CDC's might normally be subject to a takeover bid. A takeover bid cannot be mounted, however, as long as the government maintains its effective (49 percent) control of the company. As long as CDC remains a mixed enterprise as defined here, the market for corporate control will impose no discipline on its management.

The CDC is alleged to have served, or have been intended to serve, a number of public policy functions. Boardman (1984, pp. 3–4) notes that much of the discussion leading up to the formation of the CDC focussed on gaps either in the supply side of the equity market (no large Canadian pools of equity capital) or on the demand side of the market (because of foreign ownership, there were no Canadian corporations to invest in). If either of these arguments were correct, however, the CDC should have earned at least average rates of return, which it has not.

In his comments at the Royal Commission's symposium on Crown corporations, Stephen Brooks of Carleton University argued that to the extent that its goals can be inferred, Canadianization was among the more important ones. Boardman and Vining (1984) agree and conclude that CDC has achieved this goal (p. 19). They also conclude, however, that the CDC has been a costly Canadianization instrument in absolute if not in relative terms.[8]

Tarasofsky (1984) concludes that the strategy of CDC management was to invest in high-growth, export-oriented and technology-oriented industries also characterized by high rates of foreign ownership (pp. 8–9). It may be inferred that this strategy was adopted less because it would result in Canadianization than because it was thought to be profitable.[9] By this standard, both the strategy and the CDC have failed.

Conclusion: Privatization or Nationalization?

One conclusion reached in the course of writing and rewriting this paper is that despite its desirability, it is difficult to analyze government or mixed enterprises within the context of a few dominant themes. The issues are many and varied and it is often a matter of contrivance to generalize beyond individual cases. Decisions regarding increases or decreases in the government interest in an enterprise will or should turn largely on the specific circumstances of the enterprise and the purposes for which the government wishes to use it.

While broad generalizations are not defensible, some more limited generalizations are. The first would be that what may be regarded as a desirable public policy depends very much on where the examination starts. To illustrate, there is some consensus that government and private enterprises in mature industries do not differ appreciably with hold on the organization. Stakeholders normally comprise a much larger group than the more limited class of claimants known as stockholders. Stockholders are only one of many competing groups which influence an organization and whose concerns must be considered if it is to survive and grow (March and Simon, 1958).

To a considerable extent, an organization is a form of market in which influence and control are negotiated and allocated according to which participants are key to its present and future development. The stakeholders participating in an organization at any time define its activities. When key groups and individuals change the nature of their interests and goals or cease to be involved with the organization, then its strategies are modified to conform to the new concerns or to reflect those of the remaining interests. Because organizations are coalitions of interests, a central aspect of management involves handling ongoing, dynamic relationships, coping with competing and conflicting demands, and giving priority to those which are integral to the organization's survival (Cyert and March, 1963; Pfeffer and Salancik, 1978).

Proponents of the property rights and political market theories assume a deterministic view of organizational behaviour. Either there is considerable consensus among key actors about corporate goals and policies, or environmental conditions and ownership characteristics define the choices of managers and force them to behave in reactive, constrained and predictable ways. Managerial researchers assume a more pluralistic and voluntaristic perspective. Not only will stakeholders constantly disagree and redefine organizational activities, but managers often will be able to take a proactive role and autonomously choose their courses of action. Proponents of this approach acknowledge that the two other streams of research do provide insights into the conduct and performance of public corporations, but argue that each severely over-simplifies the social realities facing organizational participants by concentrating upon a small set of contingencies (see Mazzolini, 1979; Langford, 1980, 1982). Numerous organizational characteristics and external factors will interact or be exploited by managers, thereby permitting a variety of possible outcomes.

In essence, the managers of public corporations must accommodate the overlapping and often contradictory requirements of two distinct kinds of imperatives (see Figure 3-1). Like other commercial entities, they must respond to the fundamental economic imperatives of ensuring economic survival and success. These obviously encompass the need to secure and retain competitive advantages relative to existing or potential rivals; but they also include reacting to or anticipating the terms under which competition is carried out in an industry (breadth of products or services offered, degree of integration, price and non-price competition) and enhancing the processes of organizational growth and renewal (product innovation, geographic and product diversification). Even if a public corporation is granted a legally sanctioned monopoly, it may still face competition from new technologies which produce substitutes for some, or perhaps all, of its products or services (e.g., Canada Post Corporation, the telephone utilities) or political pressure on the part of those who may wish to enter the industry.

Second, a public enterprise must meet the political imperatives of government demands. As discussed earlier, these include accommodating the public policy objectives specified in its mandate, and ongoing or surprise demands made by members of government and their agencies. The managers of a public corporation will respond to the economic and political imperatives by choosing the firm's operating patterns (manufacturing and service policies, vertical integration, product diversification, foreign investment practices) and its managerial tools (organizational structure; planning, budgeting and information systems; patterns of staffing, career paths, rewards and retribution).

FIGURE 3-1   The Context of Public Enterprise Management

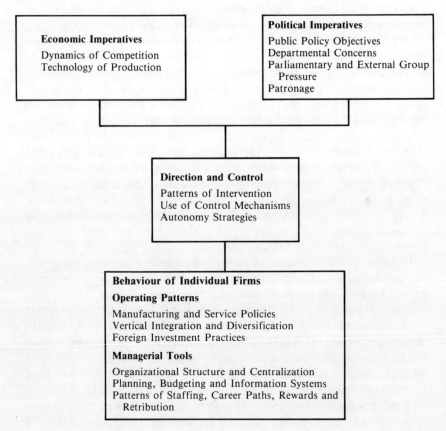

Moreover, the managers of a public corporation can be expected to have some regard for their own careers and conditions of employment. For example, if there is a competitive labour market for senior executives and public service norms prevent compensation on the basis of profit and mandate levels of compensation that are lower than those in the private sector, then Crown corporation managers can be expected to demand greater job security and higher levels of non-pecuniary income (De Alessi, 1974). If dramatic performance failures are discouraged because of the political embarrassment they might create, managers could be expected to be extremely risk averse (Davies, 1980). If there is not strong pressure to maximize profit, and if managerial compensation is based upon the size of personal empires, executives could be expected to maximize sales, subject to the constraint of achieving a minimal profit level (Borcherding, 1983). Under these circumstances, public enterprise managers also may be much more willing to use simple and convenient rules of thumb in production or pricing than their private sector counterparts (Peltzman, 1971). Of course, the extent to which these "bureaucratic" tendencies will be manifested in the behaviour of Crown corporation executives depends upon the degree to which environmental conditions compel an emphasis upon efficiency, as may occur in large private sector firms. Thus, a key assumption of this research stream is that public and private firms that operate under similar conditions may vary in the degree to which they exhibit certain behavioural traits, but not in kind.

Managerial research is also concerned with identifying and explaining the patterns by which the relationships between governments and their corporations change over time. When a public enterprise is established, the enabling legislation outlines the fundamental mission of the organization for the broader society which it serves. However, this mandate usually is made in such broad and vague terms that it cannot serve as a reliable guide to subsequent corporate actions. Responsibility for the development of detailed business and functional level policies and strategies is given to the managers, who often operate with considerable discretion within the general guidelines and informal monitoring mechanisms of the government (Mazzolini, 1979; Aharoni, 1981). The level of political intervention tends to be highest during the early years of a corporation's history, when a governing party is concerned with publicly demonstrating its commitment to a policy position and with ensuring that the managers will adhere to the government's interpretation of their mandate. As time passes, new priorities occupy the government's attention and the relationship with a Crown corporation becomes routinized. A corporation may face close scrutiny only if it suffers a dramatic performance failure or contemplates a major shift in its mission or pattern of investments (Gracey, 1978; Tupper and Doern, 1981). The number and complexity of the objectives associated with an enterprise will increase over time, and authority relationships may become fragmented. The responsibility of dealing with numerous actors and institutions may enable corporate executives to choose which they will respond to (Aharoni, 1981).

In many instances, particularly if they are facing strong private sector competition, a Crown corporation's managers may make it their personal mission to fundamentally redefine the firm's goals and activities. For example, J.L. Gray played a key role in shifting Atomic Energy of Canada Limited from a small research-oriented organization to a large producer of nuclear reactors and nuclear products (Sims and Doern, 1981). In the late 1970s Wilbert Hopper and Joel Bell redirected Petro-Canada from an initial emphasis on high-risk exploration to the creation of a fully integrated oil producer (Pratt, 1981, 1982). Causality is extremely complex in these cases, but the outcomes are partially the result of individual choices and goals, rather than just automatic reactions to irresistible environmental forces.

Like their private sector counterparts, managers of public firms prefer stable organizational behaviour and, accordingly, will seek to reduce both the degree and frequency of external intervention. They will develop autonomy strategies, courses of action geared to resisting strong government direction and to enhancing their discretion. While a number of Canadian case studies have discussed autonomy strategies, the most comprehensive research in this area has been based upon the experiences of U.S. or European firms. Walsh (1978) has documented how U.S. government corporations have attempted to construct alliances with client groups to ensure successful operations and managerial discretion. Burns (1977) has outlined how the British Broadcasting Corporation has used a tradition of non-partisan professionalism to buffer itself against political interference. Mazzolini (1979) examined the foreign investment decisions of 123 European state corporations and found that they were often undertaken as a means of protecting the autonomy and economic viability of the enterprises. He concluded that the major determinant of the success of these efforts was the relative power or influence of key individuals in the relevant firms or governments.

A lengthy discussion of this dimension of public enterprise behaviour lies outside of the scope of this paper, but the published research has indicated some of the ways in which managers of Canadian Crown corporations have attempted to enhance their discretion. As a very basic type of defence, managers may be able to restrain the development of external demands by lobbying or controlling flows of information to key units of governments. Peers (1969, 1979) has documented the extensive efforts by the Canadian Broadcasting Corporation to prevent policy makers from increasing competition from private and foreign broadcasters. Ashley and Smails (1965) and Sims and Doern (1981) have discussed the lobbying by Polysar and Atomic Energy of Canada Limited to secure approval for their investment projects from committees of the House of Commons. Bothwell and Kilbourn (1979) and McGregor (1980) have observed that the ability of executives to maintain Air Canada's status as the national airline was contingent upon the strength of their personal relationships with the ministers responsible for the corporation. Pratt (1981, 1982) and Doern and Toner (1985) have described the development of an extensive interpersonal network by Wilbert Hopper and Joel Bell which gave Petro-Canada a privileged position in the formation of federal energy policy and which buffered them against the demands of other government agencies and critics.

Proponents of property rights theory have noted that a public enterprise may be able to secure capital at a lower real cost than comparable private firms because it has access to government funds or an ability to trade upon the credit of the state in capital markets. However, from the perspective of corporate managers, long-term reliance upon government subsidies represents a form of dependence which legitimizes the imposition of demands from politicians and interest groups; and autonomy can be enhanced by minimizing the need to draw from the public trough. For example, a series of acquisitions by Petro-Canada between 1977 and 1982 advanced government objectives for increased Canadian ownership and control of the oil and gas industry; but they also provided the firm with an internal source of revenue which would enable it to become more self-sufficient and to survive if privatized (Pratt, 1981, 1982). As president of Canadian National during the 1970s, Robert Bandeen attempted to eliminate unprofitable business activities or to have the state explicitly agree to fund those undertaken to fulfill social objectives; his aggressive efforts to make the railway more profit-oriented created pressures from public officials for his resignation (Stevenson, 1981; Gratwick, 1982).

Single product companies, particularly public utilities, often enjoy very limited discretion. The costs of social objectives and proposed investments can be estimated with considerable discretion and can either be subsidized or recouped via higher prices. With product or market diversification, many of the transactions of a government enterprise become internalized beyond the sight of external interests. It can be very difficult to disaggregate the package of interdependent business activities in a multi-product firm, and to measure performance levels in particular businesses or the impact of external demands. If one product area is placed under extensive restrictions, others may remain beyond the reach of external intervention (Sexty, 1980; Aharoni, 1981). Managers may resist the imposition of external demands which would distort the balance among the business units of a diversified public enterprise. For example, executives of the Canada Development Corporation were unwilling to participate in a rescue of Massey-Ferguson Limited in 1981 because assuming an interest in the financially troubled manufacturer would adversely affect the profitability of the CDC's portfolio of investments (see Eckel and Vining, 1982). Gracey (1978) and Lambert (1979) have noted how the proliferation of subsidiaries and associated companies by diversified government corporations effectively removes much of the decision-making from direct scrutiny by representatives of the state and reduces external control. In his investigation of Air Canada, Estey (1975) has documented how all of these problems may be compounded when a public enterprise establishes investments abroad, since offshore investments lie beyond the immediate jurisdiction of the firm's government.

In recent years executives of Canadian National, Air Canada and Petro-Canada have suggested that employees or individual citizens should be allowed to invest in their corporations. Access to equity markets would permit the firms to ease the capital structure problems associated with the traditional restriction of public enterprise financing to government appropriations or debt capital. However, to a very real extent, dispersal of ownership or privatization represents an ultimate form of autonomy strategy. Even if it retains a controlling interest, a government cannot then issue directives unilaterally without taking into account the concerns of other owners. It should be recognized that these moves toward privatization and greater discretion have been undertaken by various public corporations in Canada primarily to enhance operational efficiency or competitive positions; but all also have implications for the degree of autonomy enjoyed by their managers.

The thrust of the managerial perspective can best be illustrated by two recent studies of Canadian Crown corporations (Baldwin, 1975; and Palmer, Quinn and Resendes, 1983). Research motivated by the property rights approach has been mainly statistical; but these two studies are built upon research into the managerial and institutional constraints affecting these corporations, as well as detailed examination of their internal operations, through the use of both quantitative and qualitative data. They apply the more general theories to the specific case, thereby building rigorous, indeed mathematical, models.

John Baldwin (1975) developed such a model in a detailed study of Air Canada. He suggested that the airline would meet its survival objectives by ensuring that it received support from politicians and consumer groups. This precluded simple profit maximization for two reasons. High visible profits would represent a source of potential gains to private sector firms, which would then lobby for the elimination of the public firm or for easier industry entry conditions. Large earnings would also lead users of the firm's services to demand lower prices or improvements in service and quality levels. On the other hand, losses would result in complaints from non-users about the airline's inefficiency and the increase in their tax liabilities. Thus, the best policy for the airline to pursue would be one that resulted in low but positive profits. In addition, Air Canada was required by the government to provide service on a number of unprofitable routes for political reasons.

Baldwin modelled these factors by specifying an objective function for the airline in which the two arguments were the level of the airline's profits and the difference between the per-mile fares on its profitable and unprofitable routes. The airline would attempt to minimize that difference through deliberate cross-subsidization. By providing levels of service and fares on the unprofitable routes which were comparable to those on profitable routes, it could forestall criticism from citizens who benefited from its activities. Baldwin also used the model to demonstrate theoretically how the airline would respond to such exogenous events as increases in demand, a fall in costs, and entry of competition on either its profitable or unprofitable routes. Then the theoretical projections were shown to be directionally consistent with the actual experience of the airline.

Palmer, Quinn and Resendes (1983) examined Gray Coach Lines Limited, a wholly owned subsidiary of the Toronto Transit Commission (TTC), which is a Crown corporation of the Municipality of Metropolitan Toronto. Gray Coach is the third largest bus carrier in Canada, but its assets and annual revenues from operations are less than one-sixth the size of the TTC's. The reseachers found that the institutional environment of the TTC and Gray Coach insulated managers from most political forces, enabling them to pursue some of their own goals and not just those of external interests. Neither the financial performance nor the fare structure of Gray Coach has ever been a significant issue in municipal politics, but external intervention could be expected to arise if Gray Coach ever suffered operating losses, because that would require special appropriations-in-council and call into question the organization's policies. Political market theory would suggest that local politicians should have no reason to subsidize passengers who are not based in Metropolitan Toronto and hence are not part of the electorate. In fact, Gray Coach was found to engage in extensive cross-subsidization. The chief beneficiaries have been the small group of users of its services, particularly those in other Ontario cities who commute to Toronto. The managers, in essence, have distributed income from Toronto to other Ontario residents. While this redistribution has provided highly visible benefits to the recipients, it has had a low visibility to the taxpayer-owners of Gray Coach.

A key determinant of the practices of Gray Coach and its parent firm has been the method of government subsidization of the TTC. The TTC receives a formula subsidy from the province and Metropolitan Toronto to finance deficits on its municipal operations. The revenues and costs of Gray Coach are excluded from the calculation of the subsidy, but any accounting profits on Gray Coach operations are applied against the level of subsidization. TTC executives accordingly will not wish to have Gray Coach adopt operating strategies that could have this effect, and have been able to maximize the overall revenues of the TTC by preserving the firms' separate legal identities and creating some joint operations. Through transfer pricing on integrated functions, some of the profits earned by Gray Coach can be shifted to its parent, but without realizing accounting profits or affecting subsidies.

Moreover, the imperative toward discretion and autonomy could be expected to lead managers at the TTC to prefer policies which lead to an excess of capital tied up in buses, so as to provide reserve capacity to ease scheduling difficulties. They might be expected to adopt pricing policies which are characterized by across-the-board increases, which are easy to administer, and to avoid the complications of detailed pricing calculations which a private sector firm would adopt in order to maximize profits. These assumptions were tested against, and found to be consistent with, data on the costs and fare patterns of Gray Coach.

To summarize, each of the three streams of research present various hypotheses about the behaviour of public corporations. These propositions carry direct implications for the pricing policies, output and productivity levels, costs and employment patterns of public versus private firms. The hypotheses of each stream have been expressed in very sweeping terms, but the political market and managerial perspectives have emerged only recently in the public enterprise literature and may be expected to develop much more specific and sophisticated hypotheses. We see the approach of managerial research as synthesizing and extending the insights provided by the two other streams. In particular, it adds new dimensions by considering the importance of competition (all but ignored in property rights theory), the evolution of a public corporation's relationship to government policy makers, and responses to environmental challenges by the individuals who manage a corporation. The empirical work it inspires is more holistic and does not rest after making simple statistical comparisons between two black boxes, one labelled "private" and the other "public." Rather, it compels the researcher, often through a combination of such methodologies as interviews and documentary analysis, to study the environment and incentive systems surrounding a public enterprise, and to consider theoretical constructs in the light of social realities.

Empirical Comparisons of Public and Private Firms

A number of studies have analyzed the performance of Canadian Crown corporations in terms of various measures of efficiency and effectiveness. This body of work includes both intricate methodological treatments and quick-and-dirty comparisons. Whether a given enterprise's behaviour and policies are to be viewed as good or bad involves a normative judgment. When the term "efficient" is used with respect to productivity, costs and pricing patterns, a writer is appraising behaviour according to some standard, even if the terms of that standard are not stated explicitly.

Ideally, the "efficiency" of an enterprise can be gauged properly only in the context of its overall objectives. If the role of a public corporation is not only to deliver power at cost, but also to assist regionally depressed areas, then the measurement process should take both into account. Relying solely upon an assessment of the rate of return on capital or the ratio of inputs to outputs may be entirely inappropriate. Most of the measures used by economists lack this degree of sophistication, and the problems of measurement and interpretation are immense. Their analyses typically are based upon the study of three distinct areas: productivity, costs, and profitability. Enterprises in which other goals are significant or paramount will, rightly or wrongly, often seem to be inefficient by such measures.

Productivity comparisons measure the degree to which different firms will use different volumes of resources to produce a specified set of outputs. From the perspective of economic efficiency, they reflect the varying facility with which enterprises combine and use inputs to produce outputs. If a public and a private corporation produce the same good and are known to have different output levels for a given amount of one input, it might be assumed that the two firms could be compared merely by examining output per unit of input, Y/X. However, the firms may have different output levels due to many factors, including differences in their ownership characteristics or technology of production.

Measures which gauge output per man and costs per unit of output cannot be used as reliable substitutes for the Y/X measure because they pick up factors other than productivity. For instance, if P is the price of a product, then PY/X may be measuring, in part, differences in prices received by the firms for that good. The prices may vary due to exogenous factors such as differences in the product-markets which each company serves, marginal distinctions in the attributes of the products which they provide, industry regulation, or wage and price controls. The price of labour, W, may be higher in the public enterprise than in the private sector firm. A measure of unit costs, WX/Y, will pick up costs attributable to several variables including different work locations, presence of labour organizations, or political pressure to provide better wages and working conditions. A true productivity measure, Y/X, should be independent of factor prices and these problems; and measures of value of output per man or costs per man do not necessarily reflect differences in productivity.

Productivity comparisons usually are presented in the form of growth rates or indexes of change over time. When a shift factor representing different institutional arrangements is employed, then the measure will indicate variations in the growth rate of productivity associated with the movement from one type of ownership structure to another. However, the problems of calculation and analysis can be daunting. If there is no prior information available to the researcher, then the production function for an enterprise must be estimated. A number of simple statistical measures are available in which inputs are weighted by factor shares of total costs and products by revenue shares. These can be used safely only when there are strong a priori reasons to assume constant returns to scale — that is, when a given percentage increase in inputs will yield an equal percentage increase in outputs. These conditions rarely prevail for either large public or private firms because of the wide range of inputs which they require for production and the presence of various economies of scale. Data on the volume of input supplies may not be available, and the researcher may be restricted to data on costs in different firms. Because of these problems, in most of the published research, it is the cost function of enterprises which is actually estimated (see Caves and and Christiansen, 1980).

Moreover, both the number and dimensions of outputs can be quite complex. Railways produce freight ton-miles and passenger miles; electricity may be supplied at different voltages and to different geographic areas with wide variations in terrain and population patterns. The researcher should attempt to specify these dimensions in the output measure, or the comparison may reflect issues other than productivity. If the supply of electricity to remote wilderness areas by a public corporation appears to be unprofitable or an inefficient use of national resources, this does not necessarily mean that the firm has a low productivity or cost effectiveness. The key issue of productivity analysis is whether when a public and a private firm do the same job, the public enterprise is less effective in its use of inputs than the private sector firm. Whether or not the range of outputs is socially efficient is a useful but entirely separate question.

The second type of measure examines the cost or price inefficiencies of different firms. Even though there may be no appreciable differences between a public and a private firm in terms of productivity, the public corporation may be less cost effective in its choice of inputs or may pay significantly higher prices for inputs. Cost functions are calculated by collecting data on costs, outputs and input prices for each of a sample of firms over a time period, and then examining how costs vary with prices and outputs. If outputs and prices are held constant, are costs sensitive to different institutional arrangements and higher in public than in private firms? An alternative mode of presentation may be to estimate two cost functions, one for a private enterprise and another for a comparable public sector firm, and then to consider how and in what ways they are different.

If firms face different input prices, the reasons for the variations should be examined with caution. A public firm's labour costs may exceed those of a private firm merely because a different mix of types of labour is employed, even though wage rates are the same. In an ideal measure, different categories of labour inputs would be reflected in a production function and relevant labour costs in a cost function; then it would be possible to determine whether the public firm has chosen an inferior factor combination. Similarly, a public firm with access to the resources of the state may face lower costs of capital than a private corporation. These distinctions will not show up in production or cost functions because each treats input prices as exogenous to the firm. Even if it has less expensive capital and more expensive labour, a public firm may have chosen a factor combination which is as cost effective as that which private firms would choose if faced with the same input prices.

If differences in input prices are believed to be intrinsic to ownership characteristics, then it may be necessary to revise cost measures. For example, Pryke (1971) revalued the nominal cost of capital for British public enterprises upward to a shadow cost which approximated the rates of return earned in the private sector. This type of revised measure can demonstrate that at the same cost of capital, public firms will use relatively more capital, and hence be less efficient, than private sector firms. If differences in prices can be linked to management practices (such as an inability to bargain effectively with labour unions), then the input prices should not be treated as independent variables and the differences should be incorporated in the cost measures. The key point which should be noted is that the very way in which a researcher treats input prices can markedly structure the conclusions which will be drawn from the measures. In any event, an analysis of prices and costs needs to be systematic and comprehensive; reliance upon casual empiricism, through media reports or the study of single decisions, can lead to fundamentally false conclusions.

Profitability is a third type of measure of the efficiency of public and private firms, and one commonly used by analysts in the media. Variations in profitability among a sample of companies can be attributed to three distinct elements: the productivity of each enterprise; the degree to which each is input price or cost efficient; and the volume and range of the products each produces, and the prices charged. A firm may have a lower rate of profitability than a comparable enterprise even though its productivity is higher and costs are lower; low profitability may be an outcome of factors connected with the volume and range of its products and the structure and level of its prices.

If public and private enterprises face the same set of exogenous product prices and a key objective is to enhance owner wealth, then an efficient firm will have rates of production or a range of outputs which will tend to correspond closely with the point where marginal costs and prices are equal, because that is where profits will be maximized. If firms are not price takers, than it will not be in the interest of owners for marginal costs to equate with prices and production, a situation which will occur whenever corporate practices are characterized by market power or monopolistic tendencies. In practice, the mandates of most Canadian public corporations do not emphasize profit-maximization, and specify sets of social objectives and policies which require them to make different choices than their private sector counterparts. Unfortunately, in no instance do we have any Canadian data which would indicate some of the costs of carrying out those mandates.

Each type of efficiency measure entails significant problems of calculation or has serious limitations in explanatory power. Profitability is the least satisfactory form of measurement because it encompasses any and all determinants of efficiency, and simply may not be in accord with the designated social role of a public enterprise. Few empirical studies have approached the essence of an "ideal" measure, and many have produced results which are methodologically suspect, as will be observed later in this paper. Meaningful comparisons must be carried out on an industry-by-industry basis. This, of course, assumes that there are both government and privately owned firms in an industry, and that differences can be isolated and attributed to ownership or other factors. Consequently, only a small number of studies have been generated.

The empirical evidence is limited largely to mature industries, rather than those at the early stages of the product life cycle. Thus, the data tell more about the effectiveness and efficiency of the state as a "manager," than, in the strict sense, as an "entrepreneur." This will disappoint the critics of public enterprise, since their sharpest barbs are often reserved for government attempts to become directly involved in new product development, particularly in high technology fields. Moreover, comparative studies simply have not been done for many industries. For example, the international airframe industry merits detailed analysis since it includes privately owned firms (Boeing, McDonnell Douglas, Lockheed) and government enterprises (Canadair, British Aerospace, Airbus Industrie). Recent revelations of serious management problems and large debt write-offs at both Canadair and De Havilland Aircraft would indicate that Canadian government corporations have not been among the industry leaders; but private U.S. companies, like Boeing and Lockheed, also have encountered major cost control and social conduct problems since 1970. The large aerospace firms in the United States might be characterized as "hidden Crown corporations." Despite their private ownership, they are expected to pursue policies consistent with the "national interest" and are heavily dependent upon government contracts and subsidization for survival. However, there has not been a detailed cross-national study which will enable us to draw meaningful comparisons or to go beyond the generalities outlined in media reports.

Railroads

Few comparisons of public and private enterprises have approximated the nature of "ideal" measures of productivity and cost effectiveness as closely as studies of Canadian railways by Caves and Christiansen (1980) and Caves, Christiansen, Swanson, and Tretheway (1982). The authors developed a translogarithmic production function for the two Canadian railway systems, Canadian National (CN) and Canadian Pacific (CP), and calculated the growth in total factor productivity associated with moving from one railroad to the other. Passenger miles and freight ton-miles were used as two indicators of output, while inputs included fuel, materials, equipment, structures (including rights-of-way), and four grades of labour. Outputs were not weighted by revenue shares since this would have picked up any constraints on pricing policies, such as regulatory restrictions on grain rates. Instead, the data on the cost elasticities of each product were obtained from similar U.S. research and used as product weights. Inputs were weighted not by their cost elasticities but by their shares of total costs, given that most factors were purchased in unregulated markets. The growth rate in productivity in any year as one shifts from CN TO CP was measured by the sum of the growth rates of the two inputs (aggregated by weights) minus the (weighted) sum of growth rates in inputs.

Comparing the two railroads, they found that CN had a lower productivity level than CP for the period 1956 to 1967. CN had surpassed CP by 1967, and tended to have a slightly higher growth rate until 1979, the end of the period surveyed, with the exception of 1973 to 1975. By 1979, the total factor productivity index of CN was 6 percent higher than that of CP. They then compared the growth of total factor productivity in the Canadian companies to 17 U.S. railroads for the period of 1956 to 1975. CN had a lower level of productivity than all of the other railways in 1956, while CP had a lower level than all but one of the U.S. railroads. By the mid-1960s, the Canadian firms had achieved higher levels of total factor productivity than an index of a "representative American railroad," and they continued to stay ahead for the rest of the period. In 1975, only three U.S. railroads had productivity levels exceeding that of CN and all were small, highly specialized carriers — the Santa Fe Railroad came midway between CN and CP.

The authors have argued that these outcomes can be linked to the different types of regulatory environments in the United States and Canada. The Canadian firms have had to deal with requirements to maintain western branch lines and with controls on grain rates under the Crow's Nest Pass agreement (which was abolished in 1983). (Some evidence was found indicating that these constraints affect CN more than the privately owned CP.) However, they have not been subject to the intensive regulation of pricing, entry and service conditions which has been experienced by their American counterparts. The major growth in the productivity levels of the Canadian firms occurred during the early 1960s, when the industry was partially deregulated by Canadian policy makers. The authors have argued that the existence of competition between the two railroads, even though one of them is publicly owned, has contributed to their rapid productivity growth and more efficient performance. The data also indicated that only 30 percent of the difference in productivity between Canadian and American railroads can be explained by excess capacity in the United States, resulting from regulatory constraints. Therefore, they have concluded that as long-term outcomes of deregulation, both Canadian railways have adopted better organizational design and control procedures, paid more attention to cost allocation, and used more sophisticated operating and financial management systems than their U.S. counterparts.

Their conclusions parallel those reached by Heaver and Nelson (1977) and Heaver and Waters (1982) in research on the pricing policies of Canadian railroads. These writers, however, have linked the improvements in economic performance not to deregulation in general, but specifically to the decision to deregulate railway price *and* service conditions in Canada. Managers thus secured greater latitude in the allocation of equipment and were able to make selective service arrangements with individual shippers. In particular, they have been permitted to practice value-of-service pricing, that is, to set prices according to both the ability of shippers to pay and the identifiable costs of serving traffic. This process has required managers to develop a thorough knowledge of the costs specific to the volume, routes and directions of shipments. Flexibility in setting rate and service conditions not only allows them to stress profitable types of traffic, but also to stipulate terms in service agreements which will induce shippers to use railway services in a manner which will benefit both the railways and the shippers. For example, rate concessions may be given for high volume and car utilization, while rate penalties can be exacted for small volume or shipper-induced delays in traffic. Consequently, some traffic which might otherwise not be moved can be handled profitably, and shippers have been able to realize benefits by also modifying their distribution systems (see Heaver and Nelson, 1977). In effect, the railways have been able to act as discriminating multiproduct monopolists, but the presence of inter-modal competition and/or direct market competition between the two national railways has constrained their ability to exploit this monopoly position harshly.

Gordon (1981, pp. 273–81) cites a consultant's study by R.A. Daly and Company which compares CN and CP during the period 1971 to 1976. The R.A. Daly analysis, based upon Statistics Canada data, produced information in two main categories: operating ratios, which relate to the utilization of assets and efficiency; and financial ratios, which compare operating profit margin, sales turnover and return on invested capital. The study found that the two railroads had similar growth rates in revenue and traffic, and comparable performance in terms of the utilization of rolling stock. In other areas, however, it was claimed that CP outperformed CN. CP had a higher rate of return on invested capital, averaging 7.4 percent per annum during the surveyed period, compared with CN's average of 1.6 percent per annum. In addition, CP had a higher operating profit margin, 11.7 percent per annum versus 1.8 percent per annum for CN. CP had superior performance both in absolute numbers and annual growth rates, for measures like revenue freight ton-miles per employee, railway revenue per employee, or freight revenue per employee. The Daly study argued that a key factor behind these results was CN's tendency to be overmanned and to pay higher wages and salaries than CP. In 1972, CN paid out 58 percent of its revenues in wages, while for CP the comparable figure was 47 percent. In 1976, CN had reduced its labour bill to 54 percent of revenues by trimming 5,000 jobs from its payroll between 1974 and 1976. CP's labour costs amounted to 45 percent of revenues in 1976.

These papers highlight some of the issues of efficiency measurement which were discussed earlier. From a methodological perspective, the results of the Daly study are of dubious utility. The research by Caves et al. was based upon the construction of productivity measures which control for differences in output composition or input prices. The Daly monograph not only lacks this degree of sophistication, but relies upon measures like freight revenue per employee, which will reflect factors other than productivity, including company rate structures and product mixes. Productivity is determined by the ways in which companies combine and use inputs, and even if CN is "overpaying" its workers relative to CP, this will not affect the measure of the efficiency with which it uses labour, capital, fuel and materials. The Daly study makes no attempt to explain labour variations between the firms. This may have reflected a different mix of types of labour, or social objectives which required CN to maintain branch lines and employment (see Stevenson, 1981; Gratwick, 1982). If CN is price inefficient in its labour policies, this may be a result of poor management or it may be considered an exogenous factor associated with different ownership characteristics, as labour organizations take advantage of CN's status as a Crown corporation to secure above-market compensation. Given the emphasis which we have placed upon the need for managerial research on the internal workings of public corporations, the conclusions which the Daly study attempts to draw would only be warranted if supported by data on CN's labour relations practices, comparative CN and CP wages, CN's personnel policies, and so forth.

The same issues surface with respect to the use of rates of return. Profitability, as discussed earlier, will reflect all determinants of efficiency and any corporate practices and, thus, is of limited value as an efficiency measure. Particularly disturbing has been the failure of the Daly study to consider how differences in the capital structures of the railways will impact upon rate of return analysis. Indeed, neither the research by Daly nor that by Caves et al. examine the implications for

CN's efficiency and management policies of its financial structure and the government's method of funding operations. Throughout the fifty years following the nationalization of its constituent companies in the early 1920s, CN operated with an extremely high debt burden. This, when combined with government policies to maintain money-losing operations (passenger services, little-used branch lines) made the attainment of long-term profitability improbable and the internal monitoring of activities difficult. Between 1952 and 1978, the government agreed to purchase preferred shares each year to an amount equal to 3 percent of the railway's gross revenues. Despite several restructurings, heavy borrowing to finance new equipment repeatedly raised the debt-to-equity ratio, which stood at a very high level of 62 to 38 by the mid-1970s (see Stevenson, 1981; Gratwick, 1982). Only with the passage of the Recapitalization Act of 1978 did CN secure a capital structure comparable to CP. The Act converted approximately $800 million in debt to equity, cancelled all preferred shares, and stipulated that CN should pay a dividend of at least 20 percent of net earnings to the government. Concurrently, the railway was divested of passenger services (which were given to VIA Rail Ltd.) and allowed to close many branch lines, making long-term unprofitability less likely (see Gratwick, 1982).

Airlines

Research by David Davies (1971, 1977, 1980) has frequently been cited in support of the property rights approach by its proponents. Davies compared two domestic Australian airlines, the government-owned Trans-Australian Airlines and privately owned Ansett Australian National Airlines. Davies thought that these firms represented a perfect matched pair because they operated under a tight regulatory regime which ensured that they had the same routes, charged the same prices, had identical service standards and departure times, and shared markets evenly. His data indicated that the privately owned firm had higher rates of freight tonnage, passengers and revenues per employee. Thus, according to Davies, the government-owned airline was less efficient because it was overmanned.

Davies' analysis has been critically re-examined by Forsyth and Hocking (1980) and William Jordan (1982a). These writers have pointed out that Davies incorrectly combined the data for Ansett and three of its subsidiary carriers. Only Ansett Airlines of Australia was truly comparable to the government airline. The other three carriers operated smaller aircraft on short intrastate flights. Similarly, Davies did not exclude data on operations in Papua New Guinea where the airlines have operated under significantly different circumstances.

These writers also have criticized the very legitimacy of Davies' measures. Forsyth and Hocking bluntly characterized the relevance of the revenue-per-employee-to-productivity measurement as "obscure" (1980, p. 184). In a physical sense, airlines which transport passengers, freight and mail over long distances are more productive than those which make short flights. The distance dimension of airline outputs cannot be captured by measures like freight tonnage and passengers per employee, but can be indicated by output measures such as passenger miles or freight ton-miles. Davies did not acknowledge that relationships between distance and productivity vary with alternative measures of employee productivity. Due to his choice of measures, the analysis was structured in such a fashion that short-haul intrastate carriers would appear to outperform long-haul interstate carriers — that is, that the privately owned airline would be superior to the government enterprise.

Jordan (1982a) used new data for the period of 1974 to 1979 to retest Davies' findings. In fairness, this more detailed information only became available after Davies' papers were published; but the analysis showed that the comparable productivity measures for Ansett and Trans-Australian Airlines were almost identical over the surveyed period. Jordan's results effectively quashed Davies' claim that Trans-Australian is less efficient than Ansett simply because it is government owned. This should not be surprising since, if the public and private airlines have been in such even competition, then it is unclear why the managers of the government airline would want to perform in what would easily be perceived as an inferior manner to Ansett. This almost undoubtedly would bring public investigation and revised controls or guidelines from public and regulatory officials.

Furthermore, we are troubled by the failure of Davies' research to probe causal factors, that is, its failure to indicate the various determinants of, and rationales behind, inefficiency in the government airline. Who benefits from inefficiency? What is the failure in the monitoring system that will allow such inefficiency to continue? The failure of Davies to address these issues is characteristic of the approach of many of the proponents of the property rights interpretation of public enterprise behaviour. Because these researchers operate from a deep, almost religious, commitment to the notion that private enterprise is better than state enterprise, when they secure results which appear to be consistent with their beliefs they do not trouble to ask what set of incentives and behaviours underlie those outcomes and whether there are alternative explanations.

Jordan (1982a, 1982b) examined the operations of Canadian and U.S. airlines for the period of 1975 to 1978. His sample included the two national Canadian carriers (Air Canada, CP Air), the five regional Canadian carriers (Eastern Provincial, Nordair, Pacific Western, Quebecair, and Transair), three selected U.S. trunk carriers (Delta, Northwest and Trans World), and four selected U.S. local service carriers (Allegheny, Frontier, North Central, and Southern). With the exceptions of Delta and Southern, the U.S. carriers were selected because their systemwide geographic operating areas were similar to those of the Canadian firms. Inclusion of the other two U.S. carriers permitted the study to consider whether cost variations might result from different weather conditions. As interstate and interprovincial carriers, these fourteen airlines operated under federal regulatory guidelines in the United States and Canada. They then were compared with four intrastate carriers (Air California, PSA, Air Florida, and Southwest) which operate under state regulation in competition with federally regulated companies.

Jordon compared total operating expenses per revenue ton-mile (which aggregated passenger and freight traffic) for the airlines. He controlled for the average trip length of each airline. The costs of terminal operations, system operations, takeoffs and landings are fixed with respect to trip length. Consequently, operating costs and revenues per mile taper substantially as trip length increases, a phenomenon which must be controlled for in efficiency measures.

Jordan found a high degree of comparability between the Canadian and U.S. carriers, and was able to develop regression projections for several input and output measures. Operating ratios were calculated by dividing total operating costs by total operating revenues. Low ratios, of course, would indicate low expenses relative to revenues, while high ratios would indicate small profits or losses. The intrastate U.S. carriers were significant outliers which were able to achieve substantially lower costs by specializing and running tightly-controlled operations. The operating ratios of Air Canada and CP Air were almost identical. The average operating ratio of the two airlines from 1977 to 1978 was 92.8 percent; in comparison, the average operating ratio for the three U.S. trunk carriers was 93.0 percent. The five regional carriers in Canada had a simple average operating ratio of 95 percent, as compared to 93.1 percent for the four U.S. local service carriers. Jordan found that differences in weather and population density had no material bearing upon these results.

Jordan carefully compared the two national Canadian airlines and the three U.S. trunk carriers by several productivity measures. He found that Air Canada had a relatively poor performance in terms of employee productivity and employee expenses per revenue ton-mile; but it was the best of the five large carriers in terms of fuel-related expenses. Labour and fuel accounted for slightly more than 60 percent of total operating expenses for the five airlines. Altogether, Jordan found that Air Canada ranked fourth among the five large carriers in terms of total operating expenses per revenue ton-mile, the most inclusive of the airline cost measures. Air Canada was 4.2 percent above the distance-related trend line for total operating expenses per revenue ton-mile. In comparison, Trans World was 7.0 percent above; CP Air, 1.6 percent above; Delta, 8.7 percent below; and Northwest the best at 19.2 percent below. On other measures, Air Canada did not have an unusually poor performance relative to privately owned airlines. It ranked third among the five large carriers in revenue per ton-mile load factor (tied with Trans World), and second in revenue passenger-mile load factor. The data also did not reveal a consistent pattern of price inefficiency by Air Canada in its choice of inputs.

Jordan argued that the differences in efficiency measures between CP Air and Air Canada "is not large enough to conclude that important performance differences are associated with government ownership" (1982a, p. 181). Jordan's inclusion of Delta and Northwest is noteworthy since they have been habitually considered by industry analysts to be the most efficient in the industry. Presumably, the inclusion of a number of other, less efficient, airlines would have improved Air Canada's ranking. The results which Jordan derives from his data are consistent with the more casual empiricism of industry analysts. Air Canada is not the best in the business, but it is not significantly inferior to its private sector competitors.

Like Caves et al. (1980, 1982), Jordan concludes that the key determinants of firm performance are the nature of regulation and competition. When faced with private sector competition, Crown corporations have comparable performance. Jordan claims that the efficiency of all firms probably would be enhanced on a long-term basis by deregulation.

In his analysis of Air Canada, Baldwin (1975) did not attempt to compare the performance of the Crown corporation with its privately owned competitors, whether foreign or domestic. Rather, he attempted to show the effects upon the public airline's operations of such exogenous changes as the introduction of more efficient aircraft or competition on its profitable sectors. For example, Baldwin found that the introduction of more efficient aircraft on its profitable routes enabled Air Canada to reduce its fares on its non-profitable sectors, that is, greater profitability permitted more cross-subsidization. Conversely, increases in competition were associated with lower prices and profits; with a decreased ability to cross-subsidize, the airline raised prices on non-profitable routes.

Baldwin's model of Air Canada can be used to predict and explain the airline's evolution. In the years since the book was published, the Crown corporation has faced much stronger competition (Langford, 1981), and has responded in predictable ways. It has attempted to reduce service on some non-profitable sectors, particularly those involving "show the flag" flights to other countries. Indeed, at the Canadian Transport Commission's 1982 hearings on discount fares, the then president of Air Canada, Claude Taylor, maintained that the airline covered its operating costs on all routes, although some clearly made a greater contribution to overhead than others. Air Canada also has increasingly diversified into tourism, airline servicing, and management consulting, all of which are unregulated and present opportunities for higher returns (see Estey, 1975; Langford, 1981).

At the time of writing, the government has announced its intention to undertake some deregulation of industry pricing and, possibly, entry and exit conditions. Air Canada has responded by initiating public discussion of partial or complete privatization of the airline. Air Canada's management has argued that the firm's era as an instrument of government policy is over, and that if it is to face more aggressive private sector competition, it should not be constrained by anachronistic "policy" responsibilities.

Urban Transport

The study by Palmer, Quinn and Resendes (1983) was concerned primarily with the cost allocation and pricing patterns of Gray Coach Lines Limited, but did make a number of observations about the economic performance of the bus carrier. It found that Gray Coach had an average annual return on net worth of 6.3 percent between 1969 and 1977. In comparison, Greyhound Lines of Canada Limited, the largest bus carrier in Canada, had an average return of 20.4 percent. Gray Coach's profit level was well below the "normal" rate for the industry and was below the firm's own unofficial target of 8 percent per annum. Interviews with corporate managers, however, clearly indicated that Gray Coach was expected to operate under the guideline of "breakeven plus a bit." The profit level of Greyhound was well above industry norms, and was affected by the firm's bus manufacturing subsidiary and other operations.

The difference in profitability also could be partially accounted for by the extensive cross-subsidization between Gray Coach and its parent, the Toronto Transit Commission, and there appeared to be evidence that the managers of Gray Coach and the TTC had attempted to reduce the variability of the reported rates for Gray Coach. In low-profit years, Gray Coach's profits were bolstered by the disposal of fully depreciated assets. When profits were high, payments to the TTC increased by more than when profits were low. This could be accounted for by more extensive operations and greater costs on shared functions, but it also would be consistent with the proposition that the managers will seek to avoid significant profits or losses which will attract the attention of politicians.

The authors attempted to develop indices of the technical efficiency of Gray Coach, but did not carry out a complete productivity analysis along the lines of Caves et al. They were unable to secure access to detailed data and did not have confidence in much of the publicly available information. They did find that Gray Coach appeared to be technically inefficient, and had higher maintenance costs, more mechanics and drivers per bus, and higher support and overhead expenses than industry norms. However, if payments to the TTC have been based more upon potential profits than incurred expenses, then the use of data on TTC costs which are allocated to Gray Coach for services provided by the parent firm, will yield very misleading impressions about operational efficiency. Gray Coach may be reporting certain expenses which have been overbilled by the TTC; and this would yield unfavourable performance ratios for Gray Coach relative to other carriers.

These results are consistent with the other studies if the distinctive environment of Gray Coach is taken into account. While the firm faces inter-modal competition throughout its route system, Gray Coach does not face head-to-head competition with other bus companies. The regulatory regime gives the carrier monopoly status on most bus routes, and the freedom to set prices as it deems fit. Given the ultimate accountability to metropolitan politicians, operations are conditioned by cross-subsidization practices which contribute to the overall Toronto transit system; but as a subsidiary of the TTC, the firm secures greater immunity from external monitoring than other Crown corporations. All of these conditions should be expected to lead to inefficient behaviour. Nonetheless, the authors stress that inefficiency in Gray Coach's activities is not caused by public ownership per se; rather, this is a result of the nature of the regulatory regime, which they carefully describe.

In related research, Pashigian (1976) carried out a cross-sectional analysis of 40 urban transport facilities in the United States during 1960 and 1970. He found that publicly owned transit systems had lower prices, after allowing for costs, and therefore lower profit margins. Pashigian did not attempt to determine whether this was primarily due to managerial inefficiency or to the use of public transit as a policy instrument to provide a subsidized service to its users, particularly to members of lower income groups.

Telephone Utilities

Denny, de Fontenay and Weaver (1983) compared productivity growth from 1967 to 1979 for three Canadian companies which account for over 70 percent of domestic telecommunications services: publicly owned and regulated Alberta Government Telephones (AGT), and privately owned and publicly regulated Bell Canada and British Columbia Telephone (B.C.Tel). They used translogarithmic cost functions to measure productivity growth, the same methodology employed by Caves et al. in their study of railroads. They observed that the two private firms had relatively equivalent levels of efficiency in both 1972 and 1979. In 1972, AGT had a 10 percent cost disadvantage relative to B.C.Tel, and a 7 percent disadvantage compared to Bell Canada; but, by 1978, AGT had secured a 7 percent cost advantage over both private firms. AGT was found to have made major gains in the use of labour inputs and also to have secured some gains in the use of capital and materials. Because this study was based upon aggregated publicly available data, it did not attempt to sort out the effects of regulation, competitive behaviour or economies of scale on cost functions. Nevertheless, it does show a clear case of a publicly owned utility, AGT, making major efficiency gains relative to privately owned firms.

Gordon (1981, pp. 263–70) undertook a quick comparison of the efficiency of Canada's ten telephone utilities, again based upon research carried out by R.A. Daly and Company. Three of the firms (AGT, Saskatchewan Telecommunications, and Manitoba Telephone System) are government owned, while the remainder are private sector firms. Crude efficiency comparisons such as the average number of employees per 1,000 telephones, maintenance costs per $1,000 of gross telephone plant, maintenance costs per 1,000 telephones, and traffic costs per 1,000 telephones all indicated that the three public telephone utilities were comparable with the seven private companies. The most efficient enterprise on these measures was Bell Canada, which presumably was able to take advantage of economies of scale to realize some cost advantages. The final measure, the average annual rate of change in total operating costs per 1,000 telephones from 1967 to 1976, was comparable for all ten firms. Bell Canada was the lowest at 6.5 percent, followed by Manitoba Telephone and AGT at 6.7 percent. Saskatchewan Telecommunications had a 7.2 percent rate of change and the privately owned Newfoundland Telephone was highest at 8.8 percent. Thus, Gordon concluded that the data did not indicate any significant performance differences between the public and private telephone companies.

All of the telephone companies are subject to direct regulation. Bell Canada and B.C.Tel are federally regulated, while the others come under the jurisdiction of provincial regulatory agencies. Given the wide range of regulatory guidelines which may prevail with respect to revenues, costs and profitability, managerial efficiency cannot be measured legitimately without reference to the specific regulatory regimes or demands which impinge upon individual companies. The Daly analysis makes no attempt to isolate distinctions among the companies which may be derived from differences in the size of operations, geographic conditions, or population patterns and the composition of users. At the same time, there may be sufficient comparability among the provinces and sufficient access to industry data to permit regulatory officials to investigate and take corrective action if any one company performs in a radically different manner from the others (Denning, 1982). In short, the regulatory regime again appears to be more significant than the simple fact of public or private ownership.

Electrical Utilities

Although electrical utilities constitute the largest sector among provincial Crown corporations in terms of revenues and assets, they have attracted surprisingly limited attention from Canadian researchers. In contrast, numerous studies have been made of electricity supply in the United States, where there are many public and private firms. Most of the U.S. research completed during the last decade has been based upon cross sections of data for the period of 1964 to 1973, and upon samples of companies which include all but the smallest firms.

De Alessi (1980) has claimed that a review of the literature demonstrates that public electrical utilities in the United States closely conform to the behaviour predicted by the property rights thesis. Relative to private firms, they will: charge lower and less profit-oriented prices; relate price discrimination and price changes less closely to demand and supply conditions or other economic determinants; spend more on capacity; have higher operating costs; be less likely to adopt cost-saving innovations; and exhibit greater variations in rates of return. De Alessi's assertions are open to serious challenge on several grounds. First, much of the research which he cites (1980, pp. 23–33) is concerned with the pre-1960 origins and logic of direct regulation, not with public ownership per se. Second, many of the analyses of public enterprise presented in his review relate to small municipal utilities which are heavily subsidized and constitute a very small share of aggregate production of electricity in the United States. Third, many of the studies do not make comparisons of public and private firms based upon cost and production data. Often distinctions are not made among sample firms in terms of the size of operations or type of power generation.

Indeed, much of the recent literature points in the direction opposite to that suggested by De Alessi. Hellman (1972) found that competition, where it existed, improved the performance of both public and private utilities. Primeaux (1975) discovered that public power companies were more efficient when competing with private producers than when in monopoly situations. Yunker (1975) used a sample of 24 public and 49 private utilities, and estimated costs as a function of output and the number of customers in 1969. His results indicated that costs were lower in public firms than in the private companies, although the outcomes were not statistically significant. Meyer (1975) observed data for 30 public and 30 private electricity producers over three years and found that the cost structures of the two types of firms differed significantly. Generating costs per megawatt hour declined with the number of megawatt hours and were generally lower for public utilities. Total costs for transmission were determined primarily by the number of customers, and the data indicated that public firms had lower costs. Distribution costs were affected in a complex fashion by both output and number of customers, but there appeared to be no significant differences between public and private firms. Data on the costs of maintenance per megawatt of capacity, sales and account expenses, and on general and administrative expenses, all indicated lower costs in public firms.

The studies by Yunker and Meyer are among the first efforts to examine cost efficiencies in the production of electricity while taking into account differences in output levels. Data deficiencies restricted their analyses to operating costs (labour, fuel, materials); they did not consider issues like the cost of capital. Yunker also lacked information on input prices, which would indicate whether production inefficiencies were obscured by price inefficiencies. Moreover, each study had problems of sample composition. Yunker's survey encompassed firms that just distributed electricity, along with those that generated, transmitted and distributed electricity, and Meyer included some federal government projects which dwarfed those of other companies.

Pescatrice and Trapani (1980) examined two years of cross-sectional data on 33 private and 23 public firms. A cost of capital was generated for each enterprise and variations in the technology of electricity generation were explored. They argued that capacity might be similar in age and in the general mode of production but could differ significantly in technology and, consequently, in the costs of production. Costs per megawatt hour were considered as a function of: output (the number of megawatt hours); the prices of labour, fuel and capital; the age of equipment; and the type of ownership. The results indicated that a shift from public to private ownership was associated with an increase in average costs of approximately 25 percent. Much of the difference could be attributed to the higher level of technology in public firms. Thus, none of these recent U.S. studies support the proposition that public electrical utilities have lower productivity and higher unit costs than private sector firms, once differences in output and input prices have been allowed for.

Since most of the Canadian utilities are publicly owned, it has not been possible to replicate this body of research in a Canadian context. Gordon (1981, pp. 253–60) did an extremely crude comparison of three privately owned utilities (Newfoundland Light and Power, Canadian Utilities, and Calgary Power) with the provincially owned corporations. She was able to compare only the annual average rate of change in total costs per kilowatt hour for the 1967–76 period. Gordon found that the performance of the privately owned firms fell within the range of the public firms. Manitoba Power had the best performance level with a decrease of 6.4 percent per annum, while Ontario Hydro had the worst with a cost increase of 1.5 percent per annum. Gordon's analysis failed to take into account variations in firm size, input prices, types of power generation, or regulatory regimes, and the results are therefore of little substantive value.

Much of the recent literature on Canadian electrical utilities has criticized them for their alleged failure to follow optimal pricing and investment policies specified by welfare economics. Some of the public policy debates about the pricing and investment activities of Ontario Hydro and Hydro Quebec are reflected in arguments that: electricity prices are too low; Canadian consumption is too high; exports of electricity are subsidized; and the industry is too capital-intensive (Slater, 1982). Canadian electrical utilities have followed the growth-oriented practice of pricing according to historical costs rather than peak-load pricing, which would reduce the growth of demand and flatten the load curve (Osler, 1977). Jenkins (1980) has estimated that the real rate of return in the Canadian electricity industry averaged about 3.5 percent per annum during the 1970s, while it was approximately 10 percent in other sectors. He claimed that if Canadian utilities were to impose charges sufficient to earn a return equal to the "social opportunity cost" of invested capital, rates would increase by an average of 68 percent. He also asserted that the economic waste due to the misallocation of resources in the electricity industry may amount to as much as 0.8 percent of gross national product, or a present value of about $30 billion over a ten-year period.

It also has been claimed that the provincial electrical corporations have been able to borrow at preferential interest rates, since their debts are ultimately guaranteed by provincial governments. Thus, their debt-to-equity ratios have become much higher than those of privately owned U.S. utilities. Given the availability of less expensive capital, the utilities could be expected to favour capital-intensive methods of generation with long gestation periods in plant construction (hydro, nuclear power), and to reject technologies which are more labour or fuel intensive (Berkowitz and Halpern, 1981).

These criticisms may have a great degree of economic validity, but they rest on weak factual or conceptual foundations. It is not at all obvious that such policies are uniquely attributable to the existence of government enterprise, or that even the privatization of the provincial utilities would lead to the optimally efficient behaviour which those critics favour. Systematic analyses of the investment patterns and cost efficiencies of the Canadian utilities have been conspicuous by their absence.

Canadian governments often have designated only small nominal sums for the "equity" of their corporations since ownership shares will not be traded in markets. Thus, an attempt to determine whether public firms have an inappropriate reliance upon debt by the simplistic comparison of the debt-to-equity ratios of public and private enterprises in an industry can be extremely misleading (see Berkowitz and Halpern, 1981). A detailed cost function analysis, such as that of Pescatrice and Topani (1980), would be necessary, as would the generation of a much more detailed data base than exists at the present. For example, Pryke

(1981) has conducted a detailed sector-by-sector analysis of nationalized companies in the United Kingdom and has demonstrated that the availability of cheap capital has contributed to a preference for capital-intensive projects, occasionally with disastrous consequences.

From the perspective of industrial organization theory, real rates of return are sector-specific. Not only do different industries produce entirely different goods, but many inputs (including capital, labour and technology) cannot be transferred with ease between sectors. The real rate of return in a given industry will be affected by the degree of concentration, entry and exit barriers, and the presence of scale economies. It is unreasonable, therefore, to presume that the rate of return in one industry may be unnaturally low relative to others without taking these factors into account (Shepherd, 1979, pp. 265–276).

Whether electricity supply and exports are charged to consumers at too low a price is a question of allocative efficiency, and a separate issue from the efficiency of corporate operations. The parameters of pricing policies for electrical utilities usually are stipulated by the state or its agents, and these social objectives form part of the objective function of the enterprises, regardless of whether they are publicly or privately owned. Canadian governments have long favoured the subsidization of electricity rates in order to provide a low-cost source of energy which will make Canadian industry competitive and will foster growth (Nelles, 1973). The European electrical utilities which have followed peak-load pricing are generally publicly owned. Indeed, the theory of peak-load pricing was developed by Boiteux and Masse in publicly owned Éléctricité de France. If there is public support for such practices in Canada, then lobbying might lead to appropriate changes in provincial energy policies, as well as in the mandates and incentive structures for managers of the utilities.

Steel and Oil

Gordon (1981, pp. 287–89) performed a quick comparison of Canadian steel companies. She found that Stelco, Dofasco and Algoma Steel, which are privately owned and the industry leaders, had rates of return on invested capital averaging between 7 and 9 percent per annum for the period of 1967 to 1976. Sidbec, a Quebec Crown corporation, had an average rate of return of 0.3 percent per annum, while a mixed enterprise, the Interprovincial Steel and Pipe Corporation (Ipsco), had an annual rate of return averaging 10 percent.

Ipsco is a smaller competitor which relies upon electric mills and scrap metal to produce specialty steels and steel pipe. It has been used by the governments of Alberta and Saskatchewan to develop regional manufacturing industry. Sidbec has attempted to develop an integrated steel operation along the lines of the three industry leaders but has been much too small to achieve minimum efficient scale. Like SYSCO in Nova Scotia, Sidbec originally was a weak private sector firm which was taken over by the Quebec government in order to maintain economic development and employment in the northern areas of the province. Sidbec historically has operated at a loss and has relied upon sales to Quebec-based firms or "captive markets" such as other provincial Crown corporations and government projects. The government has been willing to accept those losses as a necessary price for long-term regional development and for encouraging the "francization" of business in Quebec (Litvak and Maule, 1977). Accordingly, it cannot be considered as a commercially-oriented Crown corporation in the same sense as the others that have been discussed.

During the last two decades, government enterprises throughout the world have assumed a pre-eminent role in the oil or, more broadly defined, the energy industry. It has been very difficult for researchers to compare the efficiency of public and private oil companies because the government firms usually have been established to fulfill a wide range of public policy objectives. For example, Petro-Canada was created to: assure domestic energy supplies; act as a window on the industry; develop high-cost oil or alternative energy sources; and assist in oil exploration in less developed countries (Pratt, 1981, 1982). On the other hand, public oil companies, due to the sensitivity of their policy roles, often have gained privileges not available to their private sector counterparts. For instance, under the National Energy Program, Petro-Canada secured the use of Canadian Ownership Charge revenues to finance its acquisitions, a 25 percent back-in provision on federal lands, and possibly preferential treatment in the allocation of drilling licenses (Doern and Toner, 1985). Many government oil companies have been highly profitable but those profits, in large measure, reflect their role as collectors of economic rents, rather than their efficiency per se (Lewin, 1982).

The only comparative study of Petro-Canada and private sector firms which has been done to date was undertaken by the U.S. General Accounting Office (1981). Based upon qualitative data, it concluded that the public firm had fulfilled two of its policy objectives, accelerating the development of high-cost, high-risk reserves and serving as a window on the industry. The study found insufficient evidence to determine whether Petro-Canada was a more or less effective importer than private companies, or whether state-to-state transactions would increase energy security. While it found that Petro-Canada was comparable in efficiency to private sector firms in terms of conventional oil exploration and production, the study was based entirely upon the pre-1979 period of the company's history, that is, prior to the major expansion in the scope of its operations following the return to power of the Liberal party in early 1980. Doern and Toner (1985) do not deal directly with the efficiency of the national oil company in their study of the National Energy

Program. However, they suggest that by 1983 the federal administration was experiencing serious difficulties in scrutinizing and controlling Petro-Canada's activities and growth, despite an intensive monitoring regime.

War Industries

Borins (1982) examined the operations of Crown corporations created by the federal government during the Second World War. These enterprises included an aircraft plant (Victory Aircraft), two munitions factories (National Railway Munitions Ltd., Small Arms Ltd.), and two shipbuilding plants (Quebec Shipyards Ltd., Toronto Shipbuilding Company Ltd.). These companies served as "windows" on crucial wartime industries. Other industry participants operated under tight regulatory conditions, producing all of the outputs under contracts that gave the government exceptional powers. While the evidence is purely anecdotal, it appears that the publicly owned plants were operated just as efficiently as those in the private sector. For instance, Victory Aircraft was originally nationalized in 1941 because of its efficiency. By 1943, two directors of the British aircraft firm of Hawker Siddeley, who toured all of the Canadian aircraft plants, were so impressed with the efficiency of Victory Aircraft that they indicated their interest in purchasing the firm after the war.

Borins suggested that several special factors contributed to the performance of these public enterprises. The Crown corporations were managed by current corporate executives paid by their corporations or retired corporate executives who lived on their retirement incomes. Since they were not paid by the government, their compensation was unrelated to the size of the operation which they administered, breaking any link between personal compensation and empire-building. Many were ambitious middle-level executives, generally in their late thirties or early forties. By performing effectively, they could impress C.D. Howe, the Minister of Munitions and Supply, and thereby enhance their credentials as efficient public managers and their postwar career prospects. Finally, the nature of enterprise outputs (weapons) was readily quantifiable, and the wartime emergency emphasized production goals while minimizing political concerns. These factors, which are quite different from those that prevail in a peacetime economy, were significant in explaining why these public enterprises were run as effectively as private sector firms.

Conclusions

This review of the literature dealing with the relative efficiency of public and private enterprise in Canada suggests several interesting conclusions.

1. *There is no consistent evidence demonstrating that public enterprise is inherently less efficient than private enterprise*. At least in mature industries, the overwhelming bulk of the published research conducted in Canada and abroad, particularly the more sophisticated studies of productivity and cost efficiency, suggests that public and private firms have comparable performance levels when examined on an industry-by-industry basis. Clear differences between public and private firms do emerge, however, when pricing and profitability are concerned. Public corporations are required to fulfill certain social objectives in addition to their economic goals and activities, and often are expected to operate on a near-breakeven basis. Assessments of efficiency based upon profitability, accordingly, may use inappropriate measures and be very misleading about causality. In analyzing the behaviour of public corporations, a clear and necessary distinction must be drawn between those policies and practices derived from ownership forms or management goals, and those that are externally imposed by governments as part of their own policy objectives.

This assessment of the literature must, of course, be qualified by the patchy nature of the industries which have been examined, and by the simplistic nature of some of the studies conducted to date. Research has tended to concentrate on those sectors where government enterprise might be expected to perform well relative to private sector firms. Public corporations that operate under more turbulent industry conditions, such as the early stages of the product life cycle, may exhibit different performance characteristics, but this is largely speculative. We not only lack careful documentation of the emergence of problems experienced by firms like Canadair and De Havilland Aircraft and whether they do differ significantly from those of other industry participants, but also lack good *comparative* research on the difficulties experienced by companies like VIA Rail or Petro-Canada. There is little systematic research on vertically integrated firms in oil and natural resources, or even comparative analyses of federal and provincial corporations in the same sectors. Many measures in the studies confuse distinct issues like productivity, costs and profitability.

2. *Environment appears to be a stronger determinant of efficiency than form of ownership*. A consistent pattern which has emerged in the case studies is that performance is conditional upon the intensity and form of competition and regulation and upon the monitoring and incentive systems under which public enterprise managers work. These results are not only consistent with the thrust of research in industrial organization (see Shepherd, 1979, pp. 262–76; Porter, 1980), but also with the survey of the American literature by Denning (1982). His survey found that the existence of competition has served as an incentive to efficiency. The available research has not indicated how much competition is necessary to spur a public corporation to efficiency. Clearly, by their very nature, it is unlikely that public firms will be found in atomistic markets. Rather,

they will be located in oligopolistic industries. The extent of competition in such cases varies from market to market but often may be quite substantial. First, as in the cases of Canada Post Corporation and the telephone utilities, there is always the threat of competition from outside the market. Second, Crown corporations and their private sector competitors have very different organizational cultures, which makes collusion difficult (Porter, 1980).

Stanbury and Thompson, in the introduction to their edited volume on the management of public enterprise, also note that:

> One of the most significant themes running through this volume is that ownership per se may not matter very much. Enterprises, whether owned by governments or individuals, have to respond to their environments. Where growth and survival require responsiveness to political demands, public enterprises do, in fact, accommodate themselves to the opportunities and risks created by government action and initiatives. So do private enterprises. (1982, p. 7)

3. *We need more longitudinal case studies and sophisticated modes of analysis.* In terms of future research, we should now be long beyond the era of theoretical, and often rhetorical, debate about whether the public or private sector is more efficient. There is a need for more case studies like those of Baldwin (1975) or Palmer, Quinn and Resendes (1983), which examine the incentive systems of public enterprise managers in order to determine how they affect them in day-to-day operations. In particular, research must include more historical content in order to trace how Crown corporation managers have responded to environmental changes. Perhaps from these case studies, a more holistic and accurate theory can be constructed.

Similarly, studies should apply sophisticated measures of productivity and cost efficiencies, along the lines of Caves et al. (1980, 1982). While many writers have predicted higher input prices and unit costs in public firms for labour and materials or lower costs for capital, only a handful of studies have attempted to actually document those phenomena. We would argue that there is a need to consider total factor productivity in those analyses, and not to target isolated variables like the cost of capital alone. This will require the elaboration of much more detailed data bases than has been attempted by researchers in the past.

4. *There is a need to isolate and examine the impact of social goals on public enterprise performance levels.* Ideally, social goals for public corporations should be explicit and measured, but, as indicated both by political market theory and managerial research, political actors often have a vested interest in obscuring the role of Crown corporations in delivering benefits to client groups. One of the frustrations of this review is that in no case could we find research which attempts to measure systematically the costs of achieving policy objectives, and rarely have

researchers taken such costs into account when making assessments of performance. The comprehensive auditing movement is a useful trend, since it calls for making social goals more explicit and measuring the performance of corporations in achieving them. Analysis of performance is meaningless unless these goals are recognized as part of the objective function of a public enterprise. If goals are extremely complex and constantly changing, it will be very difficult to draw legitimate comparisons.

We would conclude by observing that Canada is not as wealthy a country as its citizens once thought, and that we can no longer afford to ignore market signals or to run public enterprises inefficiently for the benefit of either their managers or small well-organized interest groups. Although significant differences may exist between public and private enterprise on efficiency issues which have not been documented in the literature, this should not be perceived as a recommendation on our part for a proliferation of new Crown corporations. Rather, we would hope that there will be a strong public demand for greater efficiency in all sectors of the economy, and particularly in the existing public corporations.

Although the literature has not documented significant differences between public and private enterprise on efficiency issues, this finding should not be perceived as leading to a recommendation on our part for a proliferation of new Crown corporations.

Bibliography

Aharoni, Y. 1981. "Managerial Discretion." In *State-Owned Enterprises in the Western Economies*, edited by R. Vernon and Y. Aharoni, pp. 184–93. New York: St. Martin's Press.

Ahlbrandt, R. 1973. "Efficiency in the Provision of Fire Services." *Public Choice* 16: 1–15.

Aitken, H.J. 1959. "Defensive Expansionism: The State and Economic Growth in Canada." In *The State and Economic Growth*, edited by H.J. Aitken, pp. 79–114. New York: Social Science Research Council.

————. 1964. "Government and Business in Canada: An Interpretation." *Business History Review* 38: 4–21.

Alchian, A.A. 1961. *Some Economics of Property*. Study P-2316. Santa Monica: Rand Corporation.

————. 1965. "Some Economics of Property Rights." *Il Politico* 30: 816–29.

Allison, G.T. 1971. *Essence of Decision: Explaining the Cuban Missile Crisis*. Boston: Little, Brown.

Ashley, C.A. 1963. *The First Twenty-Five Years: A Study of Trans-Canada Airlines*. Toronto: Macmillan.

Ashley, C.A., and R.G. Smails. 1965. *Canadian Crown Corporations*. Toronto: Macmillan.

Baldwin, J.R. 1975. *The Regulatory Agency and the Public Corporation: The Canadian Air Transport Industry*. Cambridge, Mass.: Ballinger.

Balls, H.R. 1953. "The Financial Control and Accountability of Crown Corporations." *Public Administration* 21: 127–43.

Berkowitz, M.K., and P.J. Halpern. 1981. *The Role of Crown Corporations in the Efficient Production and Use of Electricity*. Toronto: University of Toronto, Institute for Policy Analysis.

Berle, A.A., and G. Means. 1932. *The Modern Corporation and Private Property*. New York: Macmillan.

Blakeney, A.E. 1954. "Saskatchewan Crown Corporations." In *The Public Corporation: A Comparative Symposium*, edited by W. Friedman, pp. 53–107. New York: Carswell.

Bliss, M. 1971. "Canadianizing American Business: The Roots of the Branch Plant." In *Close the 49th Parallel: The Americanization of Canada*, edited by I. Lumsden, pp. 24–42. Toronto: University of Toronto Press.

————. 1973. *A Living Profit: Studies in the Social History of Canadian Business, 1883–1911*. Toronto: McClelland and Stewart.

Borcherding, T.E. 1983. "Towards a Positive Theory of Public Sector Supply Arrangements." In *Crown Corporations in Canada: The Calculus of Instrument Choice*, edited by J.R.S. Prichard, pp. 99–184. Toronto: Butterworth.

Borins, S.F. 1982. "World War II Crown Corporations: Their Wartime Role and Peacetime Privatization." *Canadian Public Administration* 25: 380–404.

Bothwell, R. 1984. *Eldorado: Canada's National Uranium Company, 1926–1960*. Toronto: University of Toronto Press.

Bothwell, R., and W. Kilbourn. 1979. *C.D. Howe: A Biography*. Toronto: McClelland and Stewart.

Boudreaux, K.J. 1973. "Managerialism and Risk-Return Performance." *Southern Economics Journal* 29: 366–72.

Boyes, W.J., and T. Schalgenhauf. 1979. "Managerial Incentives and the Specification of Functional Forms." *Southern Economics Journal* 45: 1225–32.

Braybrooke, D., and C.E. Lindblom. 1963. *A Strategy of Decision: Policy Evaluation as a Social Process*. New York: Macmillan.

Buchanan, J., and G. Tullock. 1962. *The Calculus of Consent*. Ann Arbor: University of Michigan Press.

Burns, T. 1977. *The BBC: Public Institution and Private World*. London: Macmillan.

Canada. Commission of Inquiry into Air Canada. 1975. *Report* (Estey Commission). Ottawa: Information Canada.

———. Privy Council Office. 1977. *Crown Corporations: Direction, Control, Accountability*. Ottawa: Minister of Supply and Services Canada.

———. Royal Commission on Financial Management and Accountability. 1979. *Report* (Lambert Commission). Ottawa: Minister of Supply and Services Canada.

Caves, D.W., and L.R. Christiansen. 1980. "The Relative Efficiency of Public and Private Firms in a Competitive Environment: The Case of Canadian Railroads." *Journal of Political Economy* 88: 958–76.

Caves, D.W., L.R. Christiansen, J.A. Swanson, and M.W. Tretheway. 1982. "Economic Performance of U.S. and Canadian Railroads: The Significance of Ownership and the Regulatory Environment." In *Managing Public Enterprises*, edited by W.T. Stanbury and F. Thompson, pp. 123–60. New York: Praeger.

Ciscel, D.H. 1974. "Determinants of Executive Compensation." *Southern Economics Journal* 40: 613–17.

Coase, R. 1937. "The Nature of the Firm." *Economica* 4: 386–405.

Cooter, R., and G. Topakian. 1980. "Political Economy of a Public Corporation: Pricing Objectives of BART." *Journal of Public Economics* 13: 299–318.

Creighton, D.G. 1936. *The Empire of the St. Lawrence*. Toronto: Macmillan.

Cyert, R.M., and J.G. March. 1963. *A Behavioral Theory of the Firm*. New York: Prentice-Hall.

Davies, D.G. 1971. "The Efficiency of Public versus Private Firms: The Case of Australia's Two Airlines." *Journal of Law and Economics* 14: 149–65.

———. 1977. "Property Rights and Economic Efficiency — The Australian Airlines Revisited." *Journal of Law and Economics* 20: 223–27.

———. 1980. "Property Rights in a Regulated Environment: A Reply." *Economic Record* (June): 186–89.

De Alessi, L. 1974. "Managerial Tenure Under Private and Government Ownership in the Electric Power Industry." *Journal of Political Economy* 82: 645–53.

———. 1980. "The Economics of Property Rights: A Review of the Evidence." *Research in Law and Economics* 2: 1–47.

Denning, M. 1982. "The Public Ownership of Productive Resources: An Economic Analysis of Public Enterprise." Paper presented to the annual meeting of the Western Political Science Association, San Diego.

Dennison, M. 1960. *The People's Power: A History of Ontario Hydro*. Toronto: McClelland and Stewart.

Denny, M., A. de Fontenay, and W. Werner. 1983. "Comparing the Efficiency of Firms: Canadian Telecommunications Companies." In *Economic Analysis of Telecommunications: Theory and Applications*, edited by L. Courville, A. de Fontenay and R. Dobell. New York: Elsevier Science.

Doern, G.B., and G. Toner. 1985. *The NEP and the Politics of Energy*. Toronto: Methuen.

Downs, A. 1957. *An Economic Theory of Democracy*. New York: Harper and Row.

Eckel, C., and A. Vining. 1982. "Toward a Positive Theory of Joint Enterprise." In *Managing Public Enterprises*, edited by W.T. Stanbury and F. Thompson, pp. 209–22. New York: Praeger.

Elliott, J.W. 1972. "Control, Size, Growth and Financial Performance in the Firm." *Journal of Finance and Quantitative Analysis* 7: 1309–20.

Evans, G. 1984. *John Grierson and the National Film Board*. Toronto: University of Toronto Press.

Forsyth, P.J., and R.D. Hocking. 1980. "Property Rights and Efficiency in a Regulated Environment: The Case of Australian Airlines." *Economic Record* (June): 182–85.

Fournier, L.T. 1935. *Railroad Nationalization in Canada: The Problem of the Canadian National Railways*. Toronto: Macmillan.

Frech, H.E. 1976. "The Property Rights Theory of the Firm: Empirical Results from a Natural Experiment." *Journal of Political Economy* 84: 143–52.

————. "Property Rights, the Theory of the Firm, and Competitive Markets for Top Decision Makers." *Research in Law and Economics* 2: 49–63.

Furobotn, E.G., and S. Pejovich. 1972. "Property Rights and Economic Theory: A Survey of Recent Literature." *Journal of Economic Literature* 10: 1137–62.

Galbraith, J.K. 1973. *Economics and the Public Interest.* New York: New American Library.

Gracey, D. 1978. "Public Enterprises in Canada." In *Public Enterprise and the Public Interest*, edited by A. Gelinas, pp. 25–47. Toronto: Institute of Public Administration of Canada.

Gratwick, J. 1982. "Canadian National: Diversification and Public Responsibility in Canada's Largest Crown Corporation." In *Managing Public Enterprises*, edited by W.T. Stanbury and F. Thompson, pp. 237–49. New York: Praeger.

Gordon, M. 1981. *Government in Business.* Montreal: C.D. Howe Institute.

Hardin, H. 1974. *A Nation Unaware: The Canadian Economic Culture.* Vancouver: J.J. Douglas.

Heaver, T.D., and J.C. Nelson. 1977. *Railway Pricing Under Commercial Freedom: The Canadian Experience.* Vancouver: Centre for Transportation Studies.

Heaver, T.D., and W.G. Waters. 1982. "Public Enterprise Under Competition: A Comment on the Canadian Railways." In *Managing Public Enterprises*, edited by W.T. Stanbury and F. Thompson, pp. 152–60. New York: Praeger.

Hellman, R. 1972. *Government Competition in the Electric Utility Industry.* New York: Praeger.

Herman, E.S. 1981. *Corporate Control, Corporate Power.* New York: Cambridge University Press.

Hodgetts, J.E. 1953. "Government Enterprise." In *Proceedings of the Institute of Public Administration in Canada*, pp. 387–420. Toronto.

————. 1970. "The Public Corporation in Canada." In *Government Enterprise: A Comparative Study*, edited by W.G. Friedman and J.F. Garner, pp. 201–26. New York: Columbia University Press.

Horowitz, G. 1967. "Conservatism, Liberalism and Socialism in Canada: An Interpretation." *Canadian Journal of Economics and Political Science* 32: 348–83.

Innis, H.A. 1930. *The Fur Trade in Canada.* Toronto: University of Toronto Press.

Jenkins, G.P. 1980. "Public Utility Finance and Economic Waste." Cambridge, Mass.: Harvard University.

Jordan, W.A. 1982a. "Performance of North American and Australian Airlines: Regulation and Public Enterprise." In *Managing Public Enterprises*, edited by W.T. Stanbury and F. Thompson, pp. 161–99. New York: Praeger.

————. 1982b. *Performance of Regulated Canadian Airlines in Domestic and Transborder Operations.* Ottawa: Department of Consumer and Corporate Affairs.

Kemper, P., and J.M. Quigley. 1976. *The Economics of Refuse Collection.* Cambridge, Mass.: Ballinger.

Kitchen, H. 1976. "A Statistical Estimation of an Operating Cost Function for Municipal Refuse Collection." *Public Finance Quarterly* 4: 56–76.

Langford, J.W. 1979. "Crown Corporations as Instruments of Policy." In *Public Policy in Canada: Organization, Process, and Management*, edited by G.B. Doern and P. Aucoin. Toronto: Macmillan.

————. 1980. "The Identification and Classification of Federal Public Corporations: A Preface to Regime Building." *Canadian Public Administration* 23: 76–104.

————. 1981. "Air Canada." In *Public Corporations and Public Policy in Canada*, edited by A. Tupper and G.B. Doern, pp. 251–84. Montreal: Institute for Research on Public Policy.

————. 1982. "Public Corporations in the 1980s: Moving from Rhetoric to Analysis." *Canadian Public Administration* 25: 619–37.

Langford, J.W., and K.J. Huffman. 1983. "The Uncharted Universe of Federal Public Corporations." In *Crown Corporations in Canada: The Calculus of Instrument Choice*, edited by J.R.S. Prichard, pp. 219–302. Toronto: Butterworth.

Larner, R.J. 1970. *Management Control and the Large Corporation*. New York: Dunellen.

Lewin, A. 1982. "Public Enterprise: Purposes and Performance, a Survey of Western European Experience." In *Managing Public Enterprises*, edited by W.T. Stanbury and F. Thompson, pp. 51–78. New York: Praeger.

Lintner, J. 1981. "Economic Theory and Financial Management." In *State-Owned Enterprise in the Western Economies*, edited by R. Vernon and Y. Aharoni, pp. 23–53. New York: St. Martin's Press.

Litvak, I.A., and C.J. Maule. 1977. *Corporate Dualism and the Canadian Steel Industry*. Ottawa: Minister of Supply and Services Canada.

Lower, A.R.M. 1958. *Canadians in the Making*. Toronto: Macmillan.

MacLean, G. 1981. *Public Enterprise in Saskatchewan*. Regina: Crown Investments Corporation of Saskatchewan.

March, J.G., and H.A. Simon. 1958. *Organizations*. New York: John Wiley.

Marris, R. 1964. *The Economic Theory of Managerial Capitalism*. London: Macmillan.

Masson, H.G. 1971. "Executive Motivations, Earnings, and Consequent Equity Performance." *Journal of Political Economy* 79: 1278–92.

Mazzolini, R. 1979. *Government Controlled Corporations: International Strategic and Policy Decisions*. New York: John Wiley.

McEachern, W.A. 1978. "Ownership, Control and the Contemporary Corporation: A Comment." *Kyklos* 31: 491–96.

McGregor, G. 1980. *The Adolescence of an Airline*. Montreal: Air Canada.

Meeks, G., and G. Whittington. 1975. "Directors' Pay, Growth and Profitability." *Journal of Industrial Economics* 24: 1–14.

Meyer, R.A. 1975. "Publicly Owned versus Privately Owned Utilities: A Policy Choice." *Review of Economics and Statistics* 57: 391–99.

Monsen, R.J., J.A. Chiu, and D.E. Cooley. 1968. "The Effect of Separation of Ownership and Control on the Performance of the Large Firm." *Quarterly Journal of Economics* 82: 435–51.

Monsen, R.J., and K.A. Walters. 1984. *Nationalized Companies: A Threat to American Business*. New York: McGraw-Hill.

Morton, W. 1963. *The Kingdom of Canada*. Toronto: Macmillan.

————. 1972. *The Canadian Identity*. Toronto: University of Toronto Press.

Musolf, L.D. 1959. *Public Ownership and Accountability: The Canadian Case*. Cambridge, Mass.: Harvard University Press.

Naylor, T. 1972. *The History of Canadian Business*, volume 1. Toronto: James Lorimer.

————. 1973. *The History of Canadian Business*, volume 2. Toronto: James Lorimer.

Nelles, H.V. 1973. *The Politics of Development: Forest, Mines and Hydro-Electric Power in Ontario, 1849–1941*. Toronto: Macmillan.

Niskanen, W. 1971. *Bureaucracy and Representative Government*. Chicago: Aldine.

Olson, M. 1965. *The Logic of Collective Action*. Cambridge, Mass.: Harvard University Press.

Osler, S. 1977. "An Application of Marginal Cost Pricing Principles to B.C. Hydro." Vancouver: University of British Columbia, Programme in Natural Resources.

Palmer, J., J. Quinn, and R. Resendes. 1983. "A Case Study of Public Enterprise: Gray Coach Lines Ltd." In *Crown Corporations in Canada: The Calculus of Instrument Choice*, edited by J.R.S. Prichard, pp. 369–446. Toronto: Butterworth.

Pashigian, B.P. 1976. "Consequences and Causes of Public Ownership of Urban Transit Facilities." *Journal of Political Economy* 84: 1239–59.

Peers, F.W. 1969. *The Politics of Canadian Broadcasting, 1920–1951*. Toronto: University of Toronto Press.

_____. 1979. *The Public Eye: Television and the Politics of Canadian Broadcasting, 1952–1968*. Toronto: University of Toronto Press.

Peltzman, S. 1971. "Pricing in Public and Private Enterprises: Electric Utilities in the United States." *Journal of Law and Economics* 14: 109–47.

Pescatrice, D.R., and J.M. Trapani. 1980. "The Performance and Objectives of Public and Private Utilities in the United States." *Journal of Public Economics* 13: 259–75.

Pfeffer, J., and G.R. Salancik. 1978. *The External Control of Organizations: A Resource Dependence Perspective*. New York: Harper and Row.

Pomerehne, W.M., and B.S. Frey. 1977. "Public versus Private Production Efficiency in Switzerland: A Theoretical and Empirical Comparison." *Urban Affairs Journal* 12: 221–41.

Porter, M.E. 1980. *Competitive Strategy*. New York: Free Press.

Posner, R.A. 1971. "Taxation by Regulation." *Bell Journal of Economics and Management Science* 2: 22–50.

Pratt, L. 1981. "Petro-Canada." In *Public Corporations and Public Policy in Canada*, edited by A. Tupper and G.B. Doern, pp. 95–148. Montreal: Institute for Research on Public Policy.

_____. 1982. "Oil and State Enterprises: Assessing Petro-Canada." In *Managing Public Enterprises*, edited by W.T.Stanbury and F.Thompson, pp. 79–110. New York: Praeger.

Prichard, J.R.S., ed. 1983. *Crown Corporations in Canada: The Calculus of Instrument Choice*. Toronto: Butterworth.

Primeaux, W.J. 1975. "A Re-examination of the Monopoly Structure for Electric Utilities." In *Promoting Competition in Regulated Markets*, edited by A. Phillips. Washington, D.C.: Brookings Institution.

Pryke, R. 1971. *Public Enterprise in Practice*. London: MacGibbon and Kee.

_____. 1981. *The Nationalized Industries: Policies and Performance Since 1968*. London: Martin Robertson.

Quinn, J.B. 1980. *Strategies for Change: Logical Incrementalism*. Homewood, Ill.: Irwin.

Reed, P.W. 1973. *The Economics of Public Enterprise*. London: Butterworth.

Rees, R. 1976. *Public Enterprise Economics*. London: Weidenfeld and Nicholson.

Savas, E.S. 1977a. *Evaluating the Organization and Efficiency of Solid Waste Collection*. Boston: D.C.Heath.

_____. 1977b. "Policy Analysis for Local Government: Private versus Public Refuse Collection." *Policy Analysis* 3: 49–74.

_____. 1980. "Comparative Costs of Public and Private Enterprise in Municipal Services." In *Public and Private Enterprise in a Mixed Economy*, edited by W.J. Baumol, pp. 253–64. New York: St.Martin's Press.

Schull, J. 1979. *The Great Scot: A Biography of Donald Gordon*. Montreal: McGill-Queen's University Press.

Sexty, R.M. 1980. "Autonomy Strategies of Government Owned Business Corporations in Canada." *Strategic Management Journal* 1: 371–384.

Shepherd, W.G. 1965. *Economic Performance Under Public Ownership*. New Haven: Yale University Press.

_____. 1979. *The Economics of Industrial Organization*. New York: Prentice-Hall.

Sims, G., and G.B. Doern. 1981. "Atomic Energy of Canada Limited." In *Public Corporations and Public Policy in Canada*, edited by A. Tupper and G.B. Doern, pp. 51–94. Montreal: Institute for Research on Public Policy.

Slater, D.W. 1982. "The Production and Pricing of Electricity in Canada in the 1980s: Some Issues." Paper presented at a conference "The Impact of Regulatory Reform in Canada and the United States," Toronto, May 21, 1982.

Smyth, D.J., W.J. Boyes, and D.E. Peseau. 1975. *Size, Growth, Profits in the Large Corporation: A Study of the 500 Largest United Kingdom and United States Industrial Corporations*. New York: Holmes and Meier.

Sorenson, R. 1974. "The Separation of Ownership and Control and Firm Performance: An Empirical Analysis." *Southern Economics Journal* 41: 145–48.

Statistics Canada. 1982. *Federal Government Enterprises, Finance, 1980.* (Cat. 61-203) Ottawa.

——————. 1983. *Provincial Government Enterprises, Finance, 1980.* (Cat. 61-204) Ottawa.

——————. 1984. *Federal Government Enterprises, Finance, 1982.* (Cat. 61-203) Ottawa.

Stanbury, W.T., and F. Thompson, eds. 1982. *Managing Public Enterprises.* New York: Praeger.

Stano, M. 1975. "Executive Ownership Interests and Corporate Performance." *Southern Economics Journal* 41: 145–48.

Stevens, R. 1966. *The History of Canadian National Railways.* Toronto: Clarke Irwin.

Stevenson, G. 1981. "Canadian National Railways." In *Public Corporations and Public Policy in Canada*, edited by A.Tupper and G.B. Doern, pp. 319–52. Montreal: Institute for Research on Public Policy.

Stigler, G. 1971. "The Theory of Economic Regulation." *Bell Journal of Economics* 2: 3–21.

Trebilcock, M.J., J.R.S. Prichard, D.G. Hartle, and D.N. Dewees. 1982. *The Choice of Governing Instrument.* Ottawa: Minister of Supply and Services Canada.

Tupper, A., and G.B. Doern, eds. 1981. *Public Corporations and Public Policy in Canada.* Montreal: Institute for Research on Public Policy.

Turvey, R., ed. 1968. *Public Enterprise Economics.* London: Penguin.

——————. 1971. *Economic Analysis and Public Enterprise.* London: Allen and Unwin.

United States General Accounting Office. 1981. *Petro-Canada: The National Oil Company as a Tool of Canadian Policy.* Washington, D.C.: U.S. Government Printing Office.

Vining, A., and R. Botterell. 1983. "An Overview of the Origins, Growth, Size and Functions of Provincial Crown Corporations." In *Crown Corporations in Canada: The Calculus of Instrument Choice*, edited by J.R.S. Prichard, pp. 303–68. Toronto: Butterworth.

Walsh, A.H. 1978. *The Public's Business: The Politics and Practices of Government Corporations.* Cambridge, Mass.: MIT Press.

Ware, R.F. 1975. "Performance of Manager- versus Owner-Controlled Firms in the Food and Beverage Industry." *Quarterly Journal of Economics and Business* 15: 81–92.

Williamson, O.E. 1975. *Markets and Hierarchies: Analysis and Anti-Trust Implications.* New York: Free Press.

Yunker, J.A. 1975. "Economic Performance of Public and Private Enterprise: The Case of U.S. Electric Utilities." *Journal of Economics and Business* 28: 60–67.

4

An Agenda for Research on Financial Markets

JOHN CHANT

The Royal Commission on the Economic Union and the Development Prospects for Canada was instructed to

> inquire into and report upon the long-term economic potential, prospects and challenges facing the Canadian federation and its respective regions, as well as the implications that such prospects and challenges have for Canada's economies and governmental institutions and for the management of Canada's economic affairs.[1]

The workings of financial markets pervade every other sector and are crucial to the performance of the Canadian economy. These markets determine the overall flow of savings and investment in the economy and its distribution among competing uses. They are also the conduit through which monetary policies influence the rest of the economy. In addition, financial institutions and their activities are among the areas most regulated by government in the economy. The significance of financial markets to the economy and the extent to which they are regulated make financial markets and their functioning areas of prime concern to the Commission in fulfilling its mandate.

The purpose of this paper is to present research priorities for this Royal Commission to consider with respect to financial markets. The research areas outlined in this statement are chosen according to the needs of policy as distinct from pure academic research or even business-oriented research. The proposals are directed to those areas where there is a need for change in policy or at least a need for reaffirmation of the current approach.[2]

The research proposed in this statement emphasizes the ability of the financial system to meet the funding needs of Canadian industry. Less, but still considerable, attention is directed to the issue of safety and none to the issue of monetary control. This approach is justified on several grounds. First, at least on the safety issue, the Canadian system as a whole has achieved a superior performance over the years, despite the recent widely publicized problems of certain financial institutions.[3] Second, the issues of safety and monetary control have gained public attention through periodic revisions of financial legislation. Finally, monetary policy is the subject of a number of other studies conducted for the Royal Commission.

Within this selection of research directed toward policy issues, a distinction exists between issues of imminent concern and those directed toward a longer horizon. At present, many policies toward financial markets appear to be unsettled. Questions of jurisdiction and approach to intervention have been increasingly in the forefront of public concern. These issues are afforded considerable attention in what follows. Still, sight should not be lost of the need to plan for the issues of the future so that policy makers can be prepared to respond within a set of appropriate institutions.

The research issues identified in this study are accorded different degrees of development and emphasis. This imbalance is entirely intentional: the issue granted most attention — the separation of financial institutions — is judged to be both more pressing and more significant in the long run than any of the other issues considered.

Features of the Canadian Financial System

Before turning to research issues, several important features of Canadian financial markets and their regulation should be identified. Shaping the determination of priorities with respect to policy-directed research on financial markets are such features as:

- the separation of financial activities from each other and from real economic activity;
- federal-provincial division of responsibility;
- the variety of approaches to regulation taken by different authorities;
- the pace of technology; and
- the maintenance of Canadian ownership.

Canadian policy toward financial institutions appears to have been devoted to maintaining separations between different types of financial activities and between financial activities and real activity. The first separation, that among financial activities, has been labelled the "four pillars" principle. Since both principles involve similar issues, they are discussed together.

A number of distinct areas of activity can be distinguished in Canadian financial markets. The activities of banking, trusteeship, brokerage and insurance have been identified as separate areas of activity with a limited amount of overlap. Each activity comes under the jurisdiction of different regulatory authorities. The "four pillars" concept refers to a belief that each of these activities should be kept separate from the others. If recent hearings of the Ontario Securities Commission can be taken as a barometer of informed opinion, many people view this concept as an overriding principle governing regulatory change in the Canadian financial system.

Two arguments have been used to justify the concept. First, the types of activity covered under each pillar may be mutually compatible but may create conflict of interest when combined with the activities of another pillar. Second, it is feared by many that a breakdown of the concept would lead to increasing dominance by a few large financial institutions at the expense of others. On the other hand, others view it as a rationalization for the prevention of competition among different types of financial institutions.

The principle of separation of financial and real activity has similar motivations to preserve the separation among financial activities. Two aspects of this principle of separation need to be considered. First, the ownership, or more specifically the controlling interests, of financial institutions must be kept separate from involvement in the real sector. Second, financial institutions must limit their participation in the ownership of non-financial enterprises.

The degree to which the separation of real and financial activities is enforced varies across different sectors of the financial industry. Schedule A banks, on the one hand, are permitted to have no more than 10 percent ownership by any one interest. In contrast, such restrictions are absent for most trust and insurance companies, where many firms are controlled by single large interests.

Combination of control of financial institutions with real economic activity, some critics object, leads to a variety of problems. The potential arises for conflict between the interests of the financial institution and its customers relative to those of the enterprises involved in real activities. In addition, the present size of major Canadian financial institutions leads to a concern about the undesired dominance of the economy by these institutions.[4]

The division of responsibility for the financial sector between federal and provincial authorities serves as a major constraint on any proposal for major reform of the Canadian financial system. Some activities, such as banking, are firmly under federal jurisdiction while others, such as securities trading, credit unions and caisses populaires, are equally firmly under provincial authority. Other activities, such as the business of trust companies, have divided jurisdiction. Some companies are federally incorporated while others are provincially incorporated. Moreover, even for federally incorporated firms, such activities as estates, trusteeships and agencies are primarily provincial responsibilities.

The delineations among jurisdictions cannot be regarded as entirely unambiguous or unchanging either in the past or throughout the future. The hearings of the Ontario Securities Commission in early 1984 illustrate that provincial authorities may attempt to extend their jurisdiction to include responsibility for a federal institution — a chartered bank — engaging in a limited way in a provincially regulated activity — security trading. Moreover, from time to time the federal government has attempted to extend its authority over the supervision of securities markets since the Royal Commission on Banking and Finance recommended in 1964 that it take an initiative in this direction.[5]

Less well known in discussions of the regulation of financial markets are the vast differences of approach taken by different regulators. Historically, the regulation of the Canadian banks has been at the "hands-off" end of the spectrum. Bank powers were delineated in legislation, with little intervention by the regulator between legislative changes. On the whole, the powers granted to any bank were granted on an equal basis to any other bank qualifying under the Bank Act. To some extent, this approach has been eroded recently in a variety of ways. Between the 1967 and 1980 Bank Act revisions, the minister of finance resorted to the use of moral suasion by issuing guidelines to the chartered banks with respect to their participation in leasing and in the selling computer services. The Bank Act was supplemented for the first time in 1980 by regulations which offer greater discretion for the authorities to alter rules between Bank Act revisions. The range of discretion granted to the regulator appears to be even greater with respect to Schedule B banks.

A contrast to the "hands-off" approach which had characterized the regulation of banking can be seen in the more "interventionist" approach taken with respect to trust companies. Not all trust companies have the same powers. The legislation specifies maximum borrowing-to-capital ratios, but these set the limit to the regulator's powers and do not specify a right for any trust companies. Each trust company is assigned its own ceiling to borrowing by the regulator with the levels determined by the regulator's perception of the appropriate level.

A fairly recent concern in the regulation of financial markets has been the extent of foreign ownership of financial institutions. Historically, at various times, foreign-owned banks have operated on the same basis as domestically owned financial institutions. The Royal Commission on Banking and Finance, however, concluded that "a high degree of Canadian ownership of financial institutions is in itself healthy and desirable and that the balance of advantage is against foreign control of Canadian banks."[6] The steps taken by the First National City Bank to take over a bank that was already foreign-owned precipitated a change in Canadian policy whereby banking was declared to be a key sector in which Canadian ownership and control was to be maintained as government policy. The subsequent revision of the Bank Act in 1967 included a new provision which set a ceiling on the ownership of chartered banks. Similar constraints were placed by provincial authorities on the ownership of stock brokerage houses as a consequence of the takeover of Canadian-owned Royal Securities by Merill Lynch. The application of national ownership requirements has not been uniform throughout the financial sector. Indeed, the Study Committee on Financial Institutions reporting to the government of Quebec observed:

> We cannot see why Quebec should block a foreign group — American, say — from taking control of an institution chartered in Quebec, when an Ontario or Western Canadian group could have access to it. If our aim is to maintain control of financial institutions in Quebec hands, we do not see why a New York group should be treated differently from Toronto or Winnipeg groups. This could be answered by saying that Quebec legislation should be adapted in such a way as to prevent groups outside Quebec — rather than foreign groups — from gaining control of our financial institutions.[7]

The final factor to be taken into account in examining policy-related research issues concerns effects of changing technology on the financial industry.[8] Many of the activities in financial business involve the storage, retrieval and transferral of information, tasks which are standardized and repetitive. It is precisely this area where traditional ways of doing business are being revolutionized by the micro-chip. Most visible among these innovations are the automated teller, through which customers can carry out the majority of their transactions without access to bank personnel, and the point-of-sale terminal, at which transfers of deposit balances can be effected instantly between customer and retail merchant.

The relationship between technology and regulation is complicated by the fact that regulation can either discourage or stimulate innovation, depending on the circumstances. On the one hand, regulations which limit the behaviour of financial institutions also create incentives for financial institutions and their customers to develop new approaches to conducting the same business so as to lessen these constraints. At times, this response to regulation can be interpreted as an industry response to dated regulations which are not in accord with changing ways of performing business. Chartered banks, for example, participated in the new activity of financial leasing through subsidiaries even though their direct participation was discouraged by guidelines from the minister of finance. This constraint on bank entry into leasing was subsequently eased in the 1980 Bank Act revision.

At other times, innovation to avoid regulation may be clearly against the spirit of the regulator's intent. The development by the chartered banks of a foreign currency deposit business with Canadian residents may be interpreted as an attempt to avoid the costs of cash reserve requirements. In this case, avoidance of the regulation was restricted by the application of reserve requirements to these deposits under the 1980 Bank Act.

Regulation may also serve to inhibit technological change. For example, a financial institution may wish to develop new lines of activity which have joint economies in production with its existing services, but it may be prevented from doing so by limitations in its powers caused by the system of regulation.

Innovation can also be induced by external events other than technical changes. For example, the higher levels of inflation in the past decade have made traditional approaches to financial business more costly. Borrowers and lenders have sought out new arrangements to protect themselves from either inflation itself or uncertainties about future levels of inflation. Similarly, businesses and households have attempted to reduce their cash holdings so as to avoid the inflation "tax."

Each type of innovation must be considered in terms of its contribution to economic productivity. It may seem that innovations which reflect enhanced knowledge would clearly improve efficiency. In some cases, improved productivity is clearly the outcome. Unfortunately, in others the change in technique is directed primarily at avoiding the effects of government regulations. Innovations to overcome the effects of regulation or to ameliorate the consequences of inflation may be beneficial to the individuals who use them but may lack any social benefit. Indeed, it may be cheaper to eliminate the regulation in question. Similarly, the benefits of some innovations to overcome the costs of inflation may not persist if inflation abates significantly.

Changing technology raises three issues for framing the regulation of financial markets. First, a regulatory response may be required as changing technology fosters new activities and new ways of performing existing tasks. Regulators must determine whether the new activities lie within the scope of regulated activities and whether they alter the requirements for regulation. Second, regulators should be concerned that the framework which governs financial institutions encourages innovations which enhance economic efficiency. The ideal system of regulation for such a purpose is difficult to prescribe. Aspects of regulation which are detrimental to innovation, on the other hand, are easier to identify. A system which creates excessive uncertainty for market participants may be costly. If long delays are routine in ruling on acceptability of new forms of business, the interests of savers and lenders may be jeopardized. Existing institutions would be either precluded from supplying the new services or forced to find indirect means of meeting the needs. On the other hand, new specialized suppliers of the services may be reluctant to develop the expertise required to offer the new service if they are uncertain about the eventual entry of established institutions. Finally, innovation may alter the expectations that can be held for regulation. Certain approaches to regulation may become untenable in the face of technical change. For example, technology may reduce the ability to differentiate among demand and savings deposits when balances can be transferred at will out of savings deposits into accounts with chequing privileges. Differential reserve requirements for the two types of accounts may become effectively unenforceable. Thus the prospect of new technology may limit the possible approaches to regulation.

Approach to Research

The general approach taken in this study to outlining research priorities in the area of financial markets focuses on major participants in financial markets. The discussion starts with financial institutions, then moves to direct financial markets — the area of brokerage and underwriting -- and concludes with the regulation of issuers of securities, primarily business enterprises. The greatest attention is directed toward financial institutions because it is believed that important impending changes require the attention of policy makers.

Financial Institutions

The area of financial institutions was the major concern of the Royal Commission on Banking and Finance (the Porter Commission) and of several studies by the Economic Council of Canada. Any recommendation for research in this area must give recognition to the unfinished business of these two bodies. In addition, the present proposals will go beyond the limited scope of the Economic Council study on financial markets in two ways. The Council's study on financial institutions, *Efficiency and Regulation* (1976), was directed specifically at the imminent revision of the Bank Act, then scheduled for 1977. The passage of time since then has given greater insight into the development of technology.

The primary area of research proposed for financial institutions centres on the "four pillars" concept. The issue of separation of financial institutions has long been a subject of controversy with respect to the regulation of financial institutions. The Royal Commission on Banking and Finance recommended "that federal banking legislation must cover all private financial institutions issuing banking liabilities: that is, claims which serve as means of payment or close substitutes for them."[9]

Such a move would clearly break down the distinctions between two of the four pillars — banking and trust activities. The Economic Council, following in the same tradition, recommended a functional approach to regulation by which institutions would be subject to regulation according to the activities they undertake rather than on the basis of their incorporation.[10] Recently the issue has been the centre of attention again in the hearings of the Ontario Securities Commission with regard to the application of a chartered bank to offer and advertise security trading services.

At present, the lines of demarcation are less than distinct between the activities of the different groups among the four pillars. Figure 4-1 is taken from a study by David Petras prepared for the hearings of the Ontario Securities Commission. It portrays the legal authority for various institutions to carry out a variety of selected activities. This figure suggests that some activities are more clearly identified with specific institutions than others. Indeed, at one extreme, several activities appear to be general to a wide range of institutions. In addition, very few of the activities (insurance, securities trading and underwriting) appear to be confined mainly to a single set of institutions.

FIGURE 4-1

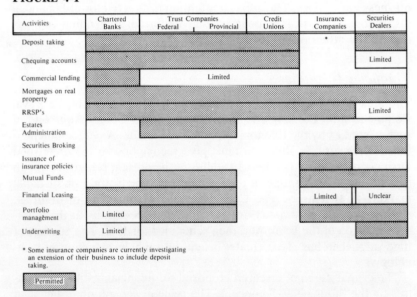

Activities	Chartered Banks	Trust Companies Federal	Provincial	Credit Unions	Insurance Companies	Securities Dealers
Deposit taking	▓	▓	▓	▓	*	▓
Chequing accounts	▓	▓	▓	▓		Limited
Commercial lending	▓	Limited				
Mortgages on real property	▓	▓	▓	▓		▓
RRSP's	▓	▓	▓	▓		Limited
Estates Administration		▓	▓			
Securities Broking						▓
Issuance of insurance policies					▓	
Mutual Funds		▓	▓		▓	
Financial Leasing	▓	▓	▓		Limited	Unclear
Portfolio management	Limited	▓	▓		▓	
Underwriting	Limited					▓

* Some insurance companies are currently investigating an extension of their business to include deposit taking.

▓ Permitted

Source: David Petras, "Financial Products and Services Provided by Financial Institutions," Ontario Securities Commission, Meeting and Hearing on Discount Brokerage and the Role of Financial Markets, Toronto, September, 1983.

The figure tends to understate the degree to which the functions of the different financial institutions overlap. Some customers may have the opportunity of choosing among the listed activities or activities not included in the figure for meeting their financial needs. For example, some businesses seeking additional funds could be able to turn to financial leasing, to borrowing through either a commercial loan or a mortgage of its real property, or even to an issue of securities. Moreover, the commercial loan may be from any of a number of different institutions including chartered banks or sales finance companies. To the extent that borrowers have these choices, the distinctions are broken down among the four pillars. The same conclusion can be drawn for any activity which has close substitutes beyond its designated pillar.

A first step in research on the issue of separation would involve an analysis of the evolution of the four pillars concept. Certain aspects of the present division of responsibility for financial activity among the four pillars may have deep-rooted precedents which have been acknowledged and respected by policy makers in shaping the past developments of the Canadian financial system. On the other hand, the principle may be the rationalization for the absence of any change that could upset the status quo, even if the present arrangements were the outcome of a series of uncoordinated decisions taken by various independent regulatory authorities.

Evidence suggests that the balance among the four pillars has changed substantially over time. From 1954 onward, participation by banks in residential lending, traditionally a preserve of other elements of the four pillars, has increased with each successive Bank Act. The deposit-taking function of trust companies has also evolved from their pure trustee function[11] to such a degree that numerous trust companies do not perform any estate, trust and agency business and act solely as deposit-taking institutions. Similarly, both chartered banks and brokerage houses have established facilities through which their customers could obtain certain services for Registered Retirement Savings Plans that they could not obtain directly. These facilities involve much the same types of arrangements as the recent proposal through which banks would offer access to brokerage services. Interestingly enough, these steps into trustee activities did not provoke the same degree of controversy as the recent proposals for offering brokerage services through banks.

The second aspect of the four pillars question consists of an assessment of the rationale for maintaining a separation of different financial activities. The arguments in favour of maintaining the separation include increased potential for conflict of interest, efficient provision of financial services to lenders and borrowers, and concentration of power. Each of these arguments is considered in more detail below.

Many of the arguments for separation are based on the potential for conflict of interest. Accordingly, the sources of the apparent conflict need to be explored. Bank entry into trust activity and trust company entry into commercial lending in each case supposedly create a source of conflict of interest. The combination of commercial lending and trustee activity apparently leads to a conflict when the financial institution lends to an enterprise that also receives finance from one of its trust accounts. The financial institution is placed into conflict with respect to information it receives in its role as lender. Is its primary responsibility to its borrowing customer to maintain confidentiality, or is it to its trust account to reveal any substantive information? Some other conflicts of interest are less obvious. The prospect of conflict of interest needs to be explored for each possible combination of activities which are currently separated under the four pillars.

It should be recognized that the potential for conflict of interest can arise even under the existing arrangements. Trust companies currently can hold mortgages on properties which also may be mortgaged to trust accounts. The exercise of priority with respect to one of these claims could jeopardize the value of the other. Alternatively, acceptance of a reorganization proposal may benefit one of the interests but be detrimental to the other interest. Similarly, a court case with respect to the role of Canadian Imperial Bank of Commerce in the struggle for control of Crown Trust suggests that conflicts may arise from the interests of different customers in conducting commercial banking by itself.[12]

Any examination of the potential for conflict must resolve a variety of issues. First, the concept of conflict of interest should be clarified. Broadly speaking, some element of conflict arises in any customer or agency relationship. Can criteria be developed to establish the point at which conflicts of interest become unacceptable? Second, once some criteria for conflicts are derived, the question to be explored is the effects of reduced separation of financial institutions on the potential for increasing the costs of conflict. One of the goals of the proposed research would be to determine whether problems of conflict of interest expand markedly when the principle of separation is breached.

The concept of conflict of interest plays an important role in the justification of both issues of separation. Therefore, before the issue can be fully assessed, the concept must be defined carefully and its economic implications must be examined. A conflict of interest arises in a relationship where one party — the principal — delegates responsibility for some aspect of his interests to another party — the agent. A conflict occurs whenever the set of actions that would give the agents maximum benefit from the relationship differs from the set of actions that would attain the maximum benefit for the principal. Such conflicts occur in most contracts, in lawyer-client and doctor-patient relationships and between shareholders and management in corporations. In many instances, the conflicts do not present any problem. Norms of behaviour have evolved by which the principal can be reasonably assured of the limits to the agent's discretion. Any remaining conflict may be too expensive for the principal to eliminate entirely. The principal often has the opportunity to avoid excessive conflict by replacing his current agent with another.

The economic consequences of conflicts of interest in financial markets also need to be considered. The costs of any conflict to the principal depend on the amount of damage which can occur before the conflict is detected and the relationship discontinued. These steps may be easier in some cases than in others. A consumer — the principal — may be able to detect that a butcher — the agent — substitutes meat of inferior quality with some ease. The cost of such a conflict of interest to the consumer consists of the consumption of inferior meat for a short period of time. In financial markets, the situation can be very different in that the principal's wealth, or a large portion of it, is at stake. Failure to limit the scope for conflict in this case would be very costly.

So far conflicts of interest have been viewed solely as a question of distribution of wealth between principals and agents. Such conflicts may be undesirable from an ethical or moral viewpoint. From this viewpoint alone, regulation governing financial institutions may be directed to limiting the scope for conflict between principals and agents.

Still, the economic argument goes farther and considers the behaviour of principals in face of the anticipation of possible losses arising from conflict. They can be expected to protect themselves against any losses arising from conflict with their agents. When these costs are perceived to be excessive, they will find alternative ways of doing business. Although the need to monitor agents may be costly, it is important to note that from the economic standpoint alternative ways of doing business may involve even greater expense. In this case, regulations reducing the scope for conflict of interest could ultimately be beneficial to both principals and their agents.

This general discussion of the consequences of conflict of interest also applies to financial markets. The possibility of losses through such conflicts may deter households or businesses from pursuing arrangements which otherwise would be most efficient. In some cases, conflict may be inherent in the activity and therefore unavoidable. At other times, conflict may arise as an effect of existing policies which determine the permitted combinations of business. Thus, policy makers must be very careful in permitting different combinations of financial activities. The conflicts of interest in some combinations may be completely innocuous. In other cases, the combination may impose excessive costs on participants in ways which discourage them from using the most efficient arrangements for fulfilling their needs for financial services.

The consequences of further de-emphasis of the separation principle for the extent of conflict of interest cannot be determined solely by Canadian experience, particularly in those areas where the principle has been upheld. International comparisons of the circumstances where substantially different approaches have been followed may be instructive for Canadians. In the United States, for example, commercial banking has been combined with other activities, most notably trusteeship functions. One study of the conflicts of interest arising from such a combination concludes:

> The potential for serious conflict would seem on its face to be considerable. And there is scattered but convincing evidence of bank abuses in past years in accommodation loans and dispositions of estate property, holdings of trust cash in excess or at less than competitive rates, discriminatory treatment of customers of different status and power, and improprieties in the allocation of trust-generated brokerage. But these abuses do not appear ever to have reached massive proportions. . . . In short, legally enforced total separation of trust and commercial banking could not now be based on the level of present abuses and anticipated benefits to customers of trust or commercial banking services.[13]

Further investigation is needed to determine whether this judgment is justified. Moreover, such investigation would reveal the types of mechanisms which may be required to limit the scope of conflict.[14] Care must be taken to ensure that the different approaches taken elsewhere do not reflect the influence of a totally different environment. For example, certain approaches may be more appropriate for an economy with many banks than for one with relatively few large banks.

So far, the separation of financial activities has been judged in terms of its benefits. Just as important, however, is the assessment of the consequences of the four pillars for Canadian enterprises. The separation of financial institutions, in addition to preventing conflicts of interest and undue concentration of power, may also impose costs on participants in financial markets. Regulations which enforce this separation may prevent use of the least-cost methods of finance. These costs must be taken into account in judging the merits of the present approach to regulation.

The traditional approach to assessing the costs of financial regulation has been to identify so-called "gaps" in the availability of finance to particular sectors or types of financial institutions. This approach is not suitable for the kind of research suggested here because the concept of a gap is quite ambiguous in itself. It does not seem possible to set any standard in order to determine the adequacy of finance to any sector. Moreover, lack of lending for any purpose does not in itself signify any shortcoming in the regulation of financial markets. Rather, lending for that purpose may simply be inherently uneconomic. The expenses of such lending, including the costs of risks of default, may exceed the interest returns gained from making the loans.

An alternative way to measure the cost of maintaining separate financial institutions is to consider the additional expense to Canadian borrowers and lenders. Certainly any comprehensive study into the workings of Canadian financial markets must be directed toward judging whether regulation adds to their cost. International comparisons of costs of lending and borrowing and the spreads between these costs for particular types of business provide one approach to this issue.[15] Such comparisons are limited in their applicability, however, because of different economic circumstances. Export finance, for example, may be more costly in one country than in another because of different risks and costs arising from the composition of exports, their destinations, and even the variability of the country's exchange rate. Any research into the costs of separation would have to rely to a large degree on indirect evidence. Do businesses incur extra costs in moving among a variety of financial institutions for different needs? Do these costs force Canadian small and medium-sized businesses to rely excessively on some forms of finance — for example, bank loans — at the expense of others? Would the Canadian business sector be stronger if greater equity participation together with infusion of management skills by financial institutions into business enterprise were possible?

While the existence of comprehensive financial institutions, offering a wide variety of different services, may have advantages to customers, there may be a cost in terms of reduced competition. Some observers fear that any further move to break down barriers between different financial services will lead to concentration of business in few comprehensive financial institutions.[16] Such an outcome is not inevitable but depends on the economies of scale in performing different financial activities and the economies of scope in combining different activities. Existing evidence on this issue of economies can be judged as no more than equivocal, on the basis of research conducted in the United States.[17] Still it seems likely that lowering barriers to each type of financial activity would increase the number of potential entrants for each activity.

A concern exists that decreased competition in financial markets might offset any other benefits to customers by leading to a higher spread between lending and borrowing rates. Such a conclusion rests on two questionable assumptions. First, the consolidation of financial activities within the scope of a few financial institutions is assumed to lead to less competition in any activity relative to the current situation, in which financial activities are separated. But any financial activity may already have less potential for competition since the present arrangements governing firms in some activities precludes them from participating in others. Second, the prospect of new entry into financial activity may become more limited as the financial system becomes consolidated into a few financial institutions. It is not clear, however, that specialized institutions would be unable to continue to compete with larger, comprehensive financial institutions. Indeed, the recent experience of trust companies and credit unions shows they can still be competitive with comprehensive institutions like chartered banks on a variety of margins.

It is difficult to conceive of research which could predict the consequences of forsaking the present separation. International comparisons could indicate whether financial services are offered as cheaply in economies with comprehensive financial institutions as in others. Still, care must be taken not to avoid extrapolating results from very different environments.

The possible consolidation of the financial system into a relatively few institutions raises one further issue which goes well beyond the scope of economics. The change may alter the political balance among different economic interests. At present, each type of financial institution represents its separate interests to legislators and policy makers. Often, as illustrated in the Ontario Securities Commission's hearings about bank entry into the securities business, the interests do not coincide among different types of institutions. Moreover, each type of institution is subject to different jurisdictions.

In contrast, with consolidation of institutions, a more uniform message would be delivered to a more limited range of policy makers, each of whom would have broader powers than at present. It may be that the prime justification for the enforcement of a separation of financial activities is based on objections to the presence of such a concentrated interest group, rather than on any purely economic argument.

The assessment of the separation approach to regulation must also take into account the future effects of changing technology, which may make it the much more difficult to maintain the existing separate powers in financial markets. The costs and benefits of the existing assignment of powers may be altered substantially over the near future. For example, at present deposits at chartered banks, trust companies, caisses populaires and credit unions all are recognized as serving as part of the means of payment. Will changing computer technology mean that balances or lines of credit at stock brokerages, insurance companies, and department stores will all perform the same role before long? Does changing computer technology mean that the costs of avoiding "department store finance" will become excessive? What aspects of "department store finance" can be adopted without jeopardizing basic principles?

In addition, it should be noted that the pressures of changing technology need not affect all the separations among powers in the same way. Experience in the United States suggests that deposit taking is now an easily entered activity. Historically, Canadian trust companies have accepted deposits for a long time. But so have insurance companies to a limited degree. U.S. investment houses offer accounts which are indistinguishable from the most comprehensive accounts offered by banks. As a first impression, it would appear that the separation of trustee, insurance, and securities business would be eroded less by technology than would deposit taking. This question still remains to be answered more thoroughly through research.

The implications for regulation of the effects of technology on the separation of powers also appears to be a priority topic for research. In particular, in what way does the movement of institutions into new areas alter the effectiveness of measures for customer safety? Will new institutions performing deposit-taking functions fit under existing deposit insurance arrangements? Alternatively, do new functions of insured institutions alter the risks of the deposit insurer? Finally, will the changing importance of different types of institutions alter the effectiveness of national ownership rules?

A wide range of approaches can be taken to the regulation of the financial industry. At one extreme, the day-to-day activities of financial institutions can be monitored and judged under authority granted by legislation. Various sanctions can be imposed, ranging from prohibition or desist orders to changed requirements in terms of capital or cash reserves. At the other extreme, broad legislative powers may be established with the regulator's role confined to assuring these powers are not exceeded. Canadian practice varies among institutions and has changed over time.[18]

The research proposed in this area would be directed toward documenting the approaches taken toward different types of financial institutions. A variety of questions would be considered. To what degree are different institutions performing similar activities subject to markedly different approaches to regulation? To what extent has the approach applied to any set of institutions evolved in recent years? Can differences in approach be explained in terms of different needs of institutions and their customers? Does the diversity of approach offer any lessons with respect to the benefits of one approach to regulation in contrast to others?

The approach to regulation is one area in which concern must be directed toward customer or depositor safety. Do differences in approach, for example, result from differences in the assumed sophistication of customers? A related question concerns the relationship of regulations governing different financial institutions to current arrangements for depositor protection through deposit insurance and similar schemes. To what degree are governments aware of the financial responsibility they have undertaken through deposit insurance?

The responsibility of government or its agents when financial institutions fail is a final aspect of the approach toward regulation which must be considered. Do deposit insurers and other regulators have established procedures or must all failures be treated on an ad hoc basis? To what extent do deposit insurers attempt to protect interests other than insured depositors? Does the protection of interests other than insured deposits increase the risks faced by the deposit insurer? If it does, are present deposit insurance arrangements appropriate and, if not, what changes should be made?

Going ahead with this proposed research does not require an identical or even similar approach for each type of financial institution. On the contrary, the approaches taken should meet the varying needs of each set of financial institutions and their customers. On the other hand, the apparent trend to more detailed oversight and intervention would appear to require scrutiny in terms of its merits.

The problem of jurisdiction differs in kind from the other research issues discussed so far. Resolving federal-provincial conflict in the area of financial institutions need not be a goal in itself; rather, it is a means by which the most appropriate framework for the regulation of financial markets can be achieved. Were the federal-provincial issue absent, each of the other issues could be considered in isolation and the preferred alternatives could be pursued by the appropriate authorities. Divided jurisdiction, or even competing jurisdiction, constrains the alternatives available to the policy makers.[19]

Differences in jurisdiction are not solely a source of conflict. Parallel jurisdictions over the same or similar activities can serve as sources of experimentation and innovation. The experience of differing jurisdictions may serve to indicate the desirability of different types of regulation.

Research into the assignment of responsibility among jurisdictions and its consequences may reveal the feasibility of alternative approaches to regulation.[20] Awareness of divided jurisdiction and its attendant problems must be an integral part of any proposal for change. In addition, identification of problems in the working of financial markets should be followed in many cases by an examination of the role of divided jurisdiction in creating them. Similarly, the feasibility of any proposals for change on the probability of their acceptance in a divided jurisdiction.

The problem of jurisdiction is especially acute in modifying the separation principle, because the pillars differ according to jurisdiction. Banks are primarily federal institutions, while brokerage is a provincial matter. Trust and insurance both face divided jurisdiction. Moreover, as the recent hearings of the Ontario Securities Commission illustrate, the question remains open whether provincial authorities have regulatory powers over federal institutions in terms of their participation in provincially regulated activities.

Both the Porter Commission and the Economic Council attached importance to the organization of the payments system. At the time the Porter Commission was being conducted, this system consisted entirely of the cheque clearing arrangements system run by the Canadian Bankers' Association. Now these arrangements have been expanded under the Canadian Payments Association to permit all deposit institutions to participate on the same basis.

The Economic Council concerned itself with the form of the "payments system of the future." Clear signs existed in the early 1970s that the computer created the potential to revolutionize the relationship between financial institutions and their customers through devices such as automated tellers and point-of-sale terminals. While the computer revolution in payments arrangement has been slower to materialize than expected, substantial changes can be foreseen in the next few years.

The evolution of the computer payments system poses a number of policy issues which parallel to some degree the former issues of the cheque clearing system. Foremost is the organizational structure of the system. At present, automated tellers are placed in branches and offer both convenience and after-hours service. The next step would appear to be de-emphasis of the branch, with independent automated tellers in public locations such as shopping centres and office complexes. The point-of-sale terminal also offers the prospect of obtaining payments services outside of banking premises. In both cases, questions of ownership and organization arise. Will common automatic tellers be developed by which customers can gain access to some or even all financial institutions? Would they be permitted under existing policies, including competition policy? Essentially the same issues are raised by the development of point-of-sale terminals.

The choices with respect to public policy are diverse. At one extreme would be a complete laissez-faire policy in which organization forms arising from private initiatives are accepted. At the other extreme, the need for government ownership of the payments mechanism might be argued on grounds parallel, say, to the Post Office or the Canadian Broadcasting Corporation. Many distrust the laissez-faire solution for fear that some institutions become excluded from the arrangements. On the other hand, the Economic Council argued strenuously against the prospect of a government-owned system because of concerns about innovation and efficiency. Between these extremes are many other possibilities. Many of the intermediate arrangements pose problems in themselves. To what extent do cooperative arrangements for payments services among certain financial institutions conflict with existing competition policy?

The vast advances in computer technology suggest that these questions should not be delayed any further, subject to the possibility that current inaction itself can be viewed as a policy. More and more institutions appear to be making commitments to future payments technologies despite uncertainties about future policies. As has been suggested earlier, uncertainties in policy may be costly in terms of discouraging the appropriate response of business to new opportunities.

Direct Financial Markets

Many of the same research issues raised with respect to financial institutions also apply to direct financial markets. Indeed, traders in securities and underwriters comprise one of the four pillars of financial markets discussed above. The institutions in direct markets also service the security issuers, discussed in the next section. Questions such as the regulation of security offerings and the rules governing takeovers are left until then. Several issues remain to be considered with respect to direct markets themselves. The most prominent include the concentration of invested funds in institutions and the role of public pension funds in financial markets.

Private pension funds and, to a lesser degree, mutual funds account for a sizable proportion of the funds invested in Canadian equities. By mid-1983, over $75 billion had been accumulated in trusteed pension funds. In many respects, these institutions resemble any other investor — they strive for the highest returns subject to maintaining acceptable levels of risk. In other respects, these funds are different. Overall, the securities that pension funds may hold are limited to securities which have met certain standards with respect to past performance.

The equities held by pension funds must meet the requirements set out in the regulation of the Pension Benefits Standards Act. Under these regulations, pension funds may hold

> the fully paid common shares of a corporation where during a period of five years that ended less than one year before the date of investment, the corporation
> i) paid in each of at least four of the five years, including the last year of that period, a dividend on its common shares, or
> ii) earned in each of at least four of the five years, including the last year of that period, an amount available for the payment of a dividend upon its common shares of at least four per cent of the average value at which the issued common shares of the corporation were carried in the capital stock account of the corporation during the year in which the dividend was paid or in which the amount was earned.[21]

These requirements are supplemented by other requirements, less important for present purposes, which limit the holdings of a pension fund in any enterprise to less than 30 percent of the outstanding shares. An additional outlet for equity investment is provided by the so-called "basket clause," which permits any pension fund to hold up to 7 percent of its portfolio in assets that are not otherwise eligible.

It has been argued that this accumulation of institutional funds, together with the eligibility requirement, has resulted in a two-tier stock market in which the institutions concentrate their equity holdings among a small array of large established corporations.[22] Firms in the second tier, whose securities are not held by these institutions, find the raising of funds through the stock more difficult, given the other characteristics of the firm. The research issues here are several. To what extent can two separate tiers be identified in the stock market? In addition, can it be determined that firms that are not held by institutional investors are at a disadvantage relative to firms in the first tier? To what extent is a division in the equity market a consequence of regulation which governs the portfolio choices of funds? If it is, to what extent can the intentions of such regulation be realized by alternative means?

The problem of the two-tier securities market, if it exists, could have been aggravated by the severe recession of the earlier 1980s. As seen above, some eligibility tests for pension investment are defined in terms of recent performance with respect to earnings and dividends. To the extent that poor economic performance causes the securities of an enterprise to lose their eligibility, the ability of the firm to finance expansion or new activities will deteriorate. Therefore, there seems to be a strong justification for conducting a study of the eligibility requirements for pension fund investment.

A parallel issue in direct financial markets is the increasing importance of public sector pensions. Unlike the case in other provinces, part of the funds collected under the Quebec Pension Plan are invested in securities issued by private firms. On a small scale, such pensions funds are like any other portfolio investment. They are made solely for investment purposes without any concern for a voice in the running of the enterprise. More recently, the body investing the QPP balances has shown an increasing interest in participating in the management of some of the enterprises in which it invests. The involvement of public pension funds in private industry raises somewhat different issues than those encountered in Crown corporations, outright nationalization or even joint ventures. In each of these cases, government intervention is explicit and well recognized. With the pension fund investment, government participation may not be as apparent to other investors. What responsibilities or limitations should public pension funds accept in the investment of their balances?

Securities Issuers

The final group of participants in financial markets are the issuers of securities — for present purposes, business enterprises. This group raises the three research issues: the regulation of security offerings, rules governing takeovers, and the tax treatment of corporate income.

Firms have a variety of choices with respect to finance. At one extreme, bank borrowing may be the simplest. Firms do not have to produce elaborate documentation of their present and proposed activities. Rather, the information requirements are met by the banks with the cooperation of the borrower. At the other extreme are public offerings where the documentation must be carried out by the securities issuer. In between are the private offerings where the securities may be issued to a limited group without the same degree of documentation as required for public issues.

The documentation requirements for public issues arise out of a concern for the "typical investor." The costs of generating such information on an individual basis may discourage investment. Documentation requirements serve to reduce the costs of scrutiny by others. Such gains come at some expense; the firm faces costs of assembling documentation and, in some cases, putting its affairs into conformity with the requirements of securities law. Research in this area would be directed toward the effects of regulations on the issues of securities. Do these regulations adequately protect shareholders? Are smaller and medium-sized firms effectively discouraged from using this means of finance?[23] To what extent do differences among jurisdictions impose excessive costs on security issuers? Can differences among jurisdictions be maintained without imposing excessive costs on security issuers? Are there more effective means for maintaining safeguards for investors at the same time as reducing costs of business?[24]

The economist views the takeovers as a device in the market economy which helps to enforce efficiency on corporate management. Economists devote considerable attention to mergers and takeovers from the standpoint of industrial organization, but less attention is directed to takeovers from the viewpoint of efficiency within the firm. In recent years, Canada has experienced many takeover initiatives, some successful and others not. Some of these takeovers have received publicity through the efforts of current management to defend against the take-over attempt — e.g, Royal Trust, Inland Transmission and Nova Scotia Trust. In some cases, agreements have been reached between bidder and target in which the bidder agrees to limit its holdings of the target company's shares. In addition, policy changes have been made which alter the prospects of successful takeovers. The Ontario Securities Commission has limited the ease of bidding for control holdings. Similarly, proposals have been made to alter the tax treatment of funds borrowed to finance takeovers.

Many of these measures appear to have had the effect of making takeovers more costly. Such measures may be understandable from the viewpoint of existing management, which tends to view the prospects of a takeover as detrimental. Yet takeovers can be in the interest of other shareholders. Steps which have limited the prospect of takeovers or have made them more expensive may be against the interests of shareholders at large.

Research in this area would be directed toward determining the workings of the takeover mechanism in Canada. Has it served to limit the inefficiencies of corporate management? What sorts of obstacles are there to the takeover mechanism and what are their effects? Do these obstacles have a rationale in terms of other objectives and are they appropriate from the standpoint of the various interests involved?

Questions of taxation cannot be ignored in examination of the workings of financial markets. Both the portfolio choices of investors and the financing decisions of borrowers are shaped by taxation. Two areas appear to have priority with respect to research. First, an unfinished agenda remains from the comprehensive recommendations of the Carter Commission with respect to the integration of the corporate and personal income tax. Recent research in the United States has documented both the limited contribution of the corporate income tax to revenue and its substantial distorting effects on corporate decisions.

It also has become increasingly apparent that the interaction of the Canadian tax system and inflation has produced a number of unanticipated effects of the tax burden on business enterprises. While it might be anticipated that inflation will cease to be such a problem in the future, it may be inappropriate to continue in the long term with a tax system which can be distorted by inflation. Indeed, the recent Lortie committee, while not analyzing "the feasibility of implementing an inflation correction of the tax system for business income," did recommend a major study on the issue.[25] While a large study of taxation is currently underway at the Economic Council and while such a topic is undoubtedly within the purview of the taxation group at this Royal Commission, emphasis is needed in terms of the impact of the tax system on financing decisions of business enterprises.

A final issue related to the corporate income tax should be mentioned. Many observers have expressed concern about the structure of liabilities of Canadian corporations — in particular, with respect to the debt service in relation to cash flow and, until recently, the relation of new debt to equity issues. To some extent, these problems have been reduced by the retreat of interest rates from the levels of recent years. Moreover, one important source of new equity for firms has been retention of earnings. The question has been raised whether the present structure of corporate liabilities is an adequate foundation for a strong economic recovery. This issue involves a number of themes already discussed. To what extent is the current situation a result of the incentives of the tax system or of recent high levels of inflation? Do the incentives arising from these sources jeopardize the stability of the corporate structure? To the extent that these concerns are judged valid, they reinforce the need to examine the effects of the corporate income tax on the financing decisions of business enterprises.

Notes

This paper was completed in June, 1984. I am indebted to Don McFetridge for his guidance and to many others for their helpful comments at various stages.

1. Royal Commission on the Economic Union and Development Prospects for Canada, *A Commission on Canada's Future* (Ottawa: Minister of Supply and Services Canada, 1983), p. 14.

2. One area which is not considered here is the finance of small business. The decision to omit this topic reflects the recent collection of research conducted under the auspices of the Small Business Financing Review section of the Department of Industry, Trade and Commerce, Ottawa. See the following working papers sponsored by them: Thorne Riddell and Thorne Stevenson and Kellog in cooperation with Canadian Facts Limited, "Small Business Venture Capital: Supply and Demand Analysis"; Facsyn Research, "Small Business Financing and Non-Bank Financial Institutions"; Edward Hughes, "The Implicit Subsidy in Federal Credit Programs"; D.G. McFetridge, "A Framework for Analysis: The Effect of Small Business Subsidies"; and James Whipp, Edward Hughes and J.R. D'Cruz, "A Profile of Small Business in Canada." See also James Hatch, Larry Wynant and Mary Jane Grant, "Federal Lending Programs for Small Business: No Longer Needed," *Canadian Public Policy* 9 (September 1983): 362–73.

3. The last bank failure in Canada was the Home Bank in 1923. Moreover, despite the much publicized failure of Greymac and associated companies in 1983, the Canadian Deposit Insurance Corporation had previously been required only twice to meet claims resulting from the failure of financial institutions. Nevertheless, it has been argued that a number of potential failures have been averted in the past through timely takeovers.

4. The five largest chartered banks account for approximately 90 percent of total bank assets. In turn, the chartered banks hold 45 percent of the assets of major financial institutions.

5. Royal Commission on Banking and Finance, *Report* (Ottawa: Queen's Printer, 1964).

6. *Ibid.*, p. 374.

7. Quebec, *Report of the Study Committee on Financial Institutions* (Quebec), pp. 203–204.

8. Some recent innovations in Canadian finance are aptly described by C. Freedman, "Financial Innovation in Canada: Causes and Consequences," *American Economic Review* 73 (May 1983) 101–106.

9. Royal Commission on Banking and Finances, *Report*, p. 378.

10. Economic Council of Canada, *Efficiency and Regulation: A Study of Deposit Institutions* (Ottawa: Minister of Supply and Services Canada, 1976), p. 60.

11. Even today these deposits are treated as legally distinct from bank deposits. Referring to deposits at federal trust companies, David Petras states that they "are in the nature of a trust as opposed to the debtor-creditor relationship established between a bank and its customers in respect to deposits accepted by the bank. . . . Subsection 113(1) of the Ontario Loan and Trust Corporations Act provides that a registered trust company does not have the power to *borrow* money by taking deposits. Section 115, however, empowers a provincial trust company . . . to *receive* deposits of money . . . and deems such companies to hold such deposits as trustee. . . ." in "Financial Product and Services Provided by Financial Institutions," a paper prepared for the meeting and hearing of the Ontario Securities Commission on Discount Brokerage and the Role of Financial Institutions, Toronto, September, 1983.

12. See Allan Robinson, "Court Tests Bank's Conflict of Interest," *Globe and Mail*, November 12, 1983, p. B1.

13. Edward S. Herman, *Conflicts of Interest: Commercial Bank Trust Departments* (Westport, Conn.: Quorum Books, 1980), pp. 123 and 126.

14. One such mechanism which should be considered is so-called "networking," by which an institution would be enabled to deliver financial services to its customers which are generated by other institutions. This compromise solution is viewed as a

way to maintain separation while permitting a range of services at one institution. The degree to which this proposal overcomes the problem of conflict of interest is not clear as many conflicts are inherent in delivery as in generation of financial services.

15. A start in this direction is provided by a study which compares bank loan yield spreads of Canadian and American banks. See George Lermer, "The Performance of Canadian Banking," *Canadian Journal of Economics* 13 (November 1980): 587–93.

16. This concern with concentration of power can be traced back as far as the Royal Commission on Banking and Finance, *Report*, 1964, p. 10. A similar concern has been expressed recently by the Joint Securities Industry Committee, *Report* (September 19, 1984), pp. 19–20.

17. In a recent article, Murray and White examine economies of scale and economies of scope in B.C. credit unions using a sample of 61 locals. They find evidence of both economies of scale and complementarity or jointness in production. See John D. Murray and Robert W. White, "Economies of Scale and Economies of Scope in Multiproduct Financial Institutions: A Study of British Columbia Credit Unions," *Journal of Finance* (June 1983): 887–902. In contrast, two studies of life insurance by Mathewson find little evidence of economies of scale but some evidence of economies of scope. See G.F. Mathewson with John Todd, *Information, Entry and Regulation in Markets for Life Insurance* (Toronto: University of Toronto Press, 1982), and S. Kellner and G.F. Mathewson, "Entry, Size Distribution and Scope Economies in the Life Insurance Industry," *Journal of Business* (January 1983): 25–44. For a different point of view, see R. Geehan, "Returns to Scale in the Life Insurance Industry," *Bell Journal of Economics* 8 (1977): 497–514.

18. The contrast in approaches to regulation can be illustrated by the comparing treatment of trust companies and chartered banks. A borrowing limit is established by regulators for each individual trust company even in the presence of a statutory limit. No formal limit exists to the borrowing powers of Schedule A chartered banks.

19. One area where divided jurisdiction appears to have created problems is the ability to change a regulatory framework. The Bank Act, which governs only federally chartered institutions, has been revised in 1954, 1967 and 1980. In addition, the ceiling to foreign bank activity was raised expeditiously in 1984. In contrast, proposed changes in trust company legislation, where some cooperation between federal and provincial authorities is required, have been delayed.

20. For further discussion of these issues, see John F. Chant, "Comment on the 1977 Bank Act," *Canadian Public Policy* 2 (Summer 1976): 380, and John F. Chant and James W. Dean, "An Approach to the Regulation of Banking Institutions in a Federal State," *Osgoode Hall Law Journal* 20 (December 1982): 721–44.

21. Canada, Pension Benefits Standard Act, *Pension Benefits Standards Regulations*, Schedule III, 1(p), as amended October 26, 1979.

22. P. Lortie, "The Case for Fixed Commission Rates in Canada," a report prepared for the Montreal Stock Exchange, April, 1975, cited by J.P. Williamson, "Canadian Financial Institutions," *Proposals for a Securities Market Law for Canada*, vol. 3 (Ottawa: Department of Consumer and Corporate Affairs Canada, 1979).

23. Economic Council of Canada finds, for example, that "the number of small initial public offerings of industrial shares (less than $2 million) in the United States in the period 1977–81 was 234 times the Canadian number. . . . Over the same period, there were no initial public offerings in Canada of less than $500,000 while there were 130 such cases in the United States. . . ." The Council notes that differences in regulation do not appear to explain this difference but suggests that either new regulations in the United States reduce the time involved in underwriting approvals or differences in capital gains taxation may be responsible. See Economic Council of Canada, *Intervention and Efficiency: A Study of Government Credit and Credit Guarantees to the Private Sector* (Ottawa: Minister of Supply and Services Canada, 1982), pp. 28–29.

24. For the discussion of a recent experiment reducing the informational requirements for firms having common shares with a market value of at least $100 million, see Allan Robinson, "New Financing Rules Pull in Major Firms," *Globe and Mail*, Monday, November 12, 1983, p. B1.

25. Ministerial Advisory Committee on Inflation and the Taxation of Personal Investment Income, *Report* (Ottawa: Minister of Supply and Services Canada, 1982), p. 44.

5

Economic Regulation in Canada
A Survey

KEITH ACHESON

If to regulate is to control and direct economic activity, then to deregulate is to return to a state of nature. Clearly, that is not the purpose of advocates of deregulation. What they do propose is replacing the present system of regulation with a system that relies more on market forces, on voluntary contractual relations, and on private decision-making. In contrast, no simple regulatory structure applicable to any and all industries is advocated in this paper. Instead, the paper assesses progress in understanding existing regulation and the ability of the political process to absorb and intelligently use any advances in reforming or modifying the system.

To examine the efficacy of the political system, traditional economic analysis is applied in a manner that may appear unconventional to some. Regulation is treated as a product, albeit an extremely complex product, for which there is an identifiable political process for determining its detailed composition. If Canadian industries are being regulated badly compared with what could be, something must be wrong with the mechanism whereby regulatory regimes are regulated.

There are two possible ways of improving that mechanism. If the political system reacts to better information about the effects of regulation by introducing socially beneficial changes, attention can be addressed to providing better information economically. If instead better information is ignored and not embodied in the regulatory product, there is no point in investing in more information. Improvement in the "product" will then require that the political process itself be reformed. I begin by developing a stylized view of the market for regulation and then examining the incentive structure for doing research and development (R&D) on improving regulation.

The other task of the paper is to survey selectively what is known about the regulatory system in Canada. Not long ago, one could have surveyed this area exhaustively in less time than it has taken to prepare this selective survey. However, within the last five years there has been a dramatic increase in competent studies of regulatory processes.

The complete economic regulatory structure is extremely complicated, encompassing all the details and nuances of the legal system, the tax and subsidy system, government expenditure, activities and decisions of government departments, Crown corporations, and rules under which clubs and cooperatives operate, as well as the structure of constraints under which private profit-oriented activities operate. Regulation in a narrower sense includes those general or specific activities that are regulated by a government-created group exercising discretion in performing its duties. This group may take the form of a regulatory commission or of a board within a government department. For the purpose of discussing the mechanism for choosing regulatory systems, my comments apply to both broad and narrow regulation. The survey of existing regulation is limited to narrow regulation.

A Stylized View of the Market for Regulation in Canada

A democratic government chooses the regulatory structure, and enforcement of the rules and provisions of the structure ultimately relies on the authority of that government. The government is elected and operates under constitutional constraints. The right to govern may be instructively viewed as a monopoly franchise that is "auctioned" in periodically held elections.

Elections are contested by parties that vie to win the exclusive right to govern.[1] Parties present slates of candidates and so a comprehensive competence can be obtained while permitting individual candidates to specialize in their areas of expertise. The party organization, its brand image, and its internal communication codes are valuable assets. Like a corporation or a club, the party offers continuity, a durability which transcends the lifetime of its present representatives and permits rewards to be reaped from current investments in terms of enhanced chances of winning over a long future period.

Parties are ranked by each voter depending on his or her expectation of what the party will do in office. In assessing the expected portfolio of regulatory policies of the parties, the voter must ascertain the effects of these policies on the attributes of life that he or she cares about. Some model of the way the world works is necessary to achieve this translation.

The typical voter has a dim awareness of the bewildering array of regulatory systems that might be put in place, and even a dimmer awareness of the consequences of any of them for fuel prices, the type of movies that will show at the local cinema, and the like. In a sense, it would be a waste if individuals studied all the arcane cases before the Canadian Radio-television and Telecommunications Commission or the Canadian Transport Commission and sifted through the economic literature for whatever nuggets of wisdom were concealed in it, instead of learning occupational skills or enjoying their leisure time.

Most voters choose a party as an agent to do the necessary study and sifting. The selection depends on an assessment of a generally described portfolio of policies, an appraisal of past performance, and any other information that helps voters predict what the party will do in various contingencies and how that will affect them. Voters are influenced in their assessments by the opinions of their peers, the cases made by the candidates, the opinions of associations to which they belong, remarks on talk shows, and information from a host of other sources.

Some groups may perceive a return from investing in informing voters, or even in misinforming them. Voters correct for the bias in information from sources known to have an interest in the outcome. Whether they overcorrect or undercorrect is not obvious. The listener knows that the message, like advertising in consumer durable markets, combines hype and selected information.

Despite the existence of partisan and impartial information sources and the fact that a voter may be better informed on policy matters connected with his or her employment, the voter is usually a very uninformed "buyer" and has little incentive to alter this status. In commercial markets, institutional arrangements often adapt, so that gains from trading occur even when buyers are at an informational disadvantage. Reputations for quality, brand names, and sunk investments, like product-specific advertising, are examples. Similarly, political institutions may be designed to ameliorate the effects of voter ignorance. Certainly, parties develop brand images and invest heavily in advertising that has no value in alternative activities.

Political competition differs from economic rivalry, and political parties differ in important ways from corporations,[2] but studying the process by which regulatory regimes are chosen from an industrial organization perspective is enlightening. In that framework, a regulatory regime would be classified as an "experience" good. Its qualities are discovered after purchase; its producers are disciplined not to take advantage of a buyer's ignorance by the desire to retain the buyer's custom.

All parties invest in selling themselves to voters as agents to be trusted and in promoting their own vision of what is socially possible and desirable. An incumbent party promotes models linking actions and outcomes that put its record in a good light, while the opposition does the opposite. Each party also attempts to discern exogenous changes in the evaluations of voters and in the causal models that they hold, so it can tailor its promises accordingly.

A party that is chosen to govern must do two things — provide a detailed regulatory structure and simultaneously translate what it is doing into a simple story that can be sold to a generally uninformed electorate. In the narrow area of regulation, the government must implicitly and explicitly decide on the discretionary scope it will give its agents, the regulators, the boundaries over which boards will have jurisdiction, the overlap with other government boards and boards of other levels of government, and the mechanisms imposed to control regulators, so that their actions will enhance the government's re-election chances. Decisions will be made on the budgetary process, the length of tenure of board members, the characteristics of regulators, the size and nature of the support staff, the career opportunities that will be open to board members when their term ends, restrictions on activities that can be undertaken while a board member or for some prescribed time after leaving office, and so on.

The detailed regulatory structure will be designed according to the idiosyncratic pattern in which industries or firms mesh in the social framework. The government may give agricultural marketing boards more extensive powers to control production and limit imports at the same time that it is relaxing entry conditions and pricing constraints in the airline industry. Both initiatives may be marketed under a slogan of "responsible regulation" or "opportunities for everyone" or some other elastic caption.

Hearings and proceedings of the boards also play an educational or marketing role in making diverse groups aware of the political constraints facing the government. By funding the representation of groups, which are politically potent but would not be represented without subsidies, and encouraging the appearance at hearings of other officials, such as the director of competition, the government permits more information about the general political support or opposition to alternative resolutions of an issue to flow not only to the regulatory board but also to organized supplier and user groups.[3]

The auction market in which the contest for the right to govern is decided is in itself a highly regulated one. The secret ballot, rules on registering to vote, processes for financing participation, reporting requirements on campaign spending, systems for allocating "free" time on radio and television are all examples of regulations that make the market for regulations perform differently than it otherwise would.

Research and Development for Better Regulatory Policies

Given this sketch of the market for regulations, what are the incentives to invest resources in conceiving and developing "better" regulatory systems rather than waiting for someone else to do it? If a political party develops a new technique, it cannot file for a patent or copyright to exclude rivals from aping the concept and incorporating the idea or its essence in their policy portfolios. Resources will not be invested in developing new policies if a benefit cannot be appropriated. Some incentive is preserved if other political parties are prevented from co-opting the idea because it clashes with their ideological roots or is not consistent with other elements of their platforms, but ideology and consistency are often loose constraints. In the commercial sector, trade secrecy can provide protection from piracy while a new product is being developed and after its introduction, if consumption or ownership of the product does not reveal the secret (for example, the aging process for a liquor). Secrecy offers protection in politics only while a policy is being developed. Once a new policy is included in a platform and revealed to the public, it is also revealed to rivals.

That there is an appropriability problem in politics is perhaps revealed by the very few resources that are visibly allocated to the research and development of new policies by the parties. Considering the magnitude of economic problems, it appears ironic that the research and development units of a firm making a personal computer would be better staffed and funded than the research wings of contending political parties.

In the commercial sector, if patents, copyright, and trade secrecy fail to provide sufficient incentive for private investment in generating new knowledge, as is the case with basic research, public investment may expand to fill the void (for example, the National Research Council). With respect to economic regulation, publicly funded research occurs in the universities, in the Economic Council of Canada, in provincial bodies such as the Ontario Economic Council, and in policy research centres (some of which are jointly funded with private concerns or charitable foundations). There is research funded by various government departments and there are reports by legislative committees, by royal commissions, and by the regulatory bodies themselves. Although much of this research is publicly funded, not all of it is publicly available. An asymmetry exists between the government and other contending parties because the former's access to resources in department and other governmental bodies gives it an advantage over other parties in developing a detailed regulatory structure.

Viewed from an industrial organization perspective, the right to govern is contestable, but not perfectly so; the incumbent has an advantage. The government can finance social R&D from the public purse and appropriate a benefit from it by restricting access to the information while policy is being formulated. Reducing this barrier would make political competition more virulent, but social innovation may be retarded since the government's incentive to fund R&D is diminished.

The above discussion is in the public choice tradition, where economic analysis is applied to political processes. This area of study has been relatively neglected in Canada. A handful of Canadian economists have made important contributions to public choice,[4] but it has not received the attention that it warrants. Citizens make extremely important economic decisions through voting. But with some exceptions, economists did not participate in the deliberations leading to recent constitutional reform in Canada, despite a widely held political and professional view that the economy was not being managed well.

If shoddy cars were being delivered to Canadians, it would be natural to call for an investigation of the automotive industry and to consider structural remedies. The first response would not be to determine through a task force whether iron engine blocks should be replaced by aluminum blocks, and then expect the industry to be reformed when its members learned the results of the investigation. If the industry already knew the comparative advantage of one metal over another for this purpose, nothing would be changed by so informing them. What should be addressed in this hypothetical example is why the industry was making the wrong choice.

To relate the analogy to the production of regulations, it should first be determined whether the problem is that governments and parties do not know what is the "best" regulatory regime, or whether they do know but would not be rewarded politically for advocating it. If the problem is a mix of the two, what is the relevant importance of each? The imperatives for research are profoundly affected by one's diagnosis of the malady. In one case, political system reforms are appropriate; in the other, better information on the causal relations in the economy are.

Unfortunately, no professional consensus exists concerning the efficiency of Canadian political processes in producing a regulatory environment for economic activity. To permit the reader to assess whether political decisions are capably reflecting the present state of economic knowledge, the next section presents a selective review of recent work. The quantity of good quality theoretical and applied research done at the universities, at think tanks, and at other institutions has increased dramatically over the last two decades. This review illustrates the complexity of many of the issues faced in designing a regulatory structure.

Basic Research

Just as basic research in the physical sciences has been concentrated in government and university laboratories, basic research with respect to the comparative advantage of different regulatory structures has been done predominately by academics. Much has been learned in the last decade; unfortunately, many of the theoretical developments have increased the information necessary to rank alternatives. Although one might wish that theoretical improvements would permit the advocacy of competition or monopoly or some standard regime as the best form for all situations, the reverse has occurred. There are many identified situations where theory suggests that welfare would be improved by removing restrictions on trade, and many where increasing the restrictions on trade would be desirable. Indeed, it is difficult to identify a trading practice or regulatory measure that would always be welfare decreasing.[5]

The theoretical developments that have had an impact on applied work in regulation are numerous. The notion of market contestability and its relationship to attributes of a multi-product cost function has had considerable influence. This analysis stresses that competitive pressures on the pricing of incumbents in an industry depend not on the number of actors in the industry but rather on the ease with which other actors can enter or leave the industry. If there are no sunk costs and an entrant has access to the same technology as an incumbent, a single producer is forced to price at the same level that an ideal regulator, constrained to break-even prices, would have chosen. In these circumstances, potential competition effectively disciplines prices by a sole supplier. No monopoly profit will be earned despite the fact that the market is supplied by one firm, and entry by inefficient producers can be determined through appropriate price decisions by the incumbent. (To accomplish the latter, different prices may have to be charged for different units of services consumed.)

By focusing attention on the conditions of entry and exit rather than concentration ratios, assessments of the need for regulation can be altered. For example, air travel between two cities may be served by a single company. With free entry, planes owned by rival companies would be diverted to the route if price was raised significantly above cost by the present supplier. No price regulation is required.

In a perfectly contestable market, cross-subsidization of competitive services by monopoly services is also not an issue since there is no monopoly profit to finance the subsidy. Contestability is never perfect but it is important to determine the extent to which potential competition disciplines incumbents before introducing detailed and costly forms of price regulation.

Although sophisticated in developing the properties of multi-product cost functions, the sources of differences in costs for different organizational modes are generally asserted, not explained, in the literature on market contestability. The transaction costs approach to comparative organizational effectiveness identifies reasons why one organizational mode may have lower costs of coordinating resources than alternatives.

Where some individuals or firms have preferential access to information, other less-informed individuals or firms may shy away from doing business with them despite the potential for gain, because of the fear of the less-informed that their ignorance will be exploited. For example, consider a firm that uses an input that may become contaminated in production. Assume that those who observe the production know when such contamination takes place but that detection of contamination by inspection is prohibitively expensive. An arm's-length supplier who is indifferent to having future commercial relations with any particular buyer (the price-taking supplier of economic theory) has a pecuniary interest in not divulging the contamination. Discovery of the defect will only occur with failure of the final product, and it may be difficult to ascertain that legal responsibility for the failure lies with the supplier of the input. Even if such liability can be ascertained, the damages awarded by a court may not compensate for the loss of wealth experienced by the manufacturer of the final product. If instead of an arm's-length supplier the input is supplied by a wholly owned subsidiary, there would be an incentive for information to be divulged, because the gain to the subsidiary of not divulging the existence of contamination would be less than the loss to the parent.[6]

Transaction cost considerations can complicate policy decisions by making restrictions on entry a possible instrument for reducing social costs. Models illustrating this phenomenon (see for example Leland, 1981) are analytically similar to common property models, which have provided a widely accepted justification for restricting entry into activities like fishing. Social policy on entry has to consider both the disciplining potential of free entry against the cost-reducing effect of entry restrictions in some informational or property-rights settings.

Much of the theoretical work in contestability involves abstract mathematical models that introduce regulation or regulatory issues in a stylized form. In contrast, much of the literature on transaction costs is more discursive.

The testing procedures that are applied reflect this difference. Theories that depict the allocative problem in terms of multi-product cost and demand functions are tested by statistical means. Although there have been impressive improvements in specifications and estimation methods, the statistical estimates of critical parameters have fluctuated considerably within the degrees of freedom permitted by alternative specifications, alternative proxies for theoretical concepts, and alternative estimation procedures.

Insights arising from considering transaction costs are typically "tested" by weaving a statistical and qualitative account that supports the theoretical story. There is a concern with the general credibility of the quantitative side of the account rather than with its rigorous econometric properties. In the story-telling approach, regulation is depicted as a process of interaction between the regulator and the industry or activity, rather than the setting of a parameter, such as an allowable rate of return.

Although purely theoretical work on regulation is concentrated in the universities, much of the applied work has been done under the auspices of the Economic Council of Canada, the Ontario Economic Council, The Institute for Research on Public Policy, the Canadian Institute of Public

Policy, the Fraser Institute, and the Department of Consumer and Corporate Affairs. In the next section of this paper, I discuss the effects of regulation on prices, quality, investment, and entry, and on productivity increases based on a selection of studies sponsored by those and other institutions.

Pricing

How are prices established in regulated industries and how should they be established? Practice varies tremendously. In some industries where entry is controlled, at least in part, price regulation is extensive and reasonably detailed (for example, telephone service, pipelines, and electricity). For another set of industries, individual prices are not a concern for the regulator, but the overall effect of the set of prices is.[7] In some instances, prices are controlled while entry is not (for example, grain handling, elevation and cleaning, taxi service in some areas); in others, entry is restricted, but price controls are cosmetic (for example, cable television services).

Some prices have to be filed and approved (for example, trucking in British Columbia, Quebec, and Ontario); in other jurisdictions, some prices for the same service are prescribed by the regulator (for example, trucking in Manitoba). It has been claimed that regulation acts to keep the fare schedule simpler than it would otherwise be.[8] Other authors claim the opposite. For example, Jordan (1982, p. 187) predicts that airline deregulation would result in a much less complicated fare structure. This prediction has not been confirmed with respect to American transcontinental routes under deregulation, where the pricing structure has been complex with complicated conditional discounts (see Ellison, 1981, p. 118).

Many of the studies analyze the characteristics of efficient prices in the circumstances facing a number of regulated industries. Because of the complexity of the issues involved, it is typical for each study to address a particular issue in isolation. Consider first the "break-even" prices that should be set by a regulator for an industry that would incur a loss if it charged marginal costs for each of its services. The prices that maximize the sum of consumer and producer surplus under these conditions are called Ramsey prices. Where there are no cross effects on demand, the markup of price over marginal cost depends inversely on the elasticity of demand. The prescription is to tax services in order to raise the funds necessary to cover costs, with the implicit tax on each service depending on demand conditions. In the past, regulated industries have often set prices according to value-of-service criteria. If value of service and inelasticities in demand are positively correlated, this pricing principle may have led to prices that approximate the Ramsey prescription.[9]

Consider, in particular, the pricing of telephone services from the Ramsey perspective. Although there is considerable disagreement on the elasticities of demand for toll and local telephone services, it is generally considered that local service is more inelastic in demand than toll service. It is also generally agreed that local service is cross-subsidized by toll service. Telephone prices then differ considerably from the Ramsey prices, since local service has a negative markup while toll service has a positive markup despite the fact that it is more elastic in demand than local service. Do we conclude from that observation that the present pricing structure is inefficient? Unfortunately, drawing a conclusion is not that easy, since many considerations are ignored in the simple Ramsey formula.

If it is considered appropriate to pursue social objectives through pricing, what is the effect on optimal prices? Breslaw and Smith (1982) address this issue for telephone services.[10] They specify demand and cost relations for Bell Canada and subject it to a break-even constraint, and then calculate the maximum of a social welfare measure that allows for income redistribution effects. The authors conclude that, because local service has a larger budget weight for lower income groups than for higher income groups, lower prices for local service have a positive effect on social utility through an income distribution effect; this offsets in part the efficiency gain from taxing the more inelastic service. Their conclusion is that toll service prices for 1978 should have been 50 percent lower and local service prices should have been raised by 19 percent. This disparity is substantially less than their estimate for the disparity between actual and Ramsey prices for that year.[11]

Another aspect of the utility pricing problem is the effect of passing on windfall gains or losses due to inflation to customers through the price structure. This problem is related to the Ramsey problem, and may invert it into a subsidy problem. Instead of having to tax in order to break even, the utility may have to make a net redistribution if it has experienced a capital gain from having equipment and low-interest debt that has become more valuable as a result of inflation. The largest subsidy should then be granted to the inelastic demand service. Quantification of the size of the gains to telephone customers from unanticipated inflation is not available. If these gains are substantial, judgments of the present pricing structure's efficiency should take them into account.

The optimal pricing of telephone services is also affected by externalities that are inherent in that service. The act of becoming a subscriber imparts a benefit to other subscribers by increasing the number of people with whom they can communicate. An external effect on the recipient is also generated by the placement of each telephone call. Some of these effects are internalized by private arrangements between individuals — for example, a parent giving an allowance for financing long-distance calls to a daughter or a son going away to college — but this internalization is far from complete. The implications of the access externality for pricing was first discussed in the Canadian literature by McManus (1973, pp. 391–94).[12] Bernstein (1980) incorporates the access externality in his specifications of demand in estimating demand and cost conditions for B.C.Tel.

Unfortunately, access is not priced separately in Canada. The optimal alteration of rates for toll and local service in order to tax existing subscribers and subsidize new ones depends on the difference between the calling patterns of the average and marginal subscriber. That information is not presently available.

The Ramsey pricing problem assumes that prices are linear, that is, that each unit is sold at the same price. If the utility can charge a different price for different units or blocks of units, the problem of raising enough revenue to cover costs is solved by charging more for the first unit than for subsequent ones (or less for initial units if the problem is to distribute to customers a capital gain from unanticipated inflation). At the margin, prices can be set at cost, with the contribution necessary to break even being supplied by taxing inframarginal use. For this reason, Helliwell (1978) advocates a rising block schedule of rates as a means of coping with redistributing to customers of electric utilities the capital gain arising from unanticipated inflation. There are many non-linearities in the telephone tariff that become obscured in the aggregated data on which the statistical studies of the industry are based, and that are ignored in most of the studies based on those data.[13] Differentiated price schedules make Ramsey prices an inappropriate benchmark.

Where a service cannot be stored and a consumer finds it costly to alter the timing of consumption, price discrimination can be practiced over time. If, by making appropriate time-of-day or time-of-year distinctions, capacity costs can be reduced, such discrimination is efficient.

Telephone rates for long-distance calls differ depending on the time of day and day of week they are made. There will be more distinctions introduced into the telephone pricing schedule if local service pricing is changed to a basis that depends on the characteristics of the call. Changes in metering costs make it feasible to measure local calls along a number of dimensions, such as time of call, number of calls made, distance of call, and parties connected. With future technology, it may be economical to signal to the user the state of congestion on trunks in the network, and make prices contingent on that state. Off-peak discounts are also permitted in the airline industry where special seasonal and weekend rates have been approved by regulators, and are ubiquitous in electricity and gas pricing schedules.

Analysts have also claimed that peak-load pricing would generate gains in areas where it has not been adopted. For example, Borins (1978) notes the absence of peak-load pricing for access to airports as a means of economizing on airport capacity. The reasons given for this failure are that:

- it would alienate general aviation from busy airports at peak-load times;
- there are transition costs;
- there is a preference for dealing with the problem internationally to cope with interrelationships between a solution for one airport aggravating the problem at another; and
- the Canadian Air Transportation Administration prefers to build airports large enough to accommodate the busiest peaks, despite the waste involved.

Harvey (1981, p. 86) argues that the capital investment in grain elevators could be reduced if multi-shift operations were introduced. The failure to do so is attributed to rigidities in the regulated prices for elevator services. With respect to the taxi industry, Papillon (1982) advocates time-of-day and area-of-city distinctions for pricing.[14]

Having identified that optimal prices depend on objectives, demand conditions, production technology and measuring technology, the following questions can be addressed. What are the social costs of setting regulated prices so that they do not effectively ration resource use? There are well-established means of estimating the values foregone as a result of inappropriate prices, using estimates of demand and cost elasticities. (This cost is subsequently referred to as the "triangle" cost because of its geometric representation in demand and supply diagrams.)

Josling (1981, p. 24), for example, calculates that the real income loss from our wheat program of subsidies to support Prairie branch lines, the Western Grains Stabilization Plan, the Crows Nest Pass Agreement, and domestic price maintenance averaged $9.12 million annually during the 1976–77 to 1978–79 period, based on a "medium" elasticity case. For the British Columbia Egg Marketing Board's policies, Borcherding (1981, p. 51) estimates a "triangle" cost of $0.3 million.

Regulation can also contribute to inefficiency by raising the cost of what is produced, and by failing to elicit the production of valuable characteristics by not rewarding their production in the pricing system. There is also a cost arising from administrative and enforcement costs and from resources invested in lobbying for political support of the program.

For example, Harvey (1981, p. 101) argues that the quota system used to control wheat production has encouraged an excessive amount of summer fallow and that the Wheat Board has not taken into account the productivity of land in assigning quotas. Both factors would raise costs. The Wheat Board has also failed to properly reward the production of better-quality, high-protein wheats. As a consequence, the average quality of Canadian wheats has been below the level that could have economically been achieved.

Borcherding (1981, p. 51) estimates many of these effects for the marketing of eggs in British Columbia. By comparing situations in British Columbia and Washington state, where egg production is not regulated in the same manner, he estimates that the size limitations on egg farms imposed under the B.C. program raised the supply price and resulted in a cost of $2 million. In addition, the costs of dumping excess supplies in the market for breaker eggs and maintaining the Board as a lobbyist and monitor were in the order of $1 million. A comparison of these sums to the $0.3 million "triangle" illustrates that these more difficult-to-measure costs can dwarf the traditional triangle measure.

An instructive way of viewing these estimates is that it is only rational to continue with existing policies if the estimates are smaller than the unmeasured benefits from external effects, beneficial quality changes, or desirable income distribution changes.

Prices and Income Distribution

The pursuit of income redistribution objectives through regulated pricing is a ubiquitous phenomenon. With respect to the price relationship between toll and local telephone service, Waverman (1982) notes that as early as 1919 the Board of Railway Governors accepted Bell Canada's proposed toll rates but reduced the increase in local rates, and comments that "keeping local rates low at the expense of toll rates is then an old and well-established practice" (p. 92).[15] Such an imbalance creates an incentive for a customer of the taxed service to avoid the tax by seeking alternatives that are uneconomic but cheaper because they are not taxed. The redistribution system is only viable if the supply of close substitutes can be economically restricted, or the "tax system" can be extended to cover the alternatives.

The cross-subsidy picture in the air travel business is not clear. There is "limited evidence" that "the international operations of the Canadian carriers are being cross-subsidized by their domestic operations"(Jordan, 1982, p. 45). On the other hand, Borins (1978) argues that CATA has set landing fees so that domestic traffic is "charged the least, transborder traffic more, and international traffic the most" (p. 139).

In trucking, Lord and Shaw (1980) report some evidence that small communities in Ontario, where trucking is regulated, receive superior service, compared with small communities in Alberta, where trucking is no longer regulated. Palmer (1974) had earlier reported that Ontario's regulated truckers held mixed portfolios of routes with different profit potential, and that the cross-subsidies were reduced by erosion of the tax base through various means of circumventing entry restrictions on the high profit lines.[16] For Manitoba, McRae and Prescott (1980) also find some evidence that service to small communities is subsidized.

In general, the ability to cross-subsidize through trucking prices is reduced by the viability of private trucking as a substitute. The intent of regulators to redistribute income through pricing is often revealed by measures taken to protect the tax base. Regulation was introduced to trucking in the 1930s, in part to protect the cross-subsidy system in rail rates. Private trucking has, in turn, been restricted to protect what little room there is for cross-subsidies in for-hire trucking.

The extent to which income is effectively redistributed through other regulated prices is unclear. For example, in the Alberta intercity bus service, Greyhound claimed that 61 percent of its routes were unprofitable based on passenger miles, but the Alberta Motor Transport Board decided that 16 percent of Greyhound's routes did not break even. An outside analyst (Reschenthaler, 1981) believes that even the 16 percent figure is inflated and concludes that "there is very little evidence of cross-subsidization" (p. 97).

It is attractive to advocate separating income redistribution from pricing on the basis that there are other more efficient means of redistributing income. Unfortunately, that premise need not be valid. There are no audits, no elaborate collection agency, no direct administrative costs of arranging the transfers through regulated prices. There are, as discussed above, distortions introduced by these pricing arrangements, as there are by any known tax system. Explicit tax and subsidy schemes also generate cost "triangles" and can cause the supply price to rise (Barzel, 1976).

What is definitely needed is identification of the income redistribution objectives and the contributions of existing regulated price schedules toward achievement of those objectives. In the absence of such information, constructive reform proposals cannot be made. With such guidance, it would be surprising if it were not possible to improve on the patchwork quilt of redistributive policies now in existence. A first step that merits exploration and political debate is to restrict redistribution to clearly identified needy groups. To subsidize consumers or producers in total seems mindless; to subsidize the poor seems reasonable.[17]

At this time, knowledge of the ultimate incidence of the cross-subsidization of services on the income of individuals in Canada is sketchy. What is the effect of the present structure of telephone rates on individuals in the economy? Despite the intense study of these rates in Canada, both because of their importance and because of the availability of data, the answer is not known. Local business rates exceed local residential rates by a factor greater than three, while costs differ by a smaller ratio. What percentage of the implied tax on business is passed on in prices and what percentage represents reductions in rents on land and other factors of production? How does the averaging within toll and local service categories affect different consumers? How does the disparity between toll and local rates affect consumers of different income, age, and family characteristics?

If income redistribution is an explicit goal in the sense that economists consider redistribution, it is surprising that the regulators have not identified more precisely the representative individual who benefits from the cross-subsidies and advertised the effects. One can understand why the representative "taxpayer" would not be identified, but not why the beneficiary would fail to be.

One possible explanation is that despite a general claim of prices being in the public interest, it is actually producers who benefit from the price structure (Jordan, 1972). The local residence-business price relationships and the toll-local rate relationship do not seem consistent with that view, although large businesses can avoid some of the "tax" with the latter by leasing private lines.

Most marketing boards distribute income to producers. For example, it has been estimated that Canadian producers benefited from dairy policies by over $1 billion and from wheat policies by over $300 million annually between the fiscal years 1976–77 and 1978–79 (Josling, 1981, p. 56). Arcus concludes that on average each producer of broilers benefited by $31,000 a year and each producer of eggs by $20,000 a year as a result of the policies of the respective marketing boards. Using a slightly different methodology, Borcherding (1981, p. 52) estimates that the net transfer to each producer from the operations of the British Columbia Egg Marketing Board was $14,000 in 1975.

The redistributions are not simply to producers. Consumers also benefit from our wheat policies, particularly in years when the world price is high. In 1974, the consumer subsidy was estimated to be $362 million and the producer subsidy $246.5 million (Josling, 1981). (The invisible taxpayer picks up the tab.)

An alternative hypothesis consistent with the pattern of subsidies resulting from wheat pricing is that regulation provides insurance against adversity (Peltzman, 1976). When exogenous events raise profits, prices are set so that consumers benefit; when profits are low, consumers are taxed to subsidize producers. The history of oil prices in Canada since 1950 conforms generally to this pattern. Since the mid-1970s, the producer prices on oil have on average been below world prices, and the industry has been heavily taxed. Before that, the opposite was true. Oil profits were significantly lower in the earlier period than in the subsequent one.[18]

Regulation may also offer insurance to subgroups among producers. The occurrence of this in regulation of the fishery has been documented (Scott and Neher, 1981, p. 11). In broadcasting, pay-TV firms are being exempted from obligations because of their tenuous financial situation. The CRTC has explicitly stated that it intends to squeeze additional

Canadian programming from more profitable television stations while relaxing constraints on the less economically viable stations.[19]

Although the costs have not been documented, regulation appears to be an expensive means of insurance. Because there is no explicit contract, industries have an incentive to mask their true financial position to avoid sharing their successes with the public purse or to encourage relief from that purse. There is an incentive for each industry to undertake costly lobbying to shift the terms of the implicit contract in its favour.

In some industries, there is a curious mix of beneficiaries from regulatory redistribution. Consumer and business travellers on core airline routes pay relatively high fares while vacationers using charters enjoy much lower rates, a situation which prompted the Consumers' Association of Canada to accuse the CTC of encouraging Canadians to vacation abroad (Ellison, 1981, p. 63). Canadian policies governing the sugar industry transfer much more income to Commonwealth producers in the Caribbean than to domestic beet producers (Josling, 1981, p. 16). In the telephone and electricity tariffs, rural residential customers benefit in comparison with their urban counterparts.

All the evidence is not consistent with a simple hypothesis. I would speculate that income distribution in the sense of redistributing income to some target group is sometimes not the motivation. From looking at pricing across a diverse set of industries, there appears to be a widely held view that some goods and services should be priced the same, despite economic inefficiencies that result. When transactions share some common characteristics, there is often political pressure for uniform prices to be charged despite the fact that efficiency would require differential prices.

For example, consider parcel service between two cities with the same variable costs for a trip between the two but different demands for the service from A to B than for service from B to A. The vehicle used to take parcels from A to B returns to A and is available to carry parcels on the return trip. In the circumstances, economically efficient pricing requires a higher price for the higher demand flow and a lower price for the lower demand flow. My guess would be that the acceptable regulated price in Canada would be the same both ways (or with a smaller disparity than would be economically justified).

There would be an economic loss from this price averaging and an inadvertent income redistribution effect. An economist who examined this situation and found that wealthy (or poor) people gained from the common prices compared with the economically efficient prices would be wrong to conclude that the wealthy (or poor) always benefited from regulation. If there were such forces operating, they might help explain the lack of an apparently coherent pattern to who benefits from regulatory pricing. Recognizing such forces does not mean that traditional redistribution is not pursued through regulatory prices, but that it shares the stage.

There is some explicit evidence that regulators are affected by such fairness considerations. For example, with respect to the regulation of bus service, Reschenthaler (1981) reports:

> in Alberta, Saskatchewan and Manitoba, equalization of fares . . . in terms of cents per mile . . . across the provinces has been a conscious objective of regulatory policy to ensure that passengers travelling between any two points, irrespective of load factors, time or distances, pay the same fare per mile. (p. 84)

Similarly, the provision of the local telephone loop may cost more to service for one house or apartment than for another, depending on the location with respect to a central office, characteristics of the residency, and the technology being employed, but each residential subscriber in a local exchange area pays the same amount.

Unfortunately, the concept of fairness differs between situations. For bus service, a common price per mile is fair and a common price per trip is not; in contrast, for telephone service, a common charge per mile of local loop is unfair and a common charge for a loop is fair.

With respect to mail service, the price is the same to send a letter to a neighbour as it is to send it across the country. My correspondence with my neighbour cross-subsidizes my letter to Vancouver.[20] If instead of writing, I telephone the same people, the communication cross-subsidy runs in the opposite direction. In my opinion, attempts to change either pricing policy would elicit vigorous political opposition. What is considered "fair" depends on the history of the industry and on the status quo in political terms, resulting in apparent economic contradictions in present pricing policies.

Incentives created by regulatory pricing can redistribute income to and from producers outside the immediate ambit of the regulated industry. One of the effects of the Crow rates was to encourage shipments of wheat through Thunder Bay rather than through Vancouver, because it lessened the burden of those rates on the railways. The effect was felt by farmers who received a lower net price for their product and by lake shippers who received a higher price for their service (Maister, 1978, p. 175).

A different concern in regulated pricing occurs when a regulated monopolist provides services in competition with other suppliers in some areas as well as being the exclusive supplier in other areas. Analysts have argued that the regulated monopolist will have an incentive to cross-subsidize its competitive services, either because the regulated monopolist likes to expand for expansion's sake, or because expansion allows the rate base to increase, permitting more profit to be earned.

To protect monopoly subscribers from being unknowingly taxed in order to finance this undesirable expansion, a number of proposals have been made. One is to prohibit the monopolist from participating in these competitive services. A second is to have the regulator ascertain by some cost test that the regulated monopolist's competitive offerings are not being subsidized. The third alternative is to ensure that the competitive services are provided by an arm's-length subsidiary of the regulated monopolist.

The best alternative depends on the efficacy of cost measurement techniques and the economies resulting from integrated production. If auditing techniques are sufficiently accurate and economical and if there are economies of scope, the second option would predominate. If there are effective costing procedures for policing the boundary between the parent and the subsidiary and determining asset prices on reorganization, and if there are no economies of scope, the third solution would be preferred. Prohibition would be justified where there is no economical means of policing the practice.

Cross-subsidization is an issue wherever Crown corporations and regulated monopolies are involved in markets that other firms serve. The CRTC has done, and is doing, the most work in developing costing procedures and in exploring their capabilities; hearings have also been scheduled by the CRTC to examine structural separation as a remedy. Where no regulatory board exists, there is no obvious focal point for resolving conflict over pricing in competitive services. The post office, for example, has become an important competitor in short-haul freight with its fourth-class mail, which includes parcel post and post pak. Competitors' concern over cross-subsidization has no obvious point of adjudication in this case.

Process vs. Statistical Models of Price Setting

In developing an economic model to describe price-setting, analysts are constrained by the analytical approach that is adopted. This imperative is well illustrated by two excellent studies of telephone regulation commissioned by the Economic Council of Canada. The first is a statistical examination of pricing and technological characteristics by Fuss and Waverman (1981) and the second is a study of telephone regulation by Waverman (1982). In the statistical study, regulated prices are established by the regulator, who sets local rates, and by the company who sets two categories of toll prices based on profit-maximization, the overall set of prices being consistent with a rate-of-return constraint. This price-setting scheme generates equations that form part of the system that is estimated.

In the study of regulation, Waverman discusses perceptively the detailed evolution of regulation federally and in two provinces. Regulation is treated as a process of discerning facts and applying remedies.[21]

The process view of regulation leads one to consider a number of different determinants of pricing that could not be encompassed by the statistical model approach. An academic economist may be content to accept that each approach reveals something of what is a complex phenomenon, but those with the responsibility to implement policy or to suggest better policies must be disappointed that so little of the total mosaic is revealed, even by "state of the art" studies.

Relaxing Regulatory Constraints on Pricing

The thrust of current thinking is that regulatory restrictions on pricing should be relaxed in the telephone and airline industries. Canadian experience with relaxing regulatory restrictions has been successful in the rail freight business. After the 1967 National Transportation Act, the railways were given almost complete freedom to make and change their rates. Section 278 of the Railway Act allows a shipper who has no effective alternative to rail to apply for a maximum rate that can be charged. The maximum is to set at 150 percent of the variable cost of providing the service. The minimum rate on freight charges is variable cost. Agreed charges can also be disallowed or altered if the CTC decides that is in the public interest. Heaver and Nelson (1978a, 1978b), who have performed the most detailed examination of pricing under this flexible regulatory umbrella, conclude that the changes have been conducive to the development of an efficient Canadian transportation system.

Between mid-1983 and December 1984, the Liquor Licensing Board of Ontario relaxed the tight pricing constraints on prices of drinks in licensed premises. Prices for drinks differed by time of day (Happy Hours), and special prices were advertised in a constrained manner. No study has been published assessing these changes.

The CRTC is also experimenting with greater price flexibility in its approach to pay-TV. It has instructed the licensed pay-TV firms to negotiate with the cable companies on appropriate rates.[22] In some cases, these are sequential monopolies. Where successive monopolies in a production chain charge what the market will bear, a substantial inefficiency can occur.[23] Only if the monopoly power of the cable companies and the pay-TV licensees is weak would the choice of this area for experimenting with flexibility appear to be a wise one. The CRTC is also refraining from exercising price regulation with respect to cellular radio service.

Additional price flexibility has also been granted to the financial sector in the last two Bank Acts. Regulation in this sector is being treated in a separate study. From the evidence available, these experiments appear to have been successful, and fears that the general public's interests would be abused by greater scope for competitive flexibility do not appear to have been warranted.[24]

Quality

Regulation directly and indirectly affects the quality of service provided. In telecommunications, the CRTC has defined eight aspects of service and the companies under its regulation must report performance according to a number of measures related to each of these aspects. Examples of measures are the percentage of service installation appointments convenient to customers and the percentage of orders for telephone service that cannot be met because the company cannot provide it. The Commission's target is a standard of performance so that 90 percent of subscribers are satisfied with the service received.[25] Some of the measures, such as convenience and satisfaction, are inherently fuzzy.

Although there was a long process of consultation, the standards appear to have been developed without any explicit consideration of the costs and benefits of compliance. Economic theory predicts that the quantity produced by a simple monopolist will be lower than it should be. However, there is no presumption that the quality will differ from the optimal.[26] If the circumstances are such that an inappropriate quality is provided, there may be excessive investment in quality rather than too little. More subtly, if quality measures are enforced, the regulated companies' efforts will predictably be allocated to achieve the measured dimensions of quality and non-measured aspects will be neglected.

In Beigie's (1973) comprehensive survey of Canadian telecommunications, the author notes that "Canadians have become accustomed to receiving superior telecommunications services" (p. 192) and there are no recommendations for regulatory surveillance of quality. Instead, Beigie advocates increased competition wherever possible. In the 1980s, terminal attachment conditions have been continuously liberalized and consumer and business options have been expanded. In addition, competition for private line configurations has been permitted and the CRTC is presently deciding on whether to allow more competition in the switched long-distance business. If quality surveillance was worthwhile under earlier conditions, scrapping it in a more competitive environment merits consideration.[27]

The CRTC has also been involved with defining and controlling quality in broadcasting. Since 1970, the Commission has established Canadian content requirements for television. In 1983 the CRTC announced its intention to use a weighted points system to define Canadian content and to make greater use of licensing powers to enforce the exhibition of a wide range of quality Canadian programs. A Byzantine set of rules is developing which includes a Canadian content credit of 50 percent for "programs produced outside Canada in languages other than English, French, Inuktitut, or Canadian Indian languages, dubbed or lip-synchronized in Canadian production facilities."[28]

Where a concept is as difficult to define as Canadianism, regulatory imposition of arbitrary measures of the concept can cause substantial distortions and can be counter productive. Canadians might be better off if viewers are allowed the freedom to choose what is Canadian, rather than having that decided for them in Ottawa. If the intent of the measures is instead to protect jobs in the production of programming, that should be made explicit.

The licensing conditions for radio control the nature of broadcasting. Language of broadcast, duration of programming in each of eight categories, community access, music plans, and so on are prescribed. Based on the common property feature of a programming type, a case can be made that unregulated broadcasting will result in excessive duplication of the more popular programming types (Steiner, 1961). This efficiency consideration could provide a rationale for quality control, but whether the actual policies are effectively designed to do so is moot.

Licensing procedures for many professions and activities prescribe quality standards. Restriction of entry may also affect the average quality of product or service offered so as to enhance welfare. It is extremely difficult to measure these quality enhancement effects and compare them to any losses due to monopoly pricing of goods and services.

In assessing the effects of deregulating Canadian airline service, Jordan (1982) predicts that quality will decline "somewhat" (p. 187) but that reduction in prices will more than compensate. Reschenthaler (1981), in reviewing hearings and decisions with respect to regulation of intercity bus service, notes that service quality and not price is the main concern of the regulator: "It is clear that the primary concerns of intervenors and of regulatory boards are frequency of service, maintenance of schedules, claims service and types of equipment used" (p. 15). It has also been claimed that regulation enhances safety by adding the sanction of licence suspension to other incentives to provide a safe service. Hirshhorn (1981b) finds that in trucking "the threat of certificate withdrawal for safety violations is so remote as to make this a realistic consideration only in respect to the most flagrant abuses of safety laws and regulations" (p. 173).

Harvey (1981) claims that the wheat marketing system has had a perverse effect on quality:

There is, within the present system, no real incentive for producers to either ascertain the exact quality of their stocks prior to delivery or to divulge the information to the marketing system or agencies. This lack of control over deliveries shows up further down the forwarding pipeline in the fact that to obtain, say, 60 cars of high protein wheat at port some 100 cars have to be allocated (and then moved from) high protein wheat areas. (p. 2)

In some areas, the government has worked in cooperation with the industry to improve quality. For example, in the Nova Scotia herring fishery, Campbell (1981) notes:

> The Bay of Fundy project has attempted to improve quality in two ways: funds have been allocated to subsidize refrigeration units on seine vessels and ice plants on shore; and the fishermen's Co-op has adopted a radio dispatch system for allocating catch to plants which have spare capacity for immediate processing. Despite these efforts of government and industry, fresh and frozen Bay of Fundy herring products are not highly regarded at the present time in the discriminating European market. (p. 14)

Concern with quality has been widespread in the fishery. Some of the quality problems in the cod fishery have resulted from the feast and famine cycles of supply to processors — cycles that have been accentuated by the regulatory encouragement of the inshore fishery and by the provisions of the unemployment insurance program (Ferris and Plourde, 1982). The second factor has been mitigated by recent changes in the unemployment insurance program.

The effects of marketing boards on product quality have not been extensively documented. Borcherding (1981, pp. 47–48) argues that the replacement of "personal" relations between producers and middlemen (graders, wholesalers, and some large retailers) by direct sales to the British Columbia Egg Marketing Board's grading stations would result in lower quality, but he does not measure the effect because of a lack of appropriate data.

Another area where regulation is explicitly concerned with quality is in pollution control. The causal relations in this area are very complex. Some emissions may be beneficial rather than harmful and, for example, restore nutrients to the soil. Many of the harmful effects on plants and animal life are subtle and reveal themselves only after a long lag. Damages may also arise from secondary effects. To illustrate, forests may be weakened by emissions so that they become more susceptible to insect damage.

An effective pollution control scheme requires a measure of pollution so that an incentive scheme for achieving the objectives can be developed and enforced. With respect to water quality, criteria for fishing, recreational use, and safety must be translated, for example, into standards of suspended solids and biochemical oxygen demand. The absorptive capacity of the water must also be determined in setting total allowable emissions. Where a number of sources of emissions exist, a system for assigning individual totals which will sum to the target is required. Scope to adjust totals and assignments should be provided to accommodate revisions that become desirable as a result of new information.

In the pulp and paper industry, the measurement problem is substantially reduced by the fact that most mills are the sole source of industrial pollution in their immediate area. The system of regulation has been to impose allowable effluent requirements for each mill.

The federal government and the provincial government share jurisdiction. Their concerns are different, the federal government having jurisdiction over fish, the provinces over water. In their study of the progress made in the last decade in Ontario, Victor et al. (1981) identify the different procedures for setting allowances by the two jurisdictions. The federal authorities calculated guidelines based on the prescribed levels for the component processes relevant to each mill, while the provincial authority based its guidelines on the mill's attributes and the absorptive capacity of the water. In both cases, the guidelines were drafted with little, if any, consideration for the costs of compliance. (The ignoring of compliance costs is also typical in product safety regulation.) There is effective cooperation between the two levels of government, with an agreement to recognize whichever set of guidelines are more stringent.

Compliance schedules were negotiated with each mill. For a period in the 1970s, special capital cost allowances were granted for pollution abatement equipment. In 1979, a condition for a mill to receive special financial assistance under a joint federal-provincial program was approval of adequate provision for pollution abatement. These were apparently weak incentives.

Since measurement for isolated mills is not difficult, the failure of such mills to meet their schedules can be accurately ascertained. Victor et al. (1981) report:

> The overall and rather strong conclusion is that, for those isolated mills where the data are sufficient for analysis, there was no significant improvement (or deterioration) in the quality of the receiving waters in the 1970–78 period. (p. 114)

A similar pattern of attempting to tailor controls to a company's situation and setting overly ambitious targets occurred with respect to sulphur dioxide emissions from the Sudbury smelter of Inco. After passage of the Air Pollution Control Act in 1967, the emissions situation at Inco was assessed. The company was required to build a new 1250-foot stack to replace three shorter chimneys. Sulphur dioxide emissions were to be reduced in four stages: 5200 tons a day by July 1, 1970; 4400 tons a day by December 31, 1974; 3600 tons a day by December 31, 1976; and 750 tons a day by December 31, 1978. Inco could not meet the third target. Extensive negotiations followed. A new directive was issued in early 1980 imposing an immediate limit of 2500 tons a day to be reduced to 1950 tons a day in 1983.

Under both federal and provincial law, the minister responsible has considerable discretion to grant exemptions and modify compliance schedules. But why were such optimistic guidelines issued, when performance is bound to be judged with reference to those guidelines? Perhaps the regulators significantly overestimated the economic prospects of the industry and would not enforce the regulations, since so doing would have put some pulp and paper mills and smelters out of business.

The tailoring of the guidelines to fit the economic viability of each mill obviously leads to variations in the quality of air and water at different sites, and to an uneven incidence of the responsibility and costs of environmental improvement. Marginal mills or smelters are not expected to do anything; profitable operations are. New mills face tougher standards than old ones. Migué (1977) argues that the tailoring of requirements and subsidies through accelerated capital cost allowances was sought by existing producers because it protected incumbents from entry.

Product safety regulation has been similar to pollution regulation in paradoxically involving close consultation between industry and governments and apparently ignoring compliance costs in making decisions except when economic viability is threatened. Hirshhorn (1981a) assesses a number of initiatives in this field and concludes that the act "has been effective in reducing the number and severity of accidents involving consumer products" (p. 105). But he also concludes that there was considerable scope for improvement in identifying the most important hazards, coping with them in a cost-efficient manner, and allocating enforcement efforts more effectively.

Investment

Analysts have been interested in the effects that regulation has on investment. Each year, in the seclusion of the classroom, the Averch-Johnson analysis of distortions in factor use resulting from rate-of-return regulation is taught to a new set of students learning the analytical power of constrained optimization techniques. Since the economists on the staff of the major regulatory bodies have all sat through those classes, one would believe that they would have developed some defences against the dissipation of wealth implied by the effect.[29]

Investment programs of regulated firms are explicitly or implicitly monitored to a varying degree. In the telephone industry, surveillance is quite detailed. In 1979, the CRTC announced that it would make an annual review of Bell Canada's five-year construction program "in light of the magnitude, detail and complexity of Bell Canada's construction program and its relationship to the financial requirements of the Company."[30] In addition, actual regulation, even in bodies that follow a rate-of-return approach, is much more complex than the stylized regulation specified in the model.

Statistical tests of the Averch-Johnson effect have been made. Fuss and Waverman (1981, ch. 3) present an elegant derivation of the theory and provide a sophisticated statistical test using Bell Canada data. The model had unreasonable values for some parameters, and no evidence of an Averch-Johnson effect was found.

In other industries, a bias to labour-intensive techniques has been attributed to the regulators. Using an estimated cost function for trucking, Kim (1984) reports that the low utilization rates caused by regulatory measures have increased the demand for labour and to a lesser extent for capital. With respect to the Nova Scotia herring fishery, Campbell (1977) comments:

> Regulation has attempted to prevent the over-capitalization of the harvesting sector by strictly limiting the seine catch and encouraging the weir and gillnet fisheries which probably tend to have higher labour cost per ton of fish landed. (p. 20)

In the fishery, controls over equipment have sometimes been motivated by a desire to protect the stock from depletion, given the absence of private incentives to do so. For example, since the 1920s the size of scallop dregs has been limited and a minimum diameter for the metal rings has been specified.

In different industries, a number of examples of distortions in investment emerge. Because of the Crow rates, the railways failed to invest in new boxcars and service deteriorated. In response to the problem, the federal government financed the acquisition of 6000 modern grain hoppers in the early 1970s. Maister (1978, p. 172) also notes that the subsidies paid by the federal government for storage of wheat on the Prairies, which began with the Temporary Wheat Reserves Act of 1956, resulted in the proliferation of elevators with low handling capacity and high storage capacity.

With respect to intercity bus service, Reschenthaler (1981) claims that without regulation smaller vehicles would be used on some routes than the standard 39-to-47-seat coaches adopted by the regulated carriers. In addition, it is estimated that the average bus fleet is 12 to 15 percent larger than it would be without regulation. With the laxness of bus service regulation in every dimension except barring entry, it is not clear what the carriers gain from this over-investment in fleet, and no convincing reason for this phenomenon is given in the study. The shoddy state of most bus terminals is also blamed on regulation, but again no analytically satisfactory reason is given for the role of regulation in causing this state of affairs.

Entry

Redistributing income through regulation requires barriers to entry or provisions to include entrants in the tax and subsidy scheme implicit in the regulated price structure. What is more difficult to determine is whether barriers to entry or licensing requirements contribute to efficiency or not.

The value of a license is often taken as evidence that regulation must be inefficient. That this inference cannot generally be drawn can be illustrated by considering the fishery problem. If rights to fish were properly restricted, they would be valuable. Their value would reflect the economic rent that could now be earned on the fishery and was previously being dissipated. Whether a restriction contributes a social gain or loss depends on circumstances.

For a restriction to be valuable, it must be enforceable. To realize the rental value of the fishery, one must exclude those fishermen who don't have a right and enforce limits on the catch of those who do. The large potential rents of the fishery have been dissipated through inefficient regulation (Scott and Neher, 1981, p. 26). Restriction always creates pressure from those who have been excluded to gain access, or from those admitted to take more than they are allowed. The same pressures to disintegration that are benign if they make an exploitative cartel fail are malignant if they make a beneficial restriction inoperative.

A number of economists have advocated replacing present direct regulation with transferable rights similar to the quotas used by some marketing boards. A limited number of rights to pollute or to catch fish would be created and distributed. These rights can have detailed conditions attached. As an illustration, Scott and Neher advocate a system of fishing rights that would specify species, time, location, and gear (p. 41).

This approach is attractive but enforcement problems and rent-seeking activities are not removed by introducing a rights system. Resources will be dissipated in attempts to influence the total number of rights to be created and their distribution. For example, Scott and Neher recommend that fishing rights be allocated initially according to historical involvement. They recognize that there would be a "socially unproductive scramble" (p. 51) to fabricate such a status, but they don't explain why the resulting dissipation would be less than that experienced under direct regulation.

One fishery where an implicit rights system appears to have been successful is the Nova Scotia herring fishery (Campbell, 1981, p. 25). Dissipation has been reduced by involving the fishermen's cooperative in the allocation.

Restrictions can generate gains in situations where there are asymmetries in information. For example, Leland (1981) argues that restricting entry into the professions could generate gains by improving the average quality of professional service that a consumer can expect to obtain at a particular price. Poorer quality professionals would be excluded until the loss from having a reduced number of professionals offsets the gain at the margin from the increased average quality of professionals.

A similar argument is made by Ferris (1982) with respect to the minimum wage. By excising the poorer jobs, the quality of the average job that a job searcher would expect to find is improved. Again there is a trade-off between the loss due to fewer jobs being available and improved job search.

The arguments depend on the government's ability to identify the lower quality types in order to exclude them — a proposition which is more credible in the employment case than in the professionals case. If the government could make the identification more economically than private parties, it would still always be preferable to grade — that is, identify the type — than to exclude, unless the costs of transmitting the grading information ruled this option out.

Informational disadvantages in identifying who the poor doctors are may result in government reliance on a professional association as its agent in establishing and enforcing a minimum standard. Since average incomes of the doctors who do qualify are higher after exclusion, the association is a willing participant.

The situation described by Leland is one in which there are too few professionals as a result of the information asymmetry and a positive correlation between an individuals's value elsewhere in the economy and his or her quality as a professional. The last individual to enter the profession is the most talented, but since people treat all professionals as equal in talent, the superiority in ability is not rewarded. It is this failure that leads to too few professionals. The same failure leads to too many, if the correlation between value in alternative pursuits and talent is negative, that is, if the last individual to enter is the least talented. He or she then gets rewarded according to the average talent in the occupation; the relative lack of talent of the individual is not reflected in lower income.

To my knowledge, there are no economic studies that examine whether quality is enhanced by professional restrictions on entry in Canada or that measure the value of the quality change. Muzondo and Pazderka (1979) provide statistical evidence that conditions of entry, fee-setting powers, advertising restrictions, and mobility restrictions raise incomes of professionals, but whether this premium is more than offset by a resulting improvement in average services provided is still moot.

The number of firms in a regulated industry also affects the quantity and quality of information flows to the regulator. A few alternate suppliers would serve this purpose well. There are many regulated duopolies in Canada. When regulators talk of competition, a restricted number is often what they appear to have in mind.

Regulators have also defended restricting entry into their industry because of a concern with industry stability. That competition would result in severe cycles of capacity utilization and prices has not been confirmed by outside analysts for the trucking, airline, and bus service industries. On the other hand, Olewiler (1981, p. 70) argues that it was a valid concern in the potash industry and that it justified introducing a prorationing scheme.

The removal of restrictions to entry redistributes income just as their creation does. This redistribution is effectively illustrated by the experience in the taxi industry in Montreal in 1946. The value of a license to operate a cab at the time was $5000. As a result of recommendations in the Asselin report, 765 new permits were issued and the value of a license dropped to nil (Papillon, 1982, p. 22).

Regardless of whether a restrictive right is socially benign or harmful, people will contest for its ownership as long as it is privately valuable. The absorption of resources in the pursuit of ownership of rights or in the effort to enhance the value of rights already obtained is referred to as rent-seeking activity. One of the challenges in designing regulatory structures is to reduce the waste resulting from rent-seeking activities.

The costs of rent-seeking activity in the regulated trucking industry in Canada have been studied by Bonsor (1980). Based on a broad survey of trucking companies, he concludes that the cost of seeking entry and of incumbents investing in deterring entry was approximately $40 million a year. One would expect the cost of obtaining a new license by application to be made equal to the cost of buying an existing one by arbitrage. It is therefore difficult to understand the relationship reported by Hirshhorn (1981b) whereby: "Carriers who obtain their licenses from a regulatory board are . . . likely to be in an advantageous position over those who purchase their license from existing carriers (p. 56).

Although it is less common, actions of a regulator may facilitate entry. In some activities, entry requires access to a facility used in common by more than one producer. For example, the interconnection of railway and telephone systems involves agreements for sharing facilities or connecting systems. A number of such agreements has been reached voluntarily. Voluntary agreements between a small number of parties may be costly to arrange, because of strategic behaviour by the parties. In instances where voluntary efforts fail but where benefits can be realized from interconnection, regulation may contribute to efficiency by imposing appropriate terms and conditions on the parties. In 1979, the CRTC ordered Bell Canada to allow a limited form of interconnection to CNCP Telecommunications. Recently, CNCP asked the CRTC to extend the domain of interconnection rights to permit CNCP to offer long-distance service. The CRTC has to assess whether there is a net benefit in allowing the extension and, if permission is granted, what the terms will be. Cost measures, distributional obligations of suppliers, costs of interconnections of different quality, and the effects of interconnection on the costs of coordinating network investment are among the more important issues that will be addressed in the hearings on this subject.

Airline travel provides another example where regulatory decisions have an important effect on the terms at which a commonly used facility will be available to potential entrants. With respect to airline deregulation, Ellison (1981) reports:

> Incumbent carriers could enjoy advantages denied new entrants in that they had ready access to the nation's airports. At many of them they held long-term contracts and they often constitute the operating committees which allocate the airport slots (p. 97).

Airports are owned and operated by the federal government in Canada. If deregulation of airlines proceeds in Canada, its success will depend on how scarce landing rights and airport space are allocated. Because of the economies of scheduling interconnecting flights from a single airport, an airport has natural monopoly features. If an open access market (or equivalent regulatory) policy for allocating landing rights is established, the stage will be appropriately set for a test of the hypothesis that competition will be beneficial in this field.

Technical Dynamism

One of the more difficult tasks in economics is to obtain a measure of productivity that is a useful guide for policy. A commonly used measure is total factor productivity (TFP). Unfortunately, TFP increases are not the result of improvements in organization or technique for which a manager has been rewarded or of a change in plant procedures which workers have accepted for more pay, or of improvements from the marginal investment in research and development. TFP is what is left over after these effects have been taken into account.

To illustrate that TFP can be a poor indicator of the firms or industries which should be encouraged to expand in order to promote progressivity, consider two firms. One is able to capture half the value created by the factors used in its R&D program in cost reductions, while the other half of the social value of its R&D is due to downward shifts in the cost function of the second firm. The second firm cannot capture any benefits of an R&D program and consequently has none. The first firm expands its R&D to the point where the marginal increases in its own wealth resulting from future cost reductions is equal to the marginal cost of the R&D resources. The first firm has no increase in total factor productivity while the second does. The first is innovative; the second is not.

A purported advantage of TFP is that the same procedure of measurement can be imposed on different industries. Nonetheless, substantially different results can be generated, depending on whether capital is treated as an intermediate good or as a primary factor of production, and on the technique used to separate scale and capacity utilization influences. Authors also differ in the method of measuring technology shifts. Some use time while others concoct technical indices that are specific to the industry in question. With these caveats made, let us turn to the evidence on TFP and regulation.

In a study on the Canadian railways, Caves and Christensen (1980) conclude that although Canadian National Railways had lower productivity than CP Rail in the late 1950s, it had closed the gap by the mid-1970s. By economy-wide standards, both railways had rapid rates of TFP growth. For Ontario Hydro, Daly and Rao (1983) find that TFP growth was above the economy average for the 1967–80 period. Denny et al. (1981) conclude that in the postwar period, Bell Canada experienced rapid increases in TFP; a subsequent study found that the British Columbia Telephone Company had slightly lower, but still high, TFP growth, while Alberta Government Telephones had higher growth than Bell (Olley and Lee, 1984).

To draw conclusions on the interaction of TFP and regulation from this evidence is difficult. The firms differ in their product mix and vertical and horizontal structures. All the corporations had rapid TFP growth. Price regulation varied considerably with railways moving from tight to loose regulatory constraints in the period studied, with Ontario Hydro pricing to cover costs, and with telecommunications carriers facing detailed price regulation.

At a more disaggregated level, Sims and Smith (1983) compare the TFP of brewery plants located in jurisdictions with regulated sewage disposal with that of plants located in unregulated areas. The growth of TFP in unregulated plants was significantly higher.

Rate-of-return regulation results in a fall in prices as costs are reduced because of innovation. Some authors (e.g., Westfield, 1970) conclude that this reduces the incentive to innovate. If R&D capital is included in the rate base and if R&D expenses are allowable expenses, this conclusion is not warranted; in this case, customers "insure" the R&D process by guaranteeing recoupment of expenses and the going rate of return on capital.

Monopoly rights also lower the costs of protecting the knowledge base from imitators and so increase the incentive to expand it. This positive effect may be more than offset by the lethargy induced by tenure in the franchise, an argument that academic economists are fond of making about all monopolists other than the one at the podium in the university lecture hall.

A monopolist's lethargy will be reduced as more competition exists in other modes — for example, in air-rail-road competition for freight and for the franchise right itself. In Canadian history, the instances where a regulated monopolist is nationalized far exceed those where a Crown corporation is "privatized."

Competitive arrangements provide no incentive to do R&D if there are no mechanisms for appropriating a private benefit from introducing a new and better idea. Patents, copyright, and trade secrecy law have evolved in response to this failure. These instruments are susceptible to many of the same problems that plague regulation. For example, with appropriation assured by a patent, competition to obtain that right can dissipate the gains from technical progress. It is not clear that regulation is at a comparative disadvantage to these other instruments in dealing with appropriability issues.

Regulation can affect the nature of change as well as its amount. Rate-of-return regulation may induce more capital-intensive innovation and, if franchises are protected when scale and scope economies are present, an incentive is created to find and develop new technologies with these characteristics. If, in controlling egg production, the number of laying hens is restricted, regulation will encourage the breeding of hens that produce more eggs. In assessing these effects, it is important to note that the patent and trade secrecy law also provide a distorted set of incentives and that, in the absence of regulation, there is an incentive to develop techniques that erect natural barriers to entry.

Some regulatory initiatives are designed to redirect innovative activity. For example, hazardous product regulation consciously alters commercial incentives to innovate. Other avenues of affecting the characteristics of future products are available, such as providing consumers directly with better information or altering liability rules. These alternatives are not costless, and the comparative advantage of one approach over another depends on the circumstances.

The anecdotal evidence on the effects of regulation on innovation illustrates how particular regulatory instruments interact with industry characteristics to influence the pace of change. Maister (1978) provides an excellent account of the regulatory barriers to introducing a more economical grain-handling and storage system in western Canada. In the 1960s, the regulation of grain-handling charges, primary elevator charges, cleaning charges, terminal elevator charges, and railway car allocations impeded the replacement of small country elevators with larger inland terminals and the shipment of grain by unit trains.

By 1970, these barriers were recognized by the federal government. In a coordinated series of legislative revisions and decisions of the Canadian Wheat Board and the Canadian Grain Commission (a group within the Department of Agriculture), these charges and practices were modified to permit the reorganization. The process of altering the regulatory structure was time-consuming, costly, and tortuous. It was not until 1974 that the Palliser Wheat Growers' Association constructed a large inland terminal at Weyland and other grain trade participants announced their intention to follow suit.

Maister's criticism is echoed by Harvey (1981), who notes that the Wheat Board failed to provide incentives to the handling companies and the railways to adjust from a market requiring storage expansion to one emphasizing throughput. At the farm level, the Board's quota system has also been blamed for low adoption rates by Canadian farmers of new high-yield varieties (see Furton and Lee, 1977).

Regulations with respect to sulphur dioxide emissions were established at levels that reflected a belief that technological changes permitting compliance would be encouraged (Olewiler, 1981, p. 57). The Ontario government's graduated targets for sulphur dioxide emissions at Inco had to be altered when a new hydrometallurgical process, which the company had hoped would allow it to meet the third and fourth stages of the order, proved not to be economically viable (Felske et al., 1981, p. 160).

Innovation by Canadian manufacturers has also been influenced by regulation in other countries. Reschenthaler (1981, p. 109) notes that MCI, a Winnipeg-based company that is North America's largest intercity bus manufacturer, could not market a large bus that it had developed because the state regulatory authorities south of the border would not approve the vehicle.

As far as the effect of regulation on the type of innovation is concerned, pollution controls illustrate that progress is affected by the content of the controls. Meeting the specified targets can be accompanied by higher emissions of other substances. For example, with respect to automobile emissions, the first controls in North America concentrated on carbon monoxide and hydrocarbons. Emissions of nitrogen oxides were not then controlled, and they increased after these early regulations. By 1970, authorities believed that nitrogen oxides represented the "most important by-product of automobile use from the viewpoint of air pollution and their abatement warrants the highest priority" (Walker, 1975, p. 3) and it was added to the controlled substances.

In the fisheries, the introduction of superior technology has often been impeded by regulation. It has not been possible to develop schemes capable of distributing the gains from adopting superior modes of production so as to improve the lot of all the affected parties. Fishermen in the halibut fishery are restricted to the use of longlines despite the greater efficiency of other methods, and in the Bay of Fundy herring fishery the seine catch has been strictly limited despite its relatively efficiency.

These restrictions have redirected innovative efforts and slowed them down rather than stopping them. In the halibut fishery, for instance, catch per unit of effort using longlines has been increased substantially by manipulating hook spacing and lines per vessel (Scott and Neher,

1981, p. 27). The size and characteristics of new vessels have also been significantly affected by input regulations.

Conclusion

There exist excellent accounts and analyses of current economic regulation in Canada. Without this work, particularly that done at the Economic Council of Canada's Regulation Reference under the energetic guidance of W.T. Stanbury, there would not be much to survey. With it, one can be more iconoclastic in doing a survey, and I have taken that liberty.

Before concluding, I want to draw attention to a tendency in regulatory analyses of maintaining different views of the informational setting while assessing different practices. Researchers tend to take the positive and normative features of competition in a setting where transactions are costless and ascribe them to competition in a world where it is costly to coordinate resources. In fact, the institutional forms, positive predictions, and normative features of competition differ significantly in the two settings. Alternatives must be compared in the same transacting environment.

To illustrate, consider the pizza delivery industry in Ottawa as viewed by an analyst from Mars whose only knowledge of Earth came from reading the literature of economic regulation. In examining its prices, the analyst would find that the stores deliver "free," or at some fixed charge, anywhere in town. Is this a cross subsidy to those who live farther away from the restaurants by those who live near, which is motivated by some social concern? Does it mean that those who live at a distance have captured the pizza industry? If the analyst explores further, it will be discovered that different dressings can be added to a basic pizza at a common price, although it is clear that the incremental cost of anchovies is dramatically different from the incremental cost of onions. Is this again conscious redistribution, or is it clever discrimination to prevent entry in the anchovy dimension? The Martian would also notice that the pizza parlours were very quiet in the middle of the afternoon, compared with the evening, but that their prices were no different. Does the failure to economize on the size of their ovens and their delivery vans reflect some form of conspiracy to overcapitalize?

The Martian would indeed be surprised when an Earthling informs him that the pizza industry is a very competitive industry. These practices reflect transactions costs and not the dictates of a regulator or of a cartel coordinator.

A final caveat needs to be made. It is tempting to conclude that market forces should be allowed to operate unencumbered by regulatory constraints unless there is clear evidence of efficiency gains from regulation or redistribution through regulation is clearly superior. That conclusion would reveal the bias of its author. Given present knowledge, it matters whether the market, the government, a particular regulatory scheme, or the status quo is given the benefit of the doubt — which organizational approach is to be the "incumbent" and be adopted unless clearly shown to be inferior to an alternative is an individual choice.

In the last decade, theoretical and applied knowledge of how regulation affects the economy has been substantially expanded. This momentum should be maintained, not through periodic surges in research that accompany a royal commission or a directive to the Economic Council of Canada, but rather on a systematic basis.

Notes

This study was completed in November 1984.

I have benefitted from discussions on the topic surveyed with my colleagues at Carleton University, Professor J. Chant of Simon Fraser University, and Professor T. Borcherding of the Claremont Graduate School.

1. The right to govern is treated here as an either-or concept. In fact, the right is less constrained the larger the majority of the winning party. See Stigler (1972).

2. An interesting discussion of the similarities and differences between political and economic competition occurs in Lectures 3 and 4 of Demsetz (1982).

3. For example, the CRTC in its *Annual Report* for 1980 made this advocacy appeal: "It seems clear that the radio broadcasters and the music industry need to have more financial assistance in the way of tax incentives or grants. There is a very close parallel between the difficulties being faced by the music recording industry and the film and television program production industries" (p. 18).

4. An indicative, but not exhaustive list of contributors would be T. Borcherding, A. Breton, D. Hartle, W. Hettich, J. Migué, A. Scott, M. Trebilcock, D. Usher, E. West, S. Winer and R. Wintrobe.

5. Some notable studies are those by Mathewson and Winter (1984); Stiglitz (1981).

6. See McManus (1975); Alchian and H. Demsetz (1972) and Williamson (1975).

7. In discussing the regulation of bus fares by the Alberta Motor Transport Board, Reschenthaler (1981) states: "The board does not interest itself in the reasonableness of individual fares, efficiency of operations, or rate of return" (p. 16).

8. Reschenthaler (1981) states with respect to bus regulation: "The company . . . feels inhibited by the regulatory apparatus from experimenting with a complex fare structure in order to increase profitability" (p. 59).

9. W.G. Waters II (1983) states: "If, as a matter of policy, we wish the railway system to be financially viable, i.e., self-sustaining without public subsidy to cover losses from decreasing cost operations, then the economically optimal pricing policy on efficiency grounds is VOSP (value of service pricing) until the overall rate of return starts to exceed competitive levels. This is known as Ramsey or Boiteux pricing in the economics literature" (p. 85).

10. In Breslaw and Smith (1982), their social measure is the integral of individuals' utilities where each individual's indirect utility function depends on the prices of the two telephone services, the prices of other goods, and income. The common utility function has decreasing marginal utility of income implying that decreases in the dispersion of income increase social utility.

11. For another estimate of the disparity between actual and Ramsey prices, see Fuss and Waverman (1981, p. 151).

12. For a more detailed modelling of the problem, see Willig (1979).
13. An exception is Fuss and Waverman (1981).
14. Papillon (1982) notes: "The ideal fare system should, in fact, establish such differences in prices, since a given price in a city with highly different levels of consumption at different times or in different areas creates waiting periods of varying lengths and a possible surplus of taxis in the downtown area" (p. 4).
15. McManus (1973) provides a more detailed history of this tendency.
16. A useful summary of studies and references on trucking regulation is provided in Hirshhorn (1981b).
17. The costs of distributions are examined and alternatives are discussed in McManus (1979).
18. Policy in the period before 1976 was described by the Department of Energy, Mines and Resources (Canada, 1980) in the following manner: "Until recently the dominant motive for this Government of Canada policy was not the security of our oil supply, because up to the mid-1970s overseas oil was not only cheaper than domestic oil, but was also considered secure. The most important reason for developing these national policies was a determination to promote the domestic oil industry, and encourage economic growth in Western Canada, even though it meant imposing higher direct costs on other parts of the country, and left the Government of Canada with little income tax revenue from the oil industry" (pp. 16–17). Policy after that time, when the industry's fortunes improved markedly, has been the mirror image.
19. CRTC — Public Notice 1983-18 — Canadian Content in Television states: "Where circumstances warrant, the Commission intends to rely to a significantly greater extent than in the past on the use of conditions of licence to stimulate improvements in Canadian television programming. This will allow much greater flexibility in taking the particular financial and human resources of each licensee into account."
20. An anonymous referee has questioned whether it is more costly to send a letter nationally than locally. I know of no published cost studies. The fact that private courier services have penetrated much more into the local mail business than the national and that their national rates are distance sensitive indicate to me that the margins are as stated in the manuscript. By and large, the pressures for entry are at the long-distance level in the telephone system and at the local level in mail.
21. Regardless of the quality of the story, economists feel uncomfortable with qualitative analysis and feel an imperative to introduce quantitative support, even when the issue does not lend itself readily to this approach. A case in point is Waverman's (1982) statistical investigation of factors influencing success in rate hearings. He concludes that: "All the evidence suggests that Bell Canada's degree of success is positively related to the number of witnesses that it calls. This result is not completely surprising since the Commissions base their decisions on the evidence before them. The result does however indicate that Bell can affect its own success rate by the amount of evidence it produces" (p. 152).
    The statistical exercise also shows that Bell Canada would benefit from having more main intervenors, a result which is dismissed as spurious by the author. The former result would appear equally spurious. That the company would bring more witnesses when its case was stronger seems credible. If so, the reported correlation would be reflecting the quality of the case, a factor which is not readily measurable and is not included in the regression. Instead of this impression, the discussion indicates that the company could increase its profits substantially by calling an additional witness. In the other study, which presents a full-blown statistical model of Bell Canada, Fuss and Waverman (1981) assume that Bell Canada is efficient in producing and marketing telephone services. Why wouldn't the company be equally efficient in presenting its case for increased rates? It is difficult to believe that a single equation would give a better prediction of the effectiveness of an additional witness than the management of the company.
22. CRTC — Public Notice 1982-44 states: "Accordingly the Commission will not at this time regulate the retail rate for pay television services. Licensees and potential exhibitors are encouraged to arrive at negotiated retail rates which compensate

exhibitors for their costs and provide them with a fair return on their investments without undermining the Commission's objectives for pay television."

23. For a readable discussion of the successive monopoly case, see Demsetz (1982, p. 48).

24. Price deregulation is generally associated with more variable profit streams. In the early 1980s, there was public concern over the "high" profits of the banks resulting in a House of Commons Committee investigation. See Canada (1982).

25. See CRTC *Annual Report* 1982–83, p. 37.

26. See Spence (1975) and Leffler (1982).

27. It seems unlikely that the Buenos Aires, Argentine experience, as reported in the *Wall Street Journal*, July 17, 1980, will be re-enacted here: "You pick up the phone, but there's no dial tone. You try another line: no dial tone. And another: no luck. What's going on here, anyway? Nothing special. It's just another day of business as usual for customers of Entel, the state-owned monopoly telephone company in this city, where phones are likely to go dead mid-conversation if they work at all, where bureaucrats boast that waiting time for repairs averages only 45 days and where the 40,000 customers a day who dare to complain are scolded: You must remain calm. You are one of many."

28. See CRTC, *Annual Report*, 1983, p. 19.

29. In a study of natural gas pipeline regulation in the United States, which incorporates an allowed rate of return, Callen (1978), finds that the method of implementation was such that no qualitatively determinate bias existed. His simulations indicate that the net benefits from regulation were within 15 percent of the maximum in all cases, and that it is "unlikely that other forms of politically acceptable regulatory procedures could do better."

30. CRTC, Public Notice, June 12, 1979.

Bibliography

Alchian, A.A., and H. Demsetz. 1972. "Production, Information Costs, andEconomic Organization." *American Economic Review* 62.

Arcus, P.L. 1981. "Broilers and Eggs." Technical Report E/13. Ottawa:Economic Council of Canada.

Barzel, Y. 1976. "An Alternative Approach to the Theory of Taxation." *Journal of Political Economy* 84.

Beigie, C.E. 1973. "An Economic Framework for Policy Action in CanadianTelecommunications." In *Telecommunications for Canada: Study 2*, edited by H.E. English. Toronto: Methuen.

Bernstein, J.I. 1980. "A Corporate Econometric Model of the British Columbia Telephone Company." In *Forecasting Public Utilities*, edited by O.D. Anderson. New York: North-Holland.

Bonsor, N.C. 1980. "The Costs of the Regulatory Process in the Canadian Trucking Industry." In *Studies of Trucking Regulation: Volume II*. Regulation Reference, Working Paper 3. Ottawa: Economic Council of Canada.

Borcherding, T.E., assisted by G.W. Dorosh. 1981. *The Egg Marketing Board: A Case Study of Monopoly and Its Social Cost*. Vancouver: Fraser Institute.

Borins, S.F. 1978. "Self-Regulation and the Canadian Air TransportationAdministration: The Case of Pickering Airport." In *Studies on Regulation in Canada*, edited by W.T. Stanbury. Ottawa: The Institute for Research on Public Policy.

Breslaw, J.A., and J.B. Smith. 1982. "Efficiency, Equity and Regulation: An Optimal Pricing Model for Bell Canada." *Canadian Journal of Economics* 15 (4).

Callen, J.L. 1978. "Production and Welfare in the Natural Gas Transmission Industry." *American Economic Review* (June).

Campbell, H.F. 1981. "The Public Regulation of Commercial Fisheries in Canada: The Bay of Fundy Herring Fishery." Technical Report 20. Ottawa: Economic Council of Canada.

Canada. 1980. Department of Energy, Mines and Resources. *The National Policy 1980.* Ottawa: The Department.

_____. 1982. House of Commons. Standing Committee on Finance, Trade and Economic Affairs. *Bank Profits.* Ottawa: Minister of Supply and Services Canada.

Caves, D.W., and L.R. Christensen. 1980. The Relative Efficiency of Public and Private Firms in a Competitive Environment: The Case of Canadian Railways." *Journal of Political Economy* 88 (October).

Daly, M.J., and P.S. Rao. 1983. "Productivity Growth, Economies of Scale, and Capacity Utilization in the Canadian Electric Power Industry: The Case of Ontario Hydro." Discussion Paper 236. Ottawa: Economic Council of Canada.

Demsetz, H. 1982. *Economic, Legal, and Political Dimensions of Competition.* Amsterdam: North-Holland.

Denny, M., C. Everson, and L. Waverman. 1981. "Estimating the Effects of Diffusion of Technical Innovations in Telecommunications: The Production Structure of Bell Canada." *Canadian Journal of Economics* 14 (1) (February).

Ellison, A.P. 1981. "U.S. Airline Deregulation: Implications for Canada." Technical Report 11. Ottawa: Economic Council of Canada.

Felske, B.E. and Associates Ltd. 1981. "Sulphur Dioxide Regulation and the Canadian Non-Ferrous Metals Industry." Technical Report 3. Ottawa: Economic Council of Canada.

Ferris, J.S. 1982. "Information and Search: An Alternative Approach to the Theory of Minimum Wages." *Economic Inquiry* 20 (October).

Ferris, J.S., and C.G. Plourde. 1982. "Labour Mobility, Seasonal Unemployment Insurance, and the Newfoundland Inshore Fishery." *Canadian Journal of Economics* 15 (August).

Furton, W.H., and G.E. Lee. 1977. "Economic Development of the Saskatchewan Wheat Economy." *Canadian Journal of Agricultural Economics* 25 (3).

Fuss, M., and L. Waverman. 1981. "The Regulation of Telecommunications in Canada." Technical Report 7. Ottawa: Economic Council of Canada.

Harvey, D.R. 1981. "Government Intervention and Regulation in the Canadian Grains Industry." Technical Report E/10. Ottawa: Economic Council of Canada.

Heaver, T.D., and J.C. Nelson. 1978a. *Railway Pricing under Commercial Freedom: The Canadian Experience.* Vancouver: University of British Columbia, Centre for Transportation Studies.

_____. 1978b. "The Roles of Competition and Regulation in Transport Markets: An Examination of Bill C-33." In *Studies on Regulation in Canada*, edited by W.T. Stanbury. Ottawa: Institute for Research on Public Policy.

Helliwell, J. 1978. "Some Emerging Issues in Utility-Regulation andRate-Making." In *Studies on Regulation in Canada*, edited by W.T. Stanbury. Ottawa: Institute for Research on Public Policy.

Hirshhorn, R. 1981a. "Product Safety Regulation and the Hazardous Products Act." Technical Report 10. Ottawa: Economic Council of Canada.

_____. 1981b. "Trucking Regulation in Canada: A Review of the Issues." Regulation Reference, Working Paper 26. Ottawa: Economic Council of Canada.

Jordan, W.A. 1972. "Producer Protection, Prior Market Structure and the Effects of Government Regulation." *Journal of Law and Economics* 15.

_____. 1982. "Performance of Regulated Canadian Airlines in Domestic and Transborder Operations." Ottawa: Department of Consumer and Corporate Affairs.

Josling, T. 1981. "Intervention and Regulation in Canadian Agriculture: A Comparison of Costs and Benefits among Sectors." Technical Report E/14. Ottawa: Economic Council of Canada.

Kim, M. 1984. "The Beneficiaries of Trucking Regulation Revisited." *Journal of Law and Economics* 27 (April).

Leffler, K.B. 1982. "Ambiguous Changes in Product Quality." *American Economic Review* (December).

Leland, H.E. 1981. "Quacks, Lemons, and Licensing: A Theory of Minimum Quality Standards." *Journal of Political Economy* 89.

Lord, R.J., and J. Shaw. 1980. "A Comparative Examination of the Impact of Regulation on the Operations and Costs of Intraprovincial Trucking Firms in Alberta and Ontario." In *Studies of Trucking Regulation: Volume II*. Regulation Reference, Working Paper 3. Ottawa: Economic Council of Canada.

Maister, David H. 1978. "Technical and Organizational Change in a Regulated Industry: The Case of Canadian Grain Transport." In *Studies on Regulation in Canada*, edited by W.T. Stanbury. Ottawa: Institute for Research on Public Policy.

Mathewson, G.F., and R.A. Winter. 1983. "Vertical Integration by Contractual Restraints in Spatial Markets." *Journal of Business* 56 (4).

————. 1984. "An Economic Theory of Vertical Restraints." *Rand Journal of Economics* 15 (1) (Spring).

————. 1985. The Economics of Vertical Restraints in Distribution." In *New Developments in the Analysis of Market Structures*, edited by Joseph Stiglitz and G.F. Mathewson. Cambridge, Mass.: MIT Press. Forthcoming.

McManus, J. 1973. "Federal Regulation of Telecommunications in Canada." In *Telecommunications for Canada*, edited by H.E. English. Toronto: Methuen.

————. 1975. "The Costs of Alternative Economic Organizations." *Canadian Journal of Economics* 13.

————. 1979. "The Role of Enforcement Costs in the Behaviour and Design of an Agricultural Marketing Board." Kingston: Queen's University, Institute for Economic Research.

McRae, J.J., and D.M. Prescott. 1980. "An Econometric Analysis of the Effect of Regulation on the Canadian Common Carrier Industry." In *Studies of Trucking Regulation: Volume II*. Regulation Reference, Working Paper 3. Ottawa: Economic Council of Canada.

Migué, J.L. 1977. "A Market Approach to Regulation." *Journal of Law and Economics* 20 (April).

Muzondo, T.R., and B. Pazderka. 1979. "Effects of Licensing on Earnings and Rates-of-Return Differentials." Ottawa: Department of Consumer and Corporate Affairs.

Olewiler, N.D. 1981. "The Regulation of Natural Resources in Canada: Theory and Practice." Technical Report 4. Ottawa: Economic Council of Canada.

Olley, R.E., and C.D. Lee. 1984. "Total Factor Productivity of Canadian Telecommunications Carriers: Project Report to the Department of Communications and to Members of the Canadian Telecommunications Carriers Association." Ottawa.

Palmer, J. 1974. "Taxation by Regulation? The Experience of Ontario Trucking Regulation." *The Logistics and Transportation Review* 10.

Papillon, B. 1982. "The Taxi Industry and Its Regulation in Canada." Regulation Reference, Working Paper 30. Ottawa: Economic Council of Canada.

Peltzman, S. 1976. "A Market Approach to Regulation." *Journal of Law and Economics* 19.

Reschenthaler, G.B. 1981. "Performance under Regulation: The Canadian Intercity Bus Industry." Ottawa: Department of Consumer and Corporate Affairs.

Scott, A., and P.A. Neher. 1981. *The Public Regulation of Commercial Fisheries in Canada*. Study prepared for the Economic Council of Canada. Ottawa: Minister of Supply and Services Canada.

Sims, W.A., and J.B. Smith. 1983. "The Impact of Environmental Regulation on Productivity Growth." Discussion Paper 241. Ottawa: Economic Council of Canada.

Spence, A.M. 1975. "Monopoly, Quality, and Regulation." *Bell Journal* 6 (Autumn).

Steiner, P.O. 1961. "Monopoly and Competition in Television: Some Policy Issues." *Manchester School* 29.

Stigler, G.J. 1972. "Economic Competition and Political Competition." *Public Choice* 13 (Fall).

Stiglitz, J.E. 1981. "Potential Competition May Reduce Welfare." *American Economic Review* 71.

Victor, P.A., and T.N. Burrell, with J. Evans and C. Figueriredo. 1981. "Environmental Protection Regulation: Water Pollution, and the Pulp and Paper Industry." Technical Report 14. Ottawa: Economic Council of Canada.

Walker, J.R. 1975. "Automobile Emmission Control: Means and Costs." Discussion Paper 41. Ottawa: Economic Council of Canada.

Waters, W.G. II. 1983. "Transportation, Transport Policies and the Future Development of Western Canada." Discussion Paper 234. Ottawa: Economic Council of Canada.

Waverman, L. 1982. "The Process of Telecommunications Regulation in Canada." Regulation Reference, Working Paper 28. Ottawa: Economic Council of Canada.

Westfield, F.M. 1971. "Innovation and Monopoly Regulation." In *Technological Change in Regulated Industries*, edited by W.M. Capron. Washington, D.C.: Brookings Institution.

Williamson, O.E. 1975. *Markets and Hierarchies*. New York: Free Press.

Willig, R.D. 1979. "The Theory of Network Access Pricing." In *Issues in Public Utility Regulation*, edited by H.M. Trebing. Ann Arbor: Michigan State University.

6

Commercial and Political Efficiency
A Comparison of Government, Mixed, and Private Enterprises

D.G. MCFETRIDGE

The purpose of this paper is to summarize some recent theoretical and empirical work on the efficiency of government enterprise. Efficiency must, of course, be measured in relative terms and defined relative to some goal. In this paper, three institutional forms are compared. They are government enterprises or Crown corporations, mixed enterprises and private enterprises.

Government enterprises are defined, for purposes of this paper, as commercial corporations which are wholly owned by a government. Mixed enterprises are defined as commercial corporations in which a government holds an equity interest sufficient to give it effective control. The proportion of the equity required for effective control will vary depending on the distribution of the non-government interest. A private enterprise is defined as any corporation in which the government does not have a controlling interest.

Not considered here, then, are distinctions involving the various organizational forms of wholly owned government enterprises, enterprises in which a government has a non-controlling interest, widely and closely held corporations, and non-corporate organizational forms. These distinctions may be important. They simply could not be considered in this paper.

Efficiency is defined relative to three different goals. The first is efficiency in the provision of commercial services. This is taken to be synonymous with what others have called managerial or firm-level commercial efficiency.

The second is efficiency in the provision of political services or what others have called efficiency as a governing or public policy instrument.

The question here is whether and under what circumstances a Crown corporation or a mixed enterprise is superior to such alternative policy instruments as subsidization, tax expenditures, regulation of various kinds, or direct expenditure by government departments for purposes of pursuing public policy goals.

The third is market efficiency, which is defined here to be an absence of monopolistic behaviour. The issue of market efficiency arises in two connections in this paper. The first is with respect to the potential role of government enterprise in increasing competition and whether government enterprises have made a contribution in this regard. The second is whether and under what circumstances the manner in which privatization occurs would reduce competition.

The paper begins with a conceptual discussion of the forces leading to efficiency in the provision of commercial and political services, respectively. Theory is of particular importance because both the data and empirical results in this area are open to a range of interpretations.

In many industries, particularly in what one might term entrepreneurial industries, which are characterized by heterogeneous and rapidly evolving products and processes, there is no benchmark of performance other than rate of return. Yet profit rates are affected by the political services a firm provides and the degree to which it is compensated for them. Neither is known with any degree of accuracy.

In other industries, which might be termed mature (because they have standardized and slowly evolving products and processes), efficiency measures in the form of input-input or input-output ratios (mechanics per bus, employees per telephone) may be available. Even here, however, the inferences drawn about efficiency are sensitive to the sophistication with which the production technology is presented. The efficiency judgments reached by various studies of railroads and airlines provide a good illustration of this point.

Another problem is that the provision of political services may take the form of an alteration of the production technology. Thus a government enterprise may be "overstaffed" or may be following a (perhaps ill-conceived) public policy directive with respect to employment creation.

Finally, as Acheson points out in his study in this volume, technologies that contribute to increased productivity may be developed at considerable cost by one firm and adopted without compensation by others. Even elaborate productivity studies may show the "free riders" to have higher productivity than the innovator. This may cut either way as far as estimates of the relative efficiency of government and private enterprises are concerned.

Therefore, in most cases, it is as much a question of the theory testing the data as of the data testing the theory. Hence, a well-reasoned set of beliefs about what "should" be efficiency under a given set of circumstances is highly desirable.

Following the discussion of the theoretical issues, there is a brief survey of the recent, largely Canadian literature on the measurement of public enterprise performance. (A more detailed survey is given in the study in this volume by Borins and Boothman.) The survey includes, first, some recent productivity comparisons of "matched pairs" of government and private enterprises. Reference is made here to preliminary results reported in some excellent studies commissioned by the Economic Council of Canada.

Second, inferences regarding commercial performance are drawn from selected recent case studies of individual Crown corporations. The firms studied here operate in what have been termed entrepreneurial industries, where simple productivity comparisons are either not possible or, if possible, are misleading. The reasons are that competing firms differ significantly with respect to the characteristics of both their products and their production technologies and that commercial performance in any case is related more closely to corporate strategy (namely, product and market selection) than to the standard input-output relationships. The discussion here is based on presentations made either to this Royal Commission's symposium on Crown corporations or to two symposia on Crown corporations organized by the Economic Council of Canada.

Third, inferences regarding the relative efficacy of government enterprises as instruments of public policy are drawn from selected case studies. While none of the surveys presented pretends to be complete, the survey of government enterprises as policy instruments is the least complete and covers only a few cases in which the public policy goals of the enterprise are explicit and have been widely debated.

Fourth, some evidence is examined with respect to the efficiency of mixed enterprises in the provision of both commercial and political services. Included in this section is a discussion of the consequences of purchases of (effective) controlling interests in private firms by public sector pension plans.

The paper concludes with a discussion of the implications of both theoretical considerations and empirical results for public policy regarding both privatization and the formation or acquisitions of new government or mixed enterprises.

Theoretical Considerations

Factors Contributing to the Efficient Provision of Commercial Services

It has been argued for more than fifty years that there will be a divergence of interests between the management and ownership of widely held corporations. In this view, the maximization of managerial utility is at the expense of the value of the firm. Efficient resource use is sacrificed in favour of managerial emoluments. The reduction in the value of the firm less the value to the managers of the perquisites they consume is called by Jensen and Meckling (1976) the net agency cost of the corporate form.

There are four types of forces at work to minimize net agency costs. They are:

- internal monitoring;
- the market for managers;
- the product market; and
- the capital market.

Internal monitoring refers to the performance incentives resulting from the internal rivalry for senior managerial positions and to the oversight provided by "outside" directors on the board of directors.

The market for managers serves to link the compensation of managers with their consumption of managerial perquisites. In essence, the competitive supply price of managers reflects the value they attach to on-the-job consumption. Some authors, such as Fama (1980), argue that the market for managers effects a full ex post "settling up" so that all agency costs are borne by managers and, under idealized conditions, they cease to exist.

Competition in the product market is thought to induce managerial efficiency for a number of reasons, none of which are particularly persuasive. First, it is thought that competition in the product market would be conducive to the evolution of superior techniques of managerial control. Second, it is argued that given competitive product markets, firms which fail to adopt techniques which minimize agency costs will disappear. In essence, the economics of natural selection is at work here.

Competition in the capital market can also reduce agency costs. The most widely cited mechanism is what is called the "market for corporate control." This is simply the purchase of a controlling interest in a corporation's voting stock by an individual or group with the intent of making changes which increase the value of the corporation. There is a corresponding increase in the value of the shares held by the controlling group, and this is the incentive to acquire control.

The market for corporate control can involve tender offers, mergers, various forms of management buy-outs, and proxy contests in which control but not ownership changes hands. The evidence is that these activities are wealth-increasing for both the parties involved and for society as a whole (Jensen and Ruback, 1983). There is also some evidence that this increase in wealth is occasionally the result of the replacement of inefficient managements or management methods, in addition to the usual economies of scale and synergistic effects.

The operation of the market for corporate control is made possible by the transferability of corporate voting stock. Transferability has other virtues as well. It allows owners to self-select with respect to task and growth orientation. As a consequence, corporations may tend to have like-minded owners.

Transferability also facilitates dispute resolution. Stockholders who are not favourable to a particular corporate investment strategy can always sell their shares to individuals who are. Thus, as circumstances change, the composition of ownership may also change.

This adaptability properly extends beyond the tastes of the owners to the distribution of ownership. The distribution of ownership always involves a trade-off between agency costs and the costs of risk-bearing. Depending on the nature of their activities, the sum of agency and risk-bearing costs may be minimized by either dispersed or concentrated share ownership. This may change over time as the nature and scale of the business change.

It might be conjectured that the trade-off will favour widely dispersed ownership in cases in which there are objective benchmarks of managerial performance. These may be related to input usage (or productivity) or perhaps to product market shares. They would be meaningful, of course, only in the case of standardized technologies and/or well-defined and stable markets — that is, in mature industries. Of course, a mature industry need not remain in that category and the ideal distribution of ownership may change.

At the other end of the spectrum are entrepreneurial industries characterized by rapidly evolving products and process technologies and a consequent absence of simple input-based or market-share performance benchmarks. The relevant inputs here are perceptiveness, judgment and timing. Failure to develop and pre-empt new markets may be more important than success in holding onto old ones. In this case, concentrated ownership on a continuing basis and the oversight associated with it may be appropriate.

Much of the foregoing is speculative in nature. It does, however, serve to emphasize that the transferability of ownership claims (residual claimant status) can be efficiency-inducing in a number of ways. Not the least of its virtues is its adaptability in that it allows for a reconfiguration of ownership structure as and when the circumstances require.

Factors Contributing to Commercial Efficiency in Government Enterprises

Government enterprises differ from private enterprises in one important respect. Ownership of the former is not transferable. As a consequence, the market for corporate control is inoperative. In addition, the identity and distribution of ownership cannot be varied as circumstances require. Owners need not be of like mind with respect to risk and growth orientation. Dispute resolution centres on what Hirschman (1970) has called the "voice" option rather than the "exit" option. Those opposing the investment strategy of a Crown corporation cannot sell out to those who favour it and vice versa. Dispute resolution is carried out via the political process.

There is a school of thought to the effect that the absence of transferable ownership rights does not constitute a significant handicap. One branch of this school argues that the principal determinant of the level of managerial efficiency is the extent of competition in the market for a firm's product. In this view, the market for corporate control is burdened conceptually by "free rider" problems and is, for practical purposes, non-existent.[1] A second branch argues that politicians have the incentive to enforce managerial efficiency on behalf of the taxpayer-owners of a Crown corporation. In this view, the Crown is the best of all worlds, combining the risk-reducing benefits of widely dispersed ownership with the detailed oversight of managerial performance.

The incentive for politicians to require managers of Crown corporations to act efficiently could come from a number of sources. First, politicians have no interest in allowing subordinates to consume, in the form of various emoluments, resources which they could use for their own purposes. Thus, the disposition of the potential surplus would be expected to occur at the political level rather than at the managerial level.

While this "solves" the immediate problem of Crown corporation efficiency, the question remains as to how the political leadership will dispose of the Crown corporation surplus. Will it be spent in the manner desired by the electorate or will it be consumed by politicians? This is what Halpern et al. (1984) call the double agency problem. Management of Crown corporations must be made to act as the government wishes and the government must be made to act as the electorate or, to interpose another step, Parliament wishes.

Some, such as Wintrobe (1984), argue that "political markets" are reasonably efficient in that the electoral process forces politicians both to require that Crown corporations operate efficiently and to distribute the resulting surplus to various segments of the community. In this view, then, the political process would ensure that a strictly commercial government enterprise is indistinguishable from a strictly commercial private enterprise.

Thus, insofar as commercial operations are concerned, there are two contending positions. One emphasizes the discipline that the capital market imposes on management and the role of transferable ownership claims in facilitating this. The other emphasizes the respective disciplinary roles of product market competition and internal monitoring by politicians, either on their own behalf or on behalf of the electorate.

In his assessment of the evidence, Borcherding (1983) concludes that both these positions have merit:

> In summary, this long and varied literature does appear to indicate that private and competitive suppliers provide cheaper contracted-for public services than do public firms not subject to competitive pressures. Further, it also appears that regulation can raise production costs of private firms, but probably not higher than their public monopoly privileged equivalents. Finally, subject to sufficient competitive pressures and absent subsidies, public and private supplying firms need not differ markedly in their efficiencies. Thus, not only does the Alchian ownership transfer mechanism influence costs but so also does the older, Smithian concern with market structure and entry regulation. (p. 136)

Efficiency in the Provision of Political Services[2]

Governments obviously purchase commercial services from firms. It is perhaps less obvious that they also want to purchase political services — that is, to induce firms to engage in activities which they would not undertake without government inducement. These activities could include the provision of goods or services on a non-compensatory basis, the use of less productive inputs or less productive combinations of inputs, or the location of activities in a less productive location than the firm would otherwise choose.

Governments can purchase political services in a number of ways. They can directly subsidize the production of goods or services, such as the shipment of grain by rail or the provision of bus services in rural areas. Governments can subsidize the use of certain inputs, such as workers drawn from socially disadvantaged groups. The location of activities in remote or otherwise high-cost locations can also be induced by direct subsidization.

A second alternative is to engage in what Stigler (1971) calls public finance regulation and what Schultz and Alexandroff (1984) more recently call planning regulation. This option involves the imposition of a regulatory regime which restricts competition in some markets, thus creating a "budget" equal to the monopoly profits of the regulated firms. This "budget" is then spent on the type of political services described above. The process is known as cross-subsidization. The existence of this practice has been documented in the case of railway transportation (McManus, 1978), air transportation (Baldwin, 1975), telecommunications (Acheson, 1985) and the petroleum industry (Baldwin, 1982), among others.

A third option exists which may contain features of the first two. In this case, the firm providing the political services is a Crown corporation. The government may again purchase political services from a Crown corporation by means of direct subsidization, as it now does with grain carried by the Canadian National Railway. The government may use planning regulation to endow a Crown corporation with monopoly profits which are then applied to the provision of political services, as it once did with Air Canada. The government may provide neither subsidies nor monopoly profits but instead accept a lower or zero return on its equity in a Crown corporation in return for the provision of political services.

An example of the latter practice is cited by McFetridge (1984). In the past, the Federal Business Development Bank has operated on a so-called "cost-recovery basis." This requires that its loan income cover its interest expenses but not the implicit (opportunity) cost of the government's equity in the FBDB. The FBDB subsidy (political services) budget is thus equal to the opportunity cost of the government's equity in it. Other examples of this practice would be the "break-even" pricing practices of at least some provincial electric utilities.

There are circumstances under which the cost of transacting in political services is lower if the supplying firm is a government enterprise. If it is costly to measure the amount and quality of services performed and the costs incurred in so doing, and if the government cannot readily turn to alternative suppliers, a private firm will have an incentive to misrepresent its performance on all these margins. A government enterprise will have less incentive to engage in this type of opportunism in that any profits derived from it ultimately accrue to the government in any case. In essence, the transaction between the government and the firm is "internalized," with all the advantages that normally entails (Williamson, 1979). This implies that regulatory or subsidy systems pursuing public policy goals which are poorly defined in one or more dimensions are less costly to administer when the participating firms are government enterprises.

Crown corporations have another advantage in the performance of political services in that, for relatively small transactions, the process of costing the service and compensating the performer can be avoided altogether. The government simply directs that the service be performed and accepts a lower return on its equity in the performing firm. Note that pursuit of this option becomes more complex in the case of a mixed enterprise when there is also a non-government equity interest in the firm. This problem is explored below.

While avoiding an explicit costing of each transaction involving political services can save resources, it does not do so without an offsetting real cost. When political services are not costed, there is some uncertainty as to whether a Crown corporation's low rate of return on equity is due to the performance of especially costly political services or to the diversion of actual or potential profits into some form of managerial consumption. Poor rates of return can always be blamed on "political constraints" when they may be due, in part, to managerial slack.[3]

This problem can be overcome, at least to some extent, in cases where there are non-profit benchmarks of managerial efficiency. In mature industries, it may be possible to discern from productivity measures (such as repairmen per telephone or mechanics per bus) or from measures of the consumption of perquisites (such as first-class air travel) whether low rates of return are the result of managerial slack or of performance of costly political services.

In sum, the use of Crown corporations to perform political services can reduce opportunism (thus saving the cost of resources devoted to it) and reduce the need to account specifically for each undertaking. One might then ask whether the performance of political services by departments of government might reduce costs still further. The answer is that it could, if departmental officials have even less to gain from opportunism than Crown corporation executives. On the basis of the performance of political services alone, one might expect the use of private firms as agents to be the most costly, Crown corporations to be less costly, and government departments to be still less costly. The observed performance of political services by all three implies that there must be some offsetting factor — namely, that political services must often be supplied jointly with commercial services. The choice of agents would then be determined by the relative proportions of commercial and political services supplied. At one end of the spectrum are private firms which supply political services only occasionally or, if continuously, in amounts which are small relative to their commercial activities. The relative importance of political services is greater in the case of Crown corporations and greater still in the case of government departments.

There are, then, essentially two dimensions in which the agent choice decision must be considered. The first is the nature of the political services to be performed. Are their costs readily ascertainable? Are the criteria for acceptable performance clear? Does this performance require a specialized commitment which leaves either party vulnerable to subsequent opportunism by the other? If measurement of cost and performance is costly and the transaction cannot be disciplined by the ability of either party to turn elsewhere, the Crown or government department will be preferred to the private firm as an agent.

The second is the importance of political services relative to the total activities of the agent. The more important the political services, the more likely their reliance on a Crown corporation or, ultimately, on a government department.

Economic Efficiency and Political Expediency

As has been suggested, governments have a number of means at their disposal for altering market outcomes. These range from measures which directly tax, regulate or subsidize individuals or groups of individuals, to measures which are applied indirectly through agents such as private firms, Crown corporations (including marketing boards) or government departments. The approach taken to this point has been to assume the existence of a desired amount of redistributive activity and then to investigate the lowest-cost means of effecting that redistribution.

Another approach is to assume that the desired amount of redistribution is itself a function of the means available to effect it. It has been argued that planning regulation and Crown corporations facilitate redistribution in that the losers are less aware of the magnitude of their losses and are therefore less inclined to oppose the transfer, while the beneficiaries remain fully cognizant of their gains.

In this view, a Crown corporation may be chosen to provide political services not because it can do so at the lowest cost but because the redistribution involved would be discerned and successfully opposed if any other mechanism were chosen.

Redistribution of various kinds can facilitate the successful adaptation of a community to new circumstances. Redistribution can also be dysfunctional in the sense that it involves the use of real resources to extract wealth from others or to prevent its extraction, rather than to produce additional wealth. Olson (1982) goes so far as to attribute the declining growth rates of the Western industrial nations to their increasing preoccupation with redistribution.

Redistribution can thus be wealth-increasing or wealth-decreasing, depending on how much and what type occurs. In this view, the fact that a Crown corporation facilitates redistribution which would not otherwise occur is neither in its favour nor against it.

This conclusion is unsatisfactory in the sense that it ignores the possibility that a government enterprise may facilitate transfers by reducing the incentive of the "victims" of these transfers to oppose them. As Trebilcock et al. (1982, pp. 30–33) argue, the losers in an income redistribution are less likely to oppose it the more costly it is to determine the amount they will lose and the less each individual loses. Government enterprise may facilitate redistribution by obscuring its magnitude from the losers, by spreading its burden more widely among them, or perhaps by concentrating its burden on a group whose opposition will not take the form of a withdrawal of political support (inframarginal voters).

There is surely some reason to argue that the facilitation of a transfer is not socially beneficial if it is a measure that society would not acquiesce to were it better understood (that is, attempted by more direct means) or were the incidence of it distributed differently. If this is the case, the contribution of government enterprise to the facilitation of redistributive activity must be held against it.

Privatization: Implications of the Theory

The privatization experiment under consideration here is the substitution of private for government enterprise. The substitution of mixed for government enterprise is discussed in the next section. What effect would privatization have on commercial efficiency, on efficiency in the provision of political services, and on the scale of political services performed?

With respect to commercial efficiency, those emphasizing the role of the capital market in ensuring efficiency would argue that the substitution of transferable for non-transferable ownership claims would result in increased efficiency. This increased efficiency would be a consequence of:

- the operation or potential operation of the market for corporate control;
- the ability of the composition and distribution of ownership to evolve in response to changing circumstances; and
- the dispute-resolving properties of transferable ownership claims.

Thus, those emphasizing the importance of transferable ownership claims would predict an increase in efficiency at the firm level regardless of the circumstances of the privatization. If the initial sale of shares involved dispersed ownership and a more concentrated ownership became appropriate, or vice versa, these forms would evolve.

Those emphasizing the role of politicians in ensuring the efficient operation of government enterprise would argue that, to the extent that privatization involves the substitution of a widely held corporation for a government enterprise, it could be efficiency-reducing. In this view, the market for corporate control and other forms of shareholder oversight will not be sufficient to replace the oversight of the political executive. This might be overcome, in part, by a concentration of ownership, but only by incurring increasing risk-bearing costs.

Those emphasizing the role of product market competition in ensuring firm-level efficiency would argue that privatization is neither necessary nor sufficient to induce an increase in efficiency. The latter can, in this view, be induced by deregulation, freer trade and a more active competition policy without changing the ownership of the firms involved.

A more subtle variant of this argument is that privatization would not increase firm-level efficiency in the context of a regulated or otherwise "protected" environment, but would do so if regulation or protection were reduced. That is, privatization and deregulation interact, the latter being necessary if the former is to have any impact.[4]

A final implication of the product-market-competition view is that some privatization arrangements could reduce competition and therefore reduce firm-level efficiency. The sale of a Crown corporation to its only competitor could, in an environment of regulatory or other entry barriers, reduce efficiency.

This raises the question of the effect of privatization on market efficiency — that is, on the extent to which the markets in which a government enterprise participates approximate a competitive norm. If a Crown corporation had been moving the market toward a competitive output level, then privatization would reduce market efficiency.

Alternatively, the sale of a Crown corporation to a prominent competitor or potential competitor could, in an environment otherwise conducive to sustained collusion, result in the cartelization of a hitherto workably competitive market.

While firm-level and market efficiency could either increase or decrease as a consequence of privatization, there would almost certainly be an increase in the cost of arranging for the performance of political services. This increase in the cost of transacting may not be significant, depending on the nature of the political services involved. It may also be either offset or reinforced by changes in the operational efficiency of the firm(s) involved.

Finally, there is both a substitution and a scale effect in operation here. In the case of privatization, politicians are obliged to substitute in favour of planning regulation, subsidization or direct expenditures as instruments. This could, in one view, also involve a substitution in favour of a less efficient instrument (in terms of resource cost). This, in turn, would imply that the marginal transfer or political service would no longer be worthwhile and would not continue.

In another view, privatization would involve the substitution of a more visible for a less visible redistributive instrument, with the consequence that transfers that were once feasible (in the sense that their magnitudes were effectively hidden from those bearing their costs) would now encounter opposition and no longer be feasible.

Thus, privatization may make it impossible to effect transfers which society genuinely wishes to make. It may also eliminate transfers which society would not have made had information about them been widely available. The larger this latter category, the more likely it is that a reduction in the amount of redistributive activity resulting from privatization will be socially beneficial.

Mixed Enterprise

While a mixed enterprise can be defined to include any firm in which a government has an equity interest, only those enterprises in which a government has a controlling or potentially controlling interest are considered here. Depending on the distribution of non-government equity holdings, a government interest of 20 percent or perhaps less may be sufficient to ensure control. Government is, of course, guaranteed control when it holds at least 51 percent of the voting stock.

A taxonomy of possible government shareholdings and distributions of the non-government interest together with conjectures regarding their respective behavioural implications is provided by Eckel, Vining and Boardman (1984). This paper assumes, strictly for the sake of simplicity, that a corporation in which the government's "steady state" equity interest does not afford it effective control can be viewed as a private enterprise so far as its efficiency in providing commercial and political services is concerned.

For mixed enterprises as defined here, the issues are the same as for conventional Crown corporations. Is a mixed enterprise likely to be more or less efficient than government or private enterprises in the provision of commercial services or in the provision of political services?

With respect to commercial or managerial efficiency, evaluation of the consequences of mixed ownership depends on the relative importance attached to the various forces disciplining management. Those holding the view that the extent of competition in the market for the firm's product is the essential determinant of managerial efficiency would argue that mixed ownership does not influence corporate commercial performance. Those holding the view that politicians have an interest in minimizing resource waste in agencies under their control would argue that a mixed enterprise is more efficient than a widely held corporation but perhaps less efficient than a closely held corporation or a government enterprise.

Those attaching importance to the role of capital market discipline operating through transferable ownership claims would argue that managerial efficiency in a mixed enterprise does not differ from that of a Crown corporation and that both are less efficient than a private firm.[5] The reason they would give is that effective government control renders the market for corporate control inoperative. Continuing government control is, by definition, incompatible with a process by which the shareholders can sell control to the managerial group valuing it most highly.

With regard to the provision of political services, some would argue that a mixed enterprise is less efficient than a Crown corporation but more efficient than a private firm. A political services transaction with a mixed enterprise is not fully internalized. To the extent that it acts on behalf of the outside (non-government) equity interest, management of a mixed enterprise is more inclined toward opportunistic behaviour vis-à-vis the government, circumstances permitting, than is Crown corporation management.

In addition, because there is a non-government equity interest, the government no longer has the option of "paying" for political services by accepting lower rates of return. If the outside interest is to be protected, political services must be costed and paid for either directly or through regulatory or other protection.

The possibility arises that the outside interest will not be protected and that reimbursement for political services will not cover the cost of providing them. If this occurs and has not been anticipated, the market value of the equity of the firm(s) involved will decline, thus imposing a capital loss on shareholders.

Anticipation by the capital market that some firms will be the targets of government buy-ins and will, as a consequence, be obliged to perform political services for which they are not fully compensated can have some destructive consequences. Consider a situation in which it is known that the government will acquire effective control of some firms and extract political services from them, but in which neither the identity of the target firms nor the excess cost of the services is known. Shares in all firms will then trade at a discount reflecting the expected excess cost of political services plus a "political risk" premium. The existence of a possible government buy-in thus results in a generalized increase in the cost of corporate capital.

In sum, a mixed enterprise is inefficient relative to a government enterprise in that transactions involving political services must be carried out at arm's length. Mixed enterprises may also entail a more general, economy-wide inefficiency in that the threat of government buy-ins for purposes of extracting political services may increase the cost of capital for all firms.[6]

Transactions in political services should be less costly with a mixed enterprise than with a private enterprise. There is a partial government interest and therefore, at least marginally, less incentive for opportunism. Given incentive effects, the government's interest may improve information flows and reduce the potential for opportunism.

Finally, the emergence of the mixed enterprise as an alternative policy instrument has both substitution and scale effects. There is some substitution away from arrangements utilizing either government or private enterprises. There may also be a scale effect in that mixed enterprises may facilitate a new set of redistributive policies. To the extent that this is a consequence of an ability to hide the magnitude of the transfers involved from those who must bear the burden of them, it is not a desirable outcome.

Empirical Studies

Commercial Efficiency: Government vs. Private Enterprise

Excellent surveys of the relative commercial performance of private and government enterprise can be found in Borcherding (1983) and in the

Borins and Boothman study in this volume. This section provides only a few illustrative comparisons and some references to the most recent Canadian work.

In regard to airlines, the work of Jordan (1982a, 1982b) indicates that there is no demonstrable efficiency difference between the government and private trunk carriers in Australia and there was no large or systematic efficiency difference between Air Canada, CP Air and three major U.S. trunk carriers prior to deregulation.

More recent work by Gillen, Oum and Tretheway (1984) employs a more sophisticated representation of airline costs and output. They conclude that Air Canada was less efficient over the period 1964–81 than CP Air, Nordair, and perhaps Pacific Western, and that this was a consequence of a greater amount of excess capacity. The latter may or may not have been due to government ownership.

Total factor productivity (TFP) in railroading is examined in a number of papers including those by Caves and Christenson (1980) and Caves, Christenson, Swanson and Tretheway (1982). The government-owned CN railway was found to have a higher rate of growth in TFP over the 1956–79 period and higher TFP after 1967 than the privately owned CP Rail. Both had higher TFP levels after the mid-1960s than all major U.S. railroads. The authors attribute this to rate deregulation in Canada in 1967, but Heaver and Waters (1982) are skeptical of this explanation. It would be of interest in this regard to see whether passage of the Staggers Act (to permit U.S. rail deregulation) has had an equally salutary effect on the productivity of U.S. railroads.

In telecommunications, Denny, de Fontenay and Werner (1983) find that, as of 1978, total factor productivity was 7 percent higher in Alberta Government Telephones (AGT) than in privately owned Bell Canada or British Columbia Telephones. In 1967, Bell was 25 percent more productive than AGT. The improvement of AGT is attributed by the authors to increases in labour efficiency, although their results (p. 121) appear to imply that the current AGT advantage lies in the more efficient use of capital. More recent simple productivity comparisons by Denny (1984) reveal no systematic private-public enterprise differences among a large number of telephone companies.

In the petroleum industry, both Pratt (1981, 1982) and Borins and Boothman (1985) cite a U.S. General Accounting Office study which concludes that prior to 1979, Petro-Canada was comparable with private sector firms in terms of oil exploration and production. A more recent study by Halpern, Plourde and Waverman (1984) concludes that "Petro Canada on most measures had inferior financial performance compared to the hypothetical industry 'benchmark'" (p. 79).

For example, the most general measure of performance — earnings before interest and taxes (EBIT) as a share of total assets — averaged

19.9 percent for the industry and 7.3 for Petro-Canada over the 1977–83 period. Some observers doubt that the performance difference is this large. They note that Petro-Canada's assets are carried on its books at their late-1970s acquisition cost whereas industry assets are carried at their earlier (on average) and hence lower acquisition cost. Two issues remain. First, an inflated acquisition cost may itself be partially the result of mismanagement. Second, in the event that, given comparable asset valuations, Petro-Canada's ratio of EBIT to total assets lies below industry levels, this may be due to the uncompensated provision of political services rather than commercial inefficiency.

In my comparison of the Federal Business Development Bank with Roynat, (McFetridge, 1984), I find that FBDB operating costs per dollar of assets averaged just under three times those of Roynat between 1980 and 1983 and conclude that this difference was in excess of that which could be explained by the FBDB's mandated emphasis on small high-risk loans. The same conclusion does not hold for the FBDB's predecessor, the Industrial Development Bank, which was deemed in earlier work to have been as efficient operationally as Roynat.

Laux and Molot (1981, 1984) make an impressionistic comparison of the efficiency of the Potash Corporation of Saskatchewan and its private sector counterparts. They conclude that neither management of the individual mines nor the basis upon which they operated changed after nationalization and that PCS is regarded by all concerned as an "aggressive and successful competitor."

Commercial Efficiency: Government Enterprise Case Studies

A second set of studies examines the operations of particular Crown corporations but does not compare them with a private sector benchmark. Many of the firms studied are in dynamic and rapidly evolving (entrepreneurial) as opposed to mature (managerial) industries. As the theoretical discussion above suggests is appropriate, evaluations of Crown corporations in entrepreneurial industries take the form of strategy assessments rather than unit cost or productivity calculations.

Government-owned De Havilland Aircraft of Canada (DHC) has been the subject of studies by White (1984a, 1984b, 1984c) and Doutriaux and Henin (1984). In his evaluation, White concludes that strategic planning at De Havilland has been poor, at least with respect to the Dash-8 decision. Part of the problem has been poor communication between the government and the firm. The government was not consulted when alternative strategies were being developed and the government ultimately chose a strategy which was different (at least with respect to financing) from any DHC management proposal.

White (1984c) concludes that some of the problems De Havilland has experienced could be remedied by the adoption of better management practices:

From my own standpoint I would like to underline one observation. Whether or not commercially-oriented Crowns, those facing competitive markets, are deemed to be successful, will to a large extent be determined by how they are administered by the Crown. The government must place these companies in an administrative context that allows for effective strategic and operating control. These skills have been well developed by large, diversified firms (principally in the U.S.) and I believe much can be learned from their experiences that could prove helpful to the government. (p. 1)

He concedes, however, that the Crown corporation may not be the appropriate organizational form for competing in entrepreneurial industries.

The essential strategic weapon in an entrepreneurial industry is pre-emption. Pre-emption involves being first to perceive and fill a market niche and then deterring subsequent entry by others. Successful entry deterrence requires that all potential entrants be convinced that there is no possibility of profitable entry. There is a great deal of literature in economics on this subject. In general, successful entry deterrence requires that a large fraction of the incumbent's assets be specific (specialized) to the market in question. In this case, potential entrants will know the incumbent has no choice but to stand and fight.

White argues that the ability of a Crown corporation to lose virtually unlimited amounts of money serves to deter potential entrants, provided that they believe the government will actually allow the Crown corporation to do so. In White's view, successful entry deterrence by the firm derives from the appearance of unwavering government support rather than the existence of market-specific assets.

The requisite appearance of government support can be sustained, in White's opinion, only by suppressing public debate on the worth of the projects in question and indeed by eliminating public accountability and public information on conditions attached to the financing of entrepreneurial Crown corporations. The problems this creates are obvious. As White (1984a) notes, "Here lies the heart of the dilemma. These companies require government support, yet subjecting them to the process of review and debate that has accompanied crown-ownership condemns them to competitive failure. . ." (p. 35). While suppression of debate is neither necessary nor sufficient for success in an entrepreneurial industry, White is on the right track.

To be successful in an entrepreneurial industry, a firm must discern and pre-empt market niches as they emerge. The capacity to do so may be impaired by requirements to perform political services such as hiring disadvantaged members of society, maintaining staff levels, and producing specific product lines or at specific production locations.

The performance of political services notwithstanding, the government enterprise, by virtue of its ownership structure, lacks some of the adaptive properties that come with transferable ownership — specifically, owner self-selection and dispute resolution. In essence, the segment of society wishing to make large risky investments cannot credibly buy out those who do not. There is no exit option, only a voice (public debate) option. As White argues, this may cripple any attempt to engage in market pre-emption.

Doutriaux and Henin are also critical of strategic decision making at DHC. They conclude that the company proceeded with the Dash-7 even though information available at the time indicated that the chances of breaking even were remote (pp. 50–51). The Dash-8 decision involved failures in the following dimensions. The airplane design did not take advantage of common cell design (as, with the Dash-7); strategic and financial planning were handled separately, by DHC and the government respectively; competitive, potentially self-serving sales forecasts were produced; and the production scheduling was inconsistent with even the most optimistic sales forecasts.

The authors conclude, like White, that the decision process at DHC has to be brought closer to that of a private company (p. 54). They appear to conclude, however, that the Crown ownership itself would continue to pose problems: "Everybody, including insiders, seems convinced that government's intervention has made DHC personnel less competitive and less performing" (p. 70). Perceptively, Doutriaux and Henin note that the problem associated with Crown ownership is not so much one of managerial sloth as of orientation:

> Government ownership also tends to encourage a technology-driven rather than a market-driven approach to strategic planning: the "person in the street" and the politicians who monitor his reactions tend to be more sensitive to technical achievements (the Canadarm is a good example of such technical leadership) than to marketing success. (p. 77)

The authors conclude that DHC has tended to design airplanes for their own sake. The same might be said of the experience of Atomic Energy of Canada Limited with CANDU reactors (see below). The implication is that insofar as commercial success in entrepreneurial industries is concerned, the ownership form does matter. Transferable ownership claims imply more flexible decision making. They may also tilt managerial incentives away from the pursuit of technological excellence for its own sake and toward the identification of profitable market niches.

Maule (1984) examines the record of the Urban Transportation Development Corporation (UTDC), owned by the government of Ontario. UTDC designs rapid transit systems and builds light rail vehicles (streetcars, subway cars). Maule notes that because the government of Ontario, either through its influence on Ontario municipal transit authorities or through provision of loan guarantees to other buyers, has stimulated if not created a demand for UTDC's products, it is difficult to make judgments regarding the company's commercial success. He finds that UTDC has been "substantially in a loss position each year" for ten years but declines to draw any conclusions from this.

Atomic Energy of Canada Limited has been the subject of a number of recent studies. An evaluation of its commercial performance necessarily involves an evaluation of its CANDU nuclear reactor program, which dwarfs all its other activities, and an investigation of the relationship, if any, between the outcome of that program and AECL's Crown corporation status.

Insofar as the CANDU program itself is concerned, a number of views have emerged. In comments made at the Commission's symposium on Crown corporations, Ross Campbell, a former AECL president, argued that the CANDU program has been a success in that Canada has developed a better reactor at a lower cost than any other nation and that many of the problems experienced by AECL have been due to government indecisiveness.

Palda (1984) calculates the R&D cost for the CANDU program at $4.7 billion 1981 dollars (assuming a zero discount rate). To this should be added the cost of carrying a heavy water inventory of close to $1 billion, write-offs of mothballed heavy water plants of $750 million and write-offs of mothballed reactors (p. 18). Palda puts the total of R&D costs and write-offs of facilities that either were unnecessary or failed to function at $6 billion (1981 dollars), which he regards as a conservative estimate (p. 19).

Included on the benefit side are such direct benefits as profits on CANDU sales abroad. The CANDU reactor has been sold to Pakistan, India, Argentina and Korea. AECL lost $130 million on the sale to Argentina (Gordon, 1981, p. 188). It would not be unreasonable to conclude that the foreign sales taken together have made no contribution at all toward covering the $6 billion which has been sunk into CANDU development. If the international sales effort as a whole, is taken into account including for example the $50 million cost (some say much more) of the failed Mexican sale, the conclusion that there has been no net benefit becomes virtually unassailable.

Domestic direct benefits from the CANDU program could be derived from the performance of the reactors installed in Canada. The benefits might be calculated as the difference between the cost per kilowatt-hour of the best alternative to CANDU and CANDU itself. Is the excess (if any) of the cost of, say, coal-fired generation over the cost of CANDU sufficient in present value terms to make a dent in the latter's $6 billion development cost? Alternatively, is the excess of what the installation of American light water reactors would cost per kilowatt-hour over the cost of CANDU sufficient to cover the development cost of the latter?

Palda (1984) did not have access to this type of evidence. He nevertheless conjectures that the program has not and will not produce a surplus of benefits over costs:

> We have what amounts to a classical declining industry; infant to geriatric in twenty-five years, like a comet leaving a trail of negative cash flow behind.

In this we are, of course, not alone among nuclear reactor producers; it is unlikely that the British, French, German and even American main contractors achieved a cumulative positive net benefit. (p. 20)

He attributes this failure to earn an economic return in part to government involvement, although not to the Crown corporation organizational form per se:

When government is a strong participant in a venture that must ultimately be justified on economic grounds, it will tend to discount market forces which will yet prove to be the stronger. (p. 21)

Evaluating the role of AECL per se in the outcome of the CANDU program, Doern (1984) concludes:

There are certainly grounds in this total web of nuclear decisions and decision-making agencies for questioning some of the decisions made. AECL was undoubtedly slow to take action in the mid to late 1970s on the uneconomic Atlantic heavy water plants. It was slow in adjusting as an organization from its predominant role in the first three decades of its existence as a research organization to the new role required by its needs in the early to mid-1970s to be a marketing and sales oriented organization. It is doubtful, however, even under the most optimistic of assumptions that the political system would have allowed it to be anything approaching an entrepreneurial firm. (p. 15)

Additional evidence on the domestic electrical generation cost savings resulting from the CANDU program has been gathered by Johnson (1984). She finds that the estimated cost advantage of the CANDU reactor over coal or light water reactors varies widely, depending on the engineering study used and the real discount rate assumed. Using generation cost estimates in Task Force Hydro (1973) and a 6 percent discount rate, she finds that the net cost advantage of CANDU over light water reactors to the year 2000 is under $1 billion (1981 dollars). At this discount rate, the R&D cost of the CANDU is over $11 billion (1981 dollars). Using the cost estimates of the OECD's Nuclear Energy Agency and a 5 percent (real) discount rate, she finds that the net cost advantage of CANDU over the most efficient light water reactor to the year 2000 is $10.8 billion (1981 dollars) — well in excess of CANDU's R&D cost, which is $9.7 billion at this discount rate. In her view, it is not obvious at all that CANDU has been the economic failure Palda deems it to be.

Lermer (1984) also compares the net saving in generation costs resulting from CANDU with the R&D cost of the program. His cost estimate, which assumes a 7.5 percent real discount rate and includes a provision for unavoidable future costs, is $16 billion (1981 dollars). Using an Energy Mines and Resources estimate that CANDU's cost advantage over a light water reactor is $153 per kilowatt, Lermer estimates that 104 gigawatts of CANDU capacity would have to be installed in Canada before total generation cost savings would be sufficient to cover the R&D costs of the program (p. 5). Predictions are that no more than 20 gigawatts will be installed by the year 2000.

Insofar as the role of AECL itself is concerned, Lermer faults AECL for focusing on the Ontario market instead of venturing abroad, particularly to western Europe and the United States during the boom years of reactor sales. The second major failing was AECL's failure to place sufficient emphasis on reducing the costs of producing heavy water and on making price and availability guarantees to potential buyers. The third failing was the delay in bringing the Douglas Point reactor on-line.

Both the failure to appreciate the importance of heavy water and to improve the technology for its production and the delay at Douglas Point are attributed by Lermer to the dominance of research (and glamorous research) over marketing concerns at AECL (pp. 15–21). This emphasis on technology over marketing and the failure to venture into industrialized foreign markets which presented sales opportunities is not unrelated, in Lermer's view, to AECL's status as a government enterprise. The implication is that had an organizational form which relied more heavily on private firms been used, the outcome of the CANDU program might have been more favourable. This, of course, begs the question of whether an alternative mode of organization was ever feasible. Lermer suggests that it might have been (pp. 17–20).

Of the studies of De Havilland, Urban Transportation Development Corporation, and Atomic Energy of Canada, those of De Havilland yield the most unambiguous conclusions. Two major products have been developed during the government's tenure as owner — the Dash-7 and Dash-8. Both are regarded as costly commercial failures which would almost certainly have been avoided had DHC not been a government enterprise.

With regard to AECL, there is uncertainty, at least in some quarters, as to whether the CANDU program has been an economic success or failure. There is uncertainty in all quarters as to whether the economic benefits of the program would have been greater had an alternative policy instrument been employed.

Efficiency in the Provision of Political Services

Government enterprises may have advantages over private enterprises with respect to the cost of arranging for the provision of political services. First, political services need not be costed and priced explicitly. The government simply accepts a lower return on its equity. Second, government enterprise management may have less incentive and/or less ability to mislead the government regarding the cost of these services.

The ideal form of empirical evidence on this issue would be a comparison of the respective costs of obtaining a particular political service from government and private enterprises. Evidence of this nature does not exist, so far as I am aware. The evidence which bears on the issue is indirect and does not admit to much in the way of generalizations.

One approach, taken by Feigenbaum (1984), is to investigate the extent to which the activities of government enterprises have deviated from the policy directions of their owners. In his survey of the European experience, Feigenbaum concludes:

> One can cite a litany of cases where public enterprise has transgressed public policy. A recent French parliamentary report noted that French national oil companies lied about access prices to crude so that state regulators would set even higher prices for retail domestic petroleum products and these same companies colluded with private firms to keep other state firms out of the oil business. During the 1973–74 oil crisis both British and French oil firms refused to divert deliveries from foreign customers to assure their home countries secure supplies of oil. (p. 23)

With respect to the Italian national oil company (ENI), Feigenbaum concludes, "Rather than ENI acting as an instrument of state policy, the relationship was, in fact, the reverse: the state became an instrument of ENI policy" (p. 30). Additional evidence on the behaviour of state holding companies and nationalized banks also implies not only that government enterprises can and do engage in opportunistic behaviours vis-à-vis their owners, but also that they can shape the political agenda itself. This cannot be taken to imply that nationalization does not reduce opportunism, only that it fails, unsurprisingly, to eliminate it.

Taking the other side of the question, one might investigate whether and under what circumstances government enterprises have contributed to the achievement of stated or inferred public policy goals. Feigenbaum cites a number of such instances in his survey of European experience.

There is a great deal of Canadian evidence on this issue, only a few examples of which are cited here. Studies of the Potash Corporation of Saskatchewan (PCS) suggest that its formation was motivated principally by the provincial government's concern with the magnitude and disposition of potash resource rents (Laux and Molot, 1981, 1984; Olewiler, 1984). These studies further suggest that the PCS may be superior to alternative methods of taxation and output control which were available to the province. This is so specifically because PCS provides the government with information on production costs and hence on potential rents, as well as providing an effective means of controlling both total industry output and the output of the remaining private producers.

Along with the power to set taxes and royalty rates, the government has the ability both to increase the total income of the industry and to appropriate a larger share of that income.

On the first issue, Laux and Molot (1981) conclude that the PCS was of material assistance to the government in the installation of the appropriate tax and royalty regime:

Although the tax conflict formally involved only the government and the private companies, it is clear that the existence of PCS was a major factor contributing to the resolution of the dispute. The presence of a government enterprise affected relations between private industry and government permitting a resolution of conflict both because it served as a learning experience for bureaucrats and because it generated a shift in the balance of bargaining power to government from industry. Experience with operating PCS quickly taught key government officials the real costs of running mines and the real impact of the reserve tax formula. (pp. 203–204)

Thus, there is at least anecdotal evidence that PCS provided the government of Saskatchewan with a "window on the industry." There are also intuitive reasons to believe that the circumstances of potash production were such as to support a "window-on-the-industry" rationale for government enterprise.

The "window on the industry" will be more beneficial to the government as the cost to outsiders of measuring industry net income increases. This cost will, in turn, be greater if some inputs (such as natural resource inputs) are unpriced and/or if the industry production technology is not widely known (that is, if it is in part proprietary). In addition, managers of closely held firms or, perhaps, of wholly owned affiliates of widely held firms might be expected to have a greater incentive to take advantage of information asymmetries to mislead the government.

These considerations lead to the conclusion that if the window-on-the-industry rationale applies anywhere, it would apply in the case of potash in Saskatchewan. The industry is characterized by an important unpriced input (potash), by production technologies that in some cases are secret (solution mining), and by firms which are almost without exception wholly owned affiliates of larger enterprises.

On the second issue, there is less evidence but it has been suggested that PCS, acting as a leader or in concert with the remaining private producers, can achieve a measure of output restriction (and thus price enhancement) more effectively than an explicit government-sponsored cartel or pro-rationing scheme.

Laux and Molot (1984) argue that PCS has provided political services in addition to cost information and output control. These include: reduction in pollution by salt wastes of agricultural land adjacent to mine sites; local sourcing of materials; additional (local) R&D; and stabilization of the rate of capacity growth (pp. 11–12). The impression is left that these outcomes are desirable from the point of view of the province but that they could not have been achieved, or at least could have been less readily achieved, by means of taxation, subsidization and regulation.

Pratt (1981, 1982) assesses the contribution of Petro-Canada toward the achievement of federal government policy goals. With respect to the "window-on-the-industry" function, Pratt (1982) concludes:

It can be plausibly argued that the company's operational experience has given Ottawa a stronger capacity to bargain with the producing provinces and the major oil companies and has diminished the ability of the companies to impose their terms by reallocating their investments. And while there certainly are grounds for questioning some aspects of federal energy policy, there can be little doubt that the national government is much more competent today in the area of energy analysis than it was, say, in early 1975 when the hurried decision was made to rescue the Syncrude project. Again it seems not unreasonable to attribute some of the growth in competence and expertise to the insights acquired from Petro-Canada's activities. (p. 107)

Waverman takes the opposite view. During an Economic Council's Conference on Government Enterprise (November, 1984), he argued that the government was using the petroleum industry as a "window on the Crown corporation." While he does not elaborate, the implication is that government ownership has not improved the latter's access to information. Halpern, Plourde and Waverman (1984) quote Petro-Canada CEO Wilbert Hopper to the effect that any potential Petro-Canada has as a window-on-the-industry has not been used by the federal government (p. 41).

Pratt (1981) also concludes that Petro-Canada's frontier exploration program and investment in synthetic fuels in the late 1970s reflect a close adherence to government energy policies:

Petro-Canada's capital spending between 1976 and 1978 was heavily skewed toward Ottawa's energy policy priorities — particularly the goal of completing a rapid appraisal of the most promising geological basins in the frontier areas. (p. 134)

Halpern, Plourde and Waverman (1984) concur in this conclusion (pp. 31–32). They argue, however, that Petro-Canada's more recent downstream acquisitions were not in response to government directives and were, indeed, incompatible with ministerial interpretations of public policy. In the view of these authors, Petro-Canada was making public policy rather than simply responding to it (pp. 41–47).

While the arguments of these authors are interesting and while they are on solid grounds in questioning the apparent integration of Petro-Canada into the energy policy making process, they do not address the issue of whether the information provided the government by Petro-Canada has been or would be less self-serving than the information which private firms might provide. Nor is there, at present, any evidence on the advantages of having a government enterprise participate directly in frontier exploration and synthetic fuel development, as opposed to relying on subsidies and tax incentives to private firms.

The public policy objectives of the Cape Breton Development Corporation (Devco) are not difficult to discern. They are maintenance of employment in the Cape Breton coal mines and encouragement of alternative economic activities in that region. Any evaluation of the activities of Devco must have two stages. The first is a cost-benefit analysis of the policy of maintaining the coal mines in operation. The second is an analysis of the policy instrument chosen by government, which would determine which policy instrument is best suited to maintaining or winding down mining employment. Existing studies by George (1981) and Trebilcock (1985) have not been able to address either issue.

George attempts to answer the following questions. Did Devco achieve the objectives set for it? Did the operation of Devco result in a smaller expenditure by the government than would have been the case under a regime of subsidies to the mines' previous owner? With respect to coal mining, George answers that Devco has achieved its mandated objectives of closing inefficient mines and introducing modern equipment and methods. Industrial development efforts came to nothing in the early years between 1968 and 1972, but there were apparently some modest achievements thereafter. Subsidy payments to Devco were close to those which were anticipated had the mines remained in private hands. George notes, however, that there was an unanticipated tripling in coal prices and some $125 million in additional capital expenditures, both of which should have resulted in lower production subsidies (pp. 380–81).

Trebilcock is also favourably disposed to both the mining and industrial development efforts of Devco. While noting that Devco has received a total of $751 million in federal subsidies to the end of 1983, he concludes that

Apart from the first four years of its existence, Devco appears to have established quite a favourable reputation compared to Dosco in terms of its ability to reassert Cape Breton coal's viability. As recently as 1968, no one would have foretold the OPEC oil price rises and the resulting quadrupling in the price of coal. Had this not happened the story of Devco may well have been different. Nevertheless one must not underrate the acceptance of the Crown corporation of this opportunity and the enthusiasm with which it appears to be proceeding.

It must be acknowledged, that the greater flexibility and cohesiveness entailed in a Crown corporation than in government departments awarding ad hoc grants of assistance appears to have served the Cape Breton region well at least better than realized through government policies in the Dosco era. (pp. 38–39).

A final empirical approach to the instrument choice problem compares the costs of alternative means (including government enterprises) of achieving particular public policy goals. A good example is provided by Baldwin (1975), who discusses the difference in the success experienced by U.S. and Canadian airline regulators in achieving redistributive goals, such as subsidizing short-haul flights by profits on long-haul flights. The Canadian regulatory regime was more successful than the

American one, but in Baldwin's opinion this cannot be attributed to the prominence of a Crown corporation, Air Canada, in the Canadian system.

American regulators failed, according to Baldwin and others, because they were unable to control entry into the long-haul market and were thus unable to preserve any surplus for distribution. Canadian regulators were able to limit entry (and flight frequencies) on surplus-generating routes. Whether their ability to do so was enhanced by the fact that the incumbent was a Crown corporation remains an unanswered question.

A much less sophisticated analysis (McFetridge, 1984) concludes that it is less costly to deliver subsidized business loans through programs administered by chartered banks, such guarantees under the Small Business Loans Act, than through the government-owned Federal Business Development Bank. However, that conclusion is based on the rather tenuous assumption that the FBDB exists only to deliver subsidized loans. It cannot be drawn if the existence of the FBDB is not contingent on its subsidized lending activity.

Mixed Enterprise

A mixed enterprise is defined in the first section as a corporation in which a government has a controlling but less than 100 percent equity interest. There it is argued that a mixed enterprise lies between a Crown corporation and a private firm as far as the cost of transacting in political services is concerned. With respect to managerial efficiency, expectations regarding the performance of mixed enterprises depend on the weights assigned to product market and capital market competition as disciplining forces. If the essential disciplining force is product market competition, then managerial efficiency will not vary appreciably across ownership forms. If it is the capital market operating through transferable ownership claims which is important, commercial performance will not differ between Crown corporations and effectively controlled mixed enterprises, and both will perform less well than private firms.

In their "world survey" of mixed enterprise performance, Boardman, Eckel and Vining (undated) cite two cross-sectional studies on the relative profitability of mixed enterprises which they regard as inconclusive in the sense that one study implies that mixed enterprises are less profitable and the other implies that they are as profitable as comparable firms (pp. 25–26). From their description, however, the studies themselves would seem not to be comparable.

Boardman, Eckel and Vining also discuss the political services required of mixed enterprises by their government part-owners. These include bail-outs, maintaining employment in the face of declining output, paying wages in excess of market or even other union scales, and diverting investment into domestic projects (p. 25). There is no discussion of whether these services are more or less readily arranged when this ownership mode is employed.

Eckel and Vermaelen (1984) attempt to draw performance inferences from observed announcement effects of government equity purchases. They calculate the weekly returns on the common stock of fourteen listed companies and test statistically whether these returns were abnormally high or low during the weeks immediately preceding and following the announcement of the government equity purchase. They find that, while there was no effect overall, the seven purchases of shares in regulated industries had a positive average announcement effect[7] while the seven purchases of shares in unregulated companies had a negative average announcement effect. They conclude that:

> The overall positive effect in the regulated sector is probably due to increased access to government policy formulation. The perception is that government policy tends to improve the profitability of the firms it operates in this sector.
>   The negative overall impact of other purchases is likely due to the expectation that firms will be forced by government to consider goals other than long-run profitability in their decision making. (p. 18)

These conclusions are perhaps somewhat stronger than is justified by the test the authors conduct. Announcement effects will depend on:

- the type of offer made (tender offer, merger, open market share purchase;
- the market's expectations regarding the ultimate holdings of the acquiring and allied government agencies in the target firm, the cost of the political services the company might be obliged to provide, and the compensation it will receive; and
- the distribution of non-government equity holdings.

Potential targets may already trade at a discount or a premium reflecting the likelihood of a government buy-in and its anticipated effect on the value of the firm. Where there is no announcement effect, it may be that government ownership has no effects, or no net effect, or merely that the market is able to distinguish the targets from the non-targets ex ante.

As was suggested in the previous section, the possibility exists that all firms trade at a discount that reflects the expected losses visited upon shareholders as a consequence of a government buy-in plus a risk premium. The increased use of mixed enterprises as a policy instrument may have the side effect of increasing the cost of corporate capital. It is worthwhile, then, to examine briefly the activities of some of the government enterprises and agencies which own mixed enterprises. These include the Alberta Heritage Fund, the Caisse de Dépot de Placement, the Société Générale de Financement, and the Canadian Development Corporation.

The activities of the Heritage Fund and the Caisse are examined by Pesando (1984). The Heritage Fund holds relatively little equity and is limited to a maximum of 5 percent of the equity of any one firm. It therefore does not pose the type of problem described above. The Caisse de Dépot may be a different matter. It is charged with the responsibility of investing the premium income of the Quebec Pension Plan and a number of Quebec public sector pension funds. It is empowered to hold up to 30 percent of the shares of any company. This is often enough to allow the Caisse to exercise effective control over a company. Fears exist that this control will be used to extract political services, perhaps in the form of the location or relocation of activities in Quebec, for which the companies concerned are not compensated. Fears that the Caisse or any other public sector pension fund might engage in this behaviour might be allayed by reducing the ceiling on public sector pension plan holdings from 30 to 10 percent of the equity of that company or by restricting these funds to hold non-voting shares. Concerns that these restrictions might impair the abilities of these funds to diversify properly and/or to protect their investments are groundless in Pesando's view.

The Société Générale de Financement is a holding company which is owned entirely by the government of Quebec. Its equity holdings are usually sufficient to give it effective control of the firms involved, and it often takes an active part in or at least influences the direction of their management. According to Martin (1984), the central objective of the SGF is to encourage locally controlled development in certain key sectors (industrial equipment, electrical generation equipment, forest products and science-based industries) of the Quebec economy. Martin finds that what he terms the financial and social rates of return on SGF investments have both been quite low. As an instrument for employment creation or for the geographic redistribution of employment, Martin feels that the SGF has been about as effective as a subsidy system. As an instrument for the establishment and maintenance of local control, however, he regards it as both appropriate and apparently successful.

The Canadian Development Corporation (CDC) is an investment company (closed end fund) formed in 1972, of which 49 percent is owned by the federal government. It is the subject of recent evaluations by Boardman (1984), Boardman and Vining (1984) and Tarasofsky (1984). All studies agree that the commercial performance of the CDC has been poor by virtually any standard. As Table 6-1 indicates, the CDC earned a lower rate of return on stockholders' equity than three other well-known holding companies (Brascan, Power Corp. and CP Enterprises) and a lower rate of return than the TSE 300 management companies' composite.

These comparisons may be unfair to the CDC in that it has concentrated its portfolio in six sectors — oil and gas, health care, petrochemical-based industries, mining, pipelines and northern trans-respect to commercial efficiency. The implication is that, given the market environment, a great burst of productivity from the privatization of Air Canada, Canadian National, or the provincial telecommunications companies should not be expected. There is thus no strong commercial efficiency case for privatization in this area. On the other hand, if these enterprises were now in private hands there would be no commercial efficiency case for nationalizing them.

Whether there would be a political efficiency case for retaining government ownership or for nationalization depends on the nature of the political services these enterprises provide or could provide. The conventional wisdom is that what political services Air Canada and CN now provide (grain transportation subsidies, provision of rail passenger transportation services to VIA) are negotiated at arm's length and that government ownership contributes little to these arrangements.

The extensive system of cross-subsidization in telecommunications seems to indicate that political services are important here. Yet there is little in the way of evidence (to my knowledge) that it is more costly to negotiate the performance of these services with privately owned Bell than with the provincially owned telecommunications companies.

There may be a temptation to draw the conclusion that ownership is not an issue and that emphasis should be placed instead on regulatory reform, competition policy, and freer trade. All firms, including government enterprises, may respond to competition by increasing their commercial efficiency. On the other hand, increasing the competitiveness of the environment may make ownership an issue where it had not been before.

There is some preliminary evidence that government enterprise is ill-suited to participation in dynamic "entrepreneurial" industries. If this is the case, privatization may well be beneficial if protection of various forms is dismantled.

There are at least some reasons to believe that government enterprise, even unencumbered by the requirement to provide political services, does not have the adaptive properties required to participate successfully in entrepreneurial industries. De Havilland provides an illustration but it should not be singled out. There are cases which are worse but have not yet been the subject of detailed studies.

Discussions about privatizing DHC have often missed the point. They have been concerned about what are essentially sunk costs. They have also equated privatization with stopping the provision of political services such as the employment of engineers in Toronto. The point to emphasize is surely that if the funds allocated to De Havilland (not to mention Canadair or AECL) had instead been allocated, for example, in part to the federal government's Industrial Research Assistance Program and in part to its special R&D tax credit policy, the so-called employment benefits might have been as great or greater. The value of the output of the resources so employed could hardly be less.[10]

Whatever decisions are made regarding the disposition of Canadair, De Havilland and others, there should be a strong presumption against the use of government enterprise as the vehicle for "high-tech" industrial strategies in other industries.

With respect to mixed enterprise, the conclusion here is that it is more likely to constitute the worst than the best of all possible worlds. It does not combine the benefits of transferable ownership with efficient provision of political services, as some have suggested. The possibility that any firm may be the target of a government buy-in and called upon to provide political services can increase the cost of capital for all firms. More stringent limitations on the equity holdings of public sector pension funds certainly have merit in this regard. Limitations on the equity purchases of the various provincial holding companies, while equally desirable, are not so easily enforced.

The Canada Development Corporation has been a major contributor to the rise of the mixed enterprise in Canada. Judgments regarding the contribution of the CDC to Canadian growth and development are as close to unanimity as occurs in the social sciences — namely, it has not made a contribution. If the low price-earnings ratio of CDC shares is in part a consequence of the large government interest in the corporation, the distribution of government shares to individual Canadians, as Boardman and Vining suggest, will itself increase their value. The "something for nothing" aspect of this strategy might be attractive to those concerned.

Notes

This study was completed in February 1985.

The first draft of this paper was a summary of the issues raised in the Royal Commission's Symposium on Crown Corporations, Ottawa, June 1984. Its revision and expansion has benefited from the comments of John Baldwin, Anthony Boardman, Sanford Borins, Aidan Vining and Rod White and from participation in symposia on Crown corporations organized for the Economic Council of Canada by Ron Hirchhorn and Patrick Robert.

1. The relationship between product market competition and managerial efficiency has been stressed by X-efficiency theorists, students of corporate strategy, and public choice theories. See De Alessi (1983), Porter (1980) and Niskanen (1975), respectively.

2. For excellent discussions of the policy instrument choice problem both in general and as it relates to Crown corporations, see Trebilcock et al. and Trebilcock and Prichard (1983).

3. The importance of this as an operational problem is emphasized by Hindle (1984).

4. In comments made at the Royal Commission's symposium on Crown corporations, Professor William Jordon noted that while he believed that Air Canada is as efficient as any regulated trunk carrier, he could not conclude that Air Canada as currently structured would necessarily do well in an unregulated environment. Others fear that because of its large size and privileged access to capital, Air Canada would do "too well" in an unregulated environment. Deregulation may thus necessitate a restructuring of ownership to ensure that a government enterprise has the ability to compete in entrepreneurial activities and that it does so on essentially the same terms as its privately owned competitors.

5. This is my own construction. Others — Eckel and Vining (1982), for example — would argue that a mixed enterprise does face more capital market discipline than a Crown corporation. The source of that discipline is not obvious when control of the enterprise is not contestable (i.e., when it remains with government) regardless of how undervalued its stock might be.

6. The cost of capital will not increase if firms are, on average, fully compensated for political services and if the risk associated with the level of compensation is fully diversifiable. The discount applied will depend on the likelihood that a firm will be targeted for a government buy-in and, perhaps, on whether a ready means of compensation exists (such as a regulatory framework). This might explain in part the positive announcement effects of buy-ins in regulated industries observed by Eckel and Vermaelen (1984).

7. The cumulative abnormal return in the case of the seven purchases of shares in regulated firms is statistically significant only at the 15 percent level.

8. The government's total investment in CDC invested at 11 percent would have been $983 million. At present market prices, the government's interest in the CDC would sell for $184 million (Boardman and Vining, 1984, p. 19).

9. This strategy continues to be recommended as one which will result in a higher than average rate of return. See Harris (1985) and Scott (1984).

10. This conclusion might be contrasted with the consensus regarding Devco to the effect that the maintenance of coal mining employment in Cape Breton could not have been accomplished at a lower cost by other means.

Bibliography

Acheson, K. 1985. "Economic Regulation in Canada: A Survey." In *Canadian Industrial Policy in Action*, volume 4 of the research studies prepared for the Royal Commission on the Economic Union and Development Prospects for Canada. Toronto: University of Toronto Press.

Baldwin, J.R. 1975. *The Regulatory Agency and the Public Corporation*. Cambridge, Mass.: Ballinger.

_____. 1982. "Federal Regulation and Public Policy in the Canadian Petroleum Industry 1958–1975." *Journal of Business Administration* 13 (1): 2.

Boardman, A. 1984. "An Evaluation of Canada Development Corporation." Paper presented to the Royal Commission Symposium on Crown Corporations, Ottawa, June.

Boardman, A., C. Eckel, and A. Vining. (undated). "The Advantages and Disadvantages of Mixed Enterprise: A World Survey." Working Paper 961. Vancouver: University of British Columbia, Faculty of Commerce and Business Administration.

Boardman, A., and A. Vining. 1984. "An Evaluation of Canada Development Corporation." Vancouver: University of British Columbia, Faculty of Commerce and Business Administration. Mimeo.

Borcherding, T.E. 1983. "Towards a Positive Theory of Public Sector Supply Arrangements." In *Crown Corporations in Canada: The Calculus of Instrument Choice*, edited by J.R.S. Prichard, pp. 99–183. Toronto: Butterworth.

Borins, Sandford F., and B. Boothman. 1985. "Crown Corporations and Economic Efficiency". In *Canadian Industrial Policy in Action*, volume 4 of the research studies prepared for the Royal Commission on the Economic Union and Development Prospects for Canada. Toronto: University of Toronto Press.

Caves, D.W., and L.R. Christenson. 1980. "The Relative Efficiency of Public and Private Firms in a Competitive Environment: The Case of Canadian Railroads." *Journal of Political Economy* 88 (October): 958–76.

Caves, D.W., L.R. Christenson, J.A. Swanson, and M. Tretheway. 1982. "Economic Performance of U.S. and Canadian Railroads: The Significance of Ownership and the Regulatory Environment." In *Managing Public Enterprise*, edited by W.T. Stanbury and Fred Thompson, pp. 123–51. New York: Praeger.

De Alessi, L. 1983. "Property Rights Transaction Costs and X-Efficiency: An Essay in Economic Theory." *American Economic Review* 73 (March): 64–81.

Denny, M. 1984. "Government Enterprises in Western Canada's Telecommunications." Paper prepared for the Economic Council of Canada's Conference on Government Enterprises, Toronto, November.

Denny, M., A. de Fontenay, and M. Werner. 1983. "Comparing the Efficiency of Firms: Canadian Telecommunications Companies." In *Economic Analysis of Telecommunications: Theory and Applications*, edited by L. Courville, A. de Fontenay and A.R. Dobell, pp. 115–30. New York: Elsevier.

Doern, G. Bruce. 1984. "Atomic Energy of Canada Ltd.: Selected Performance Issues." Paper presented to the Royal Commission Symposium on Crown Corporations, Ottawa, June.

Dotriaux, J., and C. Hennin. 1984. "Government Intervention for Employment and Technology Support: The De Havilland Case." Paper presented to the Economic Council of Canada's Conference on Government Enterprises, Toronto, November.

Eckel, Catherine, and Theo Vermaelen. 1984. "Internal Regulation: The Effects of Government Stock Ownership on the Value of the Firm." Paper presented at the annual meeting of the Canadian Economics Association, Guelph.

Eckel, Catherine, and Aidan Vining. 1982. "Towards a Positive Theory of Joint Enterprise." In *Managing Public Enterprise*, edited by W.T. Stanbury and Fred Thompson, pp. 209–22. New York: Praeger.

Eckel, C., A. Vining, and A. Boardman. 1984. "Mixed Enterprise as a Policy Instrument: Success or Failure?" Mimeo. Blacksburg: Virginia Polytechnic Institute.

Fama, E. 1980. "Agency Problems and the Theory of the Firm." *Journal of Political Economy* 88: 288–307.

Feigenbaum, H. 1984. "Politics and Public Enterprise." Paper submitted to the Royal Commission on the Economic Union and Development Prospects for Canada, Ottawa.

George, R. 1981. "The Cape Breton Development Corporation." In *Public Corporations and Public Policy in Canada*, edited by A. Tupper and G. Bruce Doern, pp. 365–88. Montreal: Institute for Research on Public Policy.

Gillen, D.W., T.H. Oum, and M.W. Tretheway. 1984. "Identifying and Measuring the

Impact of Government Ownership and Regulation of Airline Performance." Paper presented to the Economic Council of Canada's Conference on Government Enterprise, Toronto, November.

Gordon, M. 1981. *Government in Business*. Montreal, C.D. Howe Research Institute.

Halpern, P., A. Plourde, and L. Waverman. 1984. "Petro-Canada: Its Role, Control and Operations." Paper presented to the Economic Council of Canada's Conference on Government Enterprise, Toronto, November.

Harris, Richard G. 1985. *Trade, Industrial Policy and International Competition*, volume 13 of the research studies prepared for the Royal Commission on the Economic Union and Development Prospects for Canada. Toronto: University of Toronto Press.

Heaver, T.D., and W.G. Waters. 1982. "Public Enterprise Under Competition: A Comment on Canadian Railways." In *Managing Public Enterprise*, edited by W.T. Stanbury and Fred Thompson, pp. 152–59. New York: Praeger.

Hirschman, A.O. 1970. *Exit, Voice and Loyalty: Responses to Decline in Firms, Organizations and States*. Cambridge, Mass.: Harvard University Press.

Hindle, C. 1984. "Practical Problems in the Evaluation of Crown Corporation Performance." Paper presented to the Royal Commission's Symposium on Crown Corporations, Ottawa, June.

Jensen, M., and W.H. Meckling. 1976. "The Theory of the Firm: Managerial Behavior, Agency Costs and Ownership Structure." *Journal of Financial Economics* 3 (October): 305–60.

Jensen, M., and R. Ruback. 1983. "The Market for Corporate Control: The Scientific Evidence." *Journal of Financial Economics* 11: 5–50.

Johnson, S. 1984. "Some Benefit: Cost Calculations for Candu." Mimeo. Ottawa: Carleton University, Department of Economics.

Jordan, W. 1982a. "Performance on North American and Australian Airlines: Regulation and Public Enterprise." In *Managing Public Enterprise*, edited by W.T. Stanbury and Fred Thompson, pp. 161–208. New York: Praeger.

————. 1982b. "Performance of Regulated Canadian Airlines in Domestic and Transborder Operations." Ottawa: Department of Consumer and Corporate Affairs.

Laux, J., and M. Molot. 1981. "The Potash Corporation of Saskatchewan." In *Public Corporations and Public Policy in Canada*, edited by A. Tupper and G.B. Doern, pp. 189–220. Montreal: Institute for Research on Public Policy.

————. 1984. "Crown Corporation Performance: The Potash Corporation of Saskatchewan." Paper presented to the Royal Commission's Symposium on Crown Corporations, Ottawa, June.

Lermer, G. 1984. "An Evaluation of a Crown Corporation as a Strategist in an Entrepreneurial, Global Scale Industry." Paper presented to the Economic Council of Canada's Conference on Government Enterprise, Toronto, November.

Martin, F. 1984. "La S.G.F. et ses filiales: une étude de cas." Paper presented to the Economic Council of Canada's Conference on Government Enterprise, Toronto, November.

Maule, C. 1984. "The Urban Transportation Development Corporation: A Case Study of Government Enterprise." Paper presented to the Economic Council of Canada's Conference on Government Enterprise, Toronto, November.

McFetridge, D.G. 1984. "The Federal Business Development Bank." Paper presented to the Royal Commission's Symposium on Crown Corporations, Ottawa, June.

Niskanen, W. 1975. "Bureaucrats and Politicians." *Journal of Law and Economics* 18 (December): 617–44.

Olewiler, N. 1984. "Alternative Strategies for the Potash Corporation of Saskatchewan." Paper presented to the Economic Council of Canada's Conference on Government Enterprise, Toronto, November.

Olson, M. 1982. *The Rise and Decline of Nations*. New Haven: Yale University Press.

Palda, K. 1984. "AECL-CANDU." In *A Canadian Industrial Policy Toward Innovation*. Vancouver: Fraser Institute. Mimeographed.

Pesando, J. 1984. "An Economic Analysis of Government Investment Corporations with Attention to the Caisse de Dépôt et Placement du Québec and The Alberta Heritage Fund." Paper presented to the Economic Council of Canada's Conference on Government Enterprise, Toronto, November.

Porter, M. 1980. *Competitive Strategy*. New York: Basic Books.

Pratt, L. 1981. "Petro-Canada." In *Corporations and Public Policy in Canada*, edited by A. Tupper and G.B. Doern, pp. 95–148. Montreal: Institute for Research on Public Policy.

_____. 1982. "Oil and State Enterprises: Assessing Petro-Canada." In *Managing Public Enterprise*, edited by W.T. Stanbury and Fred Thompson, pp. 79–110. New York: Praeger.

Schultz, Richard, and Alan Alexandroff. 1985. *Economic Regulation and the Federal System*, volume 42 of the research studies prepared for the Royal Commission on the Economic Union and Development Prospects for Canada. Toronto: University of Toronto Press.

Scott, B. 1984. "National Strategies: Key to International Competition." Mimeo. Boston: Harvard Business School.

Stigler, G.J. 1971. "The Theory of Economic Regulation." *The Bell Journal of Economics and Management Science* 2 (Spring): 3–21.

Tarasofsky, A. 1984. "The Canada Development Corporation 1973–1983." Paper presented to the Economic Council of Canada's Conference on Government Enterprise, Toronto, November.

Task Force Hydro. 1983. "Nuclear Power in Ontario." Report prepared for the Royal Commission on Government Productivity. Toronto.

Trebilcock, Michael. 1985. *The Political Economy of Economic Adjustment: The Case of Declining Sectors*, volume 8 of the research studies prepared for the Royal Commission on the Economic Union and Development Prospects for Canada. Toronto: University of Toronto Press.

Trebilcock, M.J., D.G. Hartle, J.R.S. Prichard and D.N. Dewees. 1982. *The Choice of Governing Instrument*. Study prepared for the Economic Council of Canada. Ottawa: Minister of Supply and Services Canada.

Trebilcock, M.J., and J.R.S. Prichard. 1983. "Crown Corporations and the Calculus of Instrument Choice." In *Crown Corporations in Canada: The Calculus of Instrument Choice*, edited by J.R.S. Prichard. Toronto: Butterworth.

White, Roderick. 1984a. "Handicapped Gamesmen." *Policy Options* (May): 33–36.

_____. 1984b. "The Strategic Management of Commercially-Oriented Crown-Owned Companies." Paper presented to the Royal Commission Symposium on Crown Corporations, Ottawa, June.

_____. 1984c. Personal correspondence with the author.

Williamson, O.E. 1979. "Transaction Cost Economics: The Governance of Contractual Relations." *Journal of Law and Economics* 22 (October): 233–61.

Wintrobe, R. 1984. "Private and Public Bureaucracies." Paper presented to the Economic Council of Canada's Conference on State-Owned Enterprise, Ottawa, September.

Keith Acheson is Professor in the Department of Economics, Carleton University, Ottawa.

Barry E.C. Boothman is a graduate student in the Faculty of Administrative Studies, York University, Toronto.

Sandford F. Borins is Associate Professor of Business and Public Policy in the Faculty of Administrative Studies, York University, Toronto.

John F. Chant is Professor in the Department of Economics, Simon Fraser University, Burnaby, B.C.

Harold Crookell is Professor of Business Administration and a Founding Director of the Centre for International Business Studies, University of Western Ontario, London.

Donald G. McFetridge is Professor in the Department of Economics, Carleton University, Ottawa, and is also the Research Coordinator for the Industrial Structure section, which is part of the Economics Research Area, Royal Commission on the Economic Union and Development Prospects for Canada.

THE COLLECTED RESEARCH STUDIES

Royal Commission on the Economic Union and Development Prospects for Canada

ECONOMICS

Income Distribution and Economic Security in Canada (Vol.1), *François Vaillancourt, Research Coordinator*

Vol. 1 Income Distribution and Economic Security in Canada, *F. Vaillancourt* (C)*

Industrial Structure (Vols. 2-8), *Donald G. McFetridge, Research Coordinator*

Vol. 2 Canadian Industry in Transition, *D.G. McFetridge* (C)
Vol. 3 Technological Change in Canadian Industry, *D.G. McFetridge* (C)
Vol. 4 Canadian Industrial Policy in Action, *D.G. McFetridge* (C)
Vol. 5 Economics of Industrial Policy and Strategy, *D.G. McFetridge* (C)
Vol. 6 The Role of Scale in Canada–US Productivity Differences, *J.R. Baldwin and P.K. Gorecki* (M)
Vol. 7 Competition Policy and Vertical Exchange, *F. Mathewson and R. Winter* (M)
Vol. 8 The Political Economy of Economic Adjustment, *M. Trebilcock* (M)

International Trade (Vols. 9-14), *John Whalley, Research Coordinator*

Vol. 9 Canadian Trade Policies and the World Economy, *J. Whalley with C. Hamilton and R. Hill* (M)
Vol. 10 Canada and the Multilateral Trading System, *J. Whalley* (M)
Vol. 11 Canada–United States Free Trade, *J. Whalley* (C)
Vol. 12 Domestic Policies and the International Economic Environment, *J. Whalley* (C)
Vol. 13 Trade, Industrial Policy and International Competition, *R. Harris* (M)
Vol. 14 Canada's Resource Industries and Water Export Policy, *J. Whalley* (C)

Labour Markets and Labour Relations (Vols. 15-18), *Craig Riddell, Research Coordinator*

Vol. 15 Labour-Management Cooperation in Canada, *C. Riddell* (C)
Vol. 16 Canadian Labour Relations, *C. Riddell* (C)
Vol. 17 Work and Pay: The Canadian Labour Market, *C. Riddell* (C)
Vol. 18 Adapting to Change: Labour Market Adjustment in Canada, *C. Riddell* (C)

Macroeconomics (Vols. 19-25), *John Sargent, Research Coordinator*

Vol. 19 Macroeconomic Performance and Policy Issues: Overviews, *J. Sargent* (M)
Vol. 20 Post-War Macroeconomic Developments, *J. Sargent* (C)
Vol. 21 Fiscal and Monetary Policy, *J. Sargent* (C)
Vol. 22 Economic Growth: Prospects and Determinants, *J. Sargent* (C)
Vol. 23 Long-Term Economic Prospects for Canada: A Symposium, *J. Sargent* (C)
Vol. 24 Foreign Macroeconomic Experience: A Symposium, *J. Sargent* (C)
Vol. 25 Dealing with Inflation and Unemployment in Canada, *C. Riddell* (M)

Economic Ideas and Social Issues (Vols. 26 and 27), *David Laidler, Research Coordinator*

Vol. 26 Approaches to Economic Well-Being, *D. Laidler* (C)
Vol. 27 Responses to Economic Change, *D. Laidler* (C)

* (C) denotes a Collection of studies by various authors coordinated by the person named.
(M) denotes a Monograph.

POLITICS AND INSTITUTIONS OF GOVERNMENT

Canada and the International Political Economy (Vols. 28-30), *Denis Stairs and Gilbert R. Winham, Research Coordinators*

Vol. 28 Canada and the International Political/Economic Environment, *D. Stairs and G.R. Winham* (C)
Vol. 29 The Politics of Canada's Economic Relationship with the United States, *D. Stairs and G.R. Winham* (C)
Vol. 30 Selected Problems in Formulating Foreign Economic Policy, *D. Stairs and G.R. Winham* (C)

State and Society in the Modern Era (Vols. 31 and 32), *Keith Banting, Research Coordinator*

Vol. 31 State and Society: Canada in Comparative Perspective, *K. Banting* (C)
Vol. 32 The State and Economic Interests, *K. Banting* (C)

Constitutionalism, Citizenship and Society (Vols. 33-35), *Alan Cairns and Cynthia Williams, Research Coordinators*

Vol. 33 Constitutionalism, Citizenship and Society in Canada, *A. Cairns and C. Williams* (C)
Vol. 34 The Politics of Gender, Ethnicity and Language in Canada, *A. Cairns and C. Williams* (C)
Vol. 35 Public Opinion and Public Policy in Canada, *R. Johnston* (M)

Representative Institutions (Vols. 36-39), *Peter Aucoin, Research Coordinator*

Vol. 36 Party Government and Regional Representation in Canada, *P. Aucoin* (C)
Vol. 37 Regional Responsiveness and the National Administrative State, *P. Aucoin* (C)
Vol. 38 Institutional Reforms for Representative Government, *P. Aucoin* (C)
Vol. 39 Intrastate Federalism in Canada, *D.V. Smiley and R.L. Watts* (M)

The Politics of Economic Policy (Vols. 40-43), *G. Bruce Doern, Research Coordinator*

Vol. 40 The Politics of Economic Policy, *G.B. Doern* (C)
Vol. 41 Federal and Provincial Budgeting, *A.M. Maslove, M.J. Prince and G.B. Doern* (M)
Vol. 42 Economic Regulation and the Federal System, *R. Schultz and A. Alexandroff* (M)
Vol. 43 Bureaucracy in Canada: Control and Reform, *S.L. Sutherland and G.B. Doern* (M)

Industrial Policy (Vols. 44 and 45), *André Blais, Research Coordinator*

Vol. 44 Industrial Policy, *A. Blais* (C)
Vol. 45 The Political Sociology of Industrial Policy, *A. Blais* (M)

LAW AND CONSTITUTIONAL ISSUES

Law, Society and the Economy (Vols. 46-51), *Ivan Bernier and Andrée Lajoie, Research Coordinators*

Vol. 46 Law, Society and the Economy, *I. Bernier and A. Lajoie* (C)
Vol. 47 The Supreme Court of Canada as an Instrument of Political Change, *I. Bernier and A. Lajoie* (C)
Vol. 48 Regulations, Crown Corporations and Administrative Tribunals, *I. Bernier and A. Lajoie* (C)
Vol. 49 Family Law and Social Welfare Legislation in Canada, *I. Bernier and A. Lajoie* (C)
Vol. 50 Consumer Protection, Environmental Law and Corporate Power, *I. Bernier and A. Lajoie* (C)
Vol. 51 Labour Law and Urban Law in Canada, *I. Bernier and A. Lajoie* (C)

The International Legal Environment (Vols. 52-54), *John Quinn, Research Coordinator*

Vol. 52 The International Legal Environment, *J. Quinn* (C)
Vol. 53 Canadian Economic Development and the International Trading System, *M.M. Hart* (M)
Vol. 54 Canada and the New International Law of the Sea, *D.M. Johnston* (M)

Harmonization of Laws in Canada (Vols. 55 and 56), *Ronald C.C. Cuming, Research Coordinator*

Vol. 55 Perspectives on the Harmonization of Law in Canada, *R. Cuming* (C)
Vol. 56 Harmonization of Business Law in Canada, *R. Cuming* (C)

Institutional and Constitutional Arrangements (Vols. 57 and 58), *Clare F. Beckton and A. Wayne MacKay, Research Coordinators*

Vol. 57 Recurring Issues in Canadian Federalism, *C.F. Beckton and A.W. MacKay* (C)
Vol. 58 The Courts and The Charter, *C.F. Beckton and A.W. MacKay* (C)

FEDERALISM AND THE ECONOMIC UNION

Federalism and The Economic Union (Vols. 58-72), *Mark Krasnick, Kenneth Norrie and Richard Simeon, Research Coordinators*

Vol. 59 Federalism and Economic Union in Canada, *K. Norrie, R. Simeon and M. Krasnick* (M)
Vol. 60 Perspectives on the Canadian Economic Union, *M. Krasnick* (C)
Vol. 61 Division of Powers and Public Policy, *R. Simeon* (C)
Vol. 62 Case Studies in the Division of Powers, *M. Krasnick* (C)
Vol. 63 Intergovernmental Relations, *R. Simeon* (C)
Vol. 64 Disparities and Interregional Adjustment, *K. Norrie* (C)
Vol. 65 Fiscal Federalism, *M. Krasnick* (C)
Vol. 66 Mobility of Capital in the Canadian Economic Union, *N. Roy* (M)
Vol. 67 Economic Management and the Division of Powers, *T.J. Courchene* (M)
Vol. 68 Regional Aspects of Confederation, *J. Whalley* (M)
Vol. 69 Interest Groups in the Canadian Federal System, *H.G. Thorburn* (M)
Vol. 70 Canada and Quebec, Past and Future: An Essay, *D. Latouche* (M)
Vol. 71 The Political Economy of Canadian Federalism: 1940-1984, *R. Simeon and I. Robinson* (M)

THE NORTH

Vol. 72 The North, *Michael S. Whittington, Coordinator* (C)

COMMISSION ORGANIZATION

Chairman
Donald S. Macdonald

Commissioners

Clarence L. Barber	William M. Hamilton	Daryl K. Seaman
Albert Breton	John R. Messer	Thomas K. Shoyama
M. Angela Cantwell Peters	Laurent Picard	Jean Casselman-Wadds
E. Gérard Docquier	Michel Robert	Catherine T. Wallace

Senior Officers

Executive Director
J. Gerald Godsoe

Director of Policy	*Senior Advisors*	*Directors of Research*
Alan Nymark	David Ablett	Ivan Bernier
Secretary	Victor Clarke	Alan Cairns
Michel Rochon	Carl Goldenberg	David C. Smith
	Harry Stewart	
Director of Administration	*Director of Publishing*	*Co-Directors of Research*
Sheila-Marie Cook	Ed Matheson	Kenneth Norrie
		John Sargent

Research Program Organization

Economics	Politics and the Institutions of Government	Law and Constitutional Issues
Research Director	*Research Director*	*Research Director*
David C. Smith	Alan Cairns	Ivan Bernier
Executive Assistant & Assistant Director (Research Services)	*Executive Assistant*	*Executive Assistant & Research Program Administrator*
I. Lilla Connidis	Karen Jackson	Jacques J.M. Shore
Coordinators	*Coordinators*	*Coordinators*
David Laidler	Peter Aucoin	Clare F. Beckton
Donald G. McFetridge	Keith Banting	Ronald C.C. Cuming
Kenneth Norrie*	André Blais	Mark Krasnick
Craig Riddell	Bruce Doern	Andrée Lajoie
John Sargent*	Richard Simeon	A. Wayne MacKay
François Vaillancourt	Denis Stairs	John J. Quinn
John Whalley	Cynthia Williams	
	Gilbert R. Winham	
Research Analysts	*Research Analysts*	*Administrative and Research Assistant*
Caroline Digby	Claude Desranleau	Nicolas Roy
Mireille Ethier	Ian Robinson	
Judith Gold		
Douglas S. Green	*Office Administration*	*Research Analyst*
Colleen Hamilton	Donna Stebbing	Nola Silzer
Roderick Hill		
Joyce Martin		

*Kenneth Norrie and John Sargent co-directed the final phase of Economics Research with David Smith